MW01628558

V. V. Vereshchagin

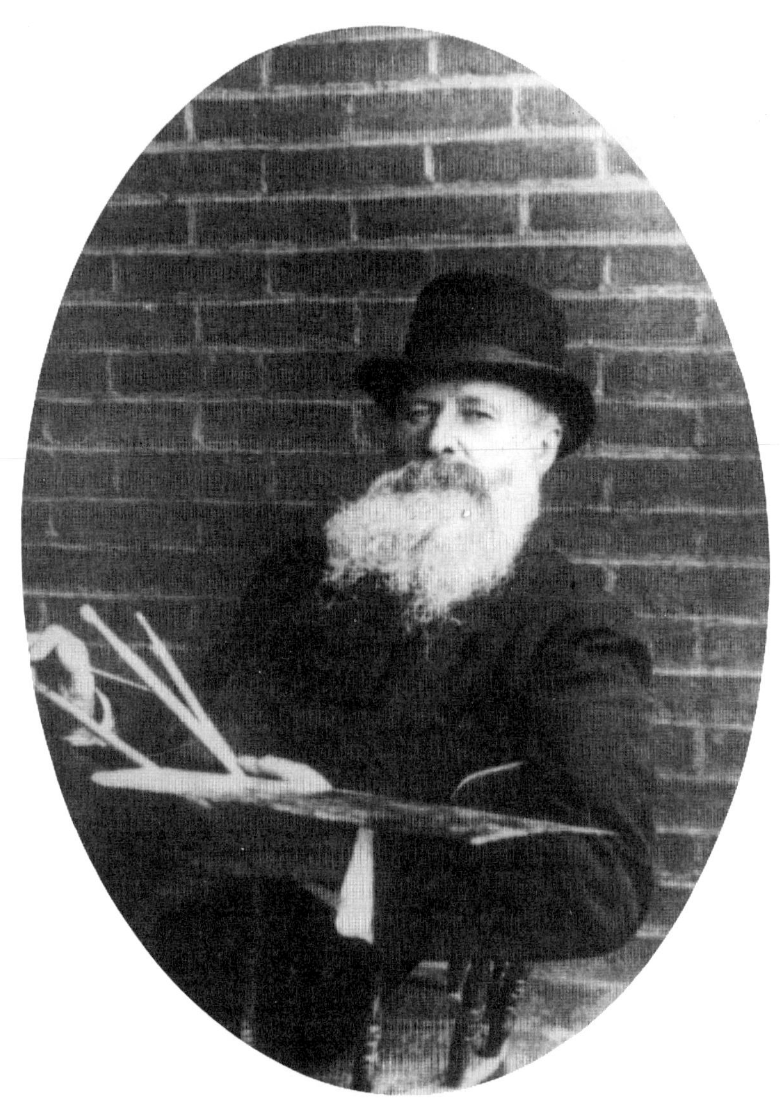

V. V. Vereshchagin, ca. 1900.

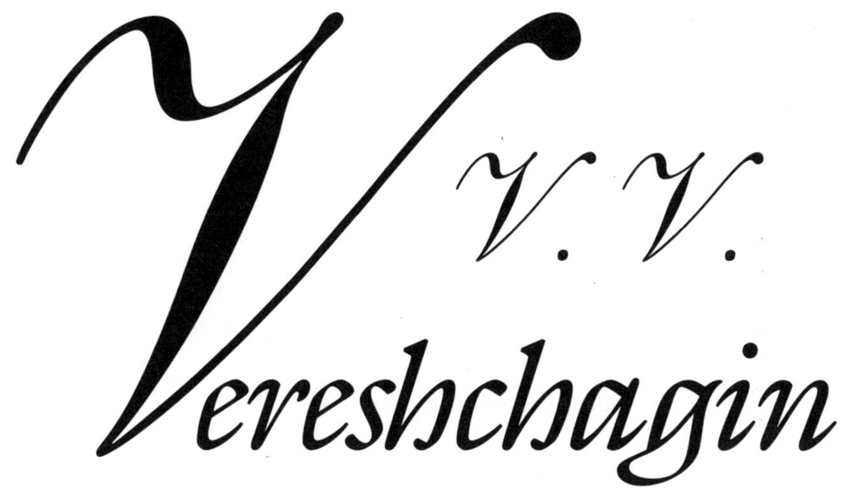

V. V. Vereshchagin

ARTIST AT WAR

Vahan D. Barooshian

UNIVERSITY PRESS OF FLORIDA

Gainesville/Tallahassee/Tampa/Boca Raton/Pensacola

Orlando/Miami/Jacksonville

Printed in the United States of America on acid-free paper ♾

Design by Betty Palmer McDaniel

Library of Congress Cataloging-in-Publication Data
Barooshian, Vahan D.
V. V. Vereshchagin: artist at war / Vahan D. Barooshian.
p. cm.
Includes bibliographical references and index.
ISBN 0-8130-1178-7
1. Vereshchagin, Vasilii Vasilevich, 1842–1904—Criticism and interpretation. 2. War in art. 3. Realism in art—Russia.
I. Title.
ND699.V5B37 1993
759.7—dc20 92-32515

The reproduction of the color plates in this book was made possible in part by funds awarded by Wells College from a grant in support of faculty research from the Bristol-Myers Squibb Foundation.

The University Press of Florida is the scholarly publishing agency for the State University System of Florida, comprised of Florida A & M University, Florida Atlantic University, Florida International University, Florida State University, University of Central Florida, University of Florida, University of North Florida, University of South Florida, and University of West Florida.

University Press of Florida
15 Northwest 15th Street
Gainesville, FL 32611

To the memory of my mother, Shamirám,
who knew only peace and love

CONTENTS

ILLUSTRATIONS

Color Plates (following page 110)

ACKNOWLEDGMENTS

I am indebted to a number of people and institutions for making this book possible. My greatest debt is to my friends and colleagues, particularly Professor John Nesselhof, with whom I held many fruitful discussions about Vereshchagin and who read the entire manuscript and provided me with judicious advice and suggestions. I also extend my gratitude to Arthur J. Bellinzoni, Jr., for his valuable comments and critical eye. I am grateful to my cousin, Martin Barooshian, a professional artist and a consultant for Swann Galleries, New York City, with whom I held prolonged discussions in examining many of Vereshchagin's paintings and who enriched my understanding and appreciation of them. During her extended tour of the Soviet Union in 1988, Dominique Corbett sent me valuable materials about Vereshchagin, some from the Tretiakov Gallery, whose collection of Vereshchagin's works aroused my initial interest. I cannot express enough appreciation to her. I kindly thank the staffs of the Fogg Art and the Widener libraries at Harvard University and of the Olin and Art libraries at Cornell University for their cooperation. I am very grateful to Wells College, to Robert Plane, president, and to Linda Rinker, dean, for granting me a stipend to cover costs of travel and research. Louise Rossmann of Long Library was always gracious and helpful in locating obscure references for me. I am lovingly grateful to my wife, Barbara, and to my daughter and son, Sarah and Daniel, for their help, patience, and understanding while I worked on the book. To all others who contributed in some way to this study, my sincere gratitude. I hope that my system of transliterating Russian into English will present no difficulties, least of all to those who know Russian. Finally, I alone am responsible for the contents of the book.

INTRODUCTION

Vasily Vasilevich Vereshchagin is a fascinating phenomenon of nineteenth-century history and art. Although he has been largely forgotten in the West, the recent publication of four books about him in the Soviet Union, where his works have been considered classics since the Revolution, attest to his enduring legacy and unmistakable significance in the history of Russian and world art. The foremost artist of nineteenth-century realism in Russia, Ilia Repin (1844–1930), called Vereshchagin "a colossus, a great artist," "a real Hercules," "to a high degree an immense phenomenon in our life," "a genius, a superman."[1] Even Vereshchagin's enemies called him a "pioneer" in his time and could not deny him an "honourable place in the history of Russian art" and culture, since his works "conceal a great power, a great artistic potentiality" of universal relevance.[2] During the last quarter of the nineteenth century, he was one of the great, dominant personalities, the most compelling and famous Russian artist in the Western world, where his numerous exhibits in Paris, London, Berlin, Vienna, New York, Chicago, Philadelphia, Baltimore, and other major cities attracted hundreds of thousands of viewers and often caused a sensation. The paintings he exhibited usually created a lasting impression, for they were "inspired by a genuine, real, and powerful talent, by a talent that knows no rest or fatigue."[3]

In America of the 1880s and after, Vereshchagin's art was seen as the foundation of an American school of painting. In this country, his works are included in the collections of the Brooklyn Museum and the Boston Museum of Fine Arts. These institutions, among others, own several of Vereshchagin's paintings, which were bought at auction in New York in 1892 and 1902. He was, perhaps, the most widely traveled of all nineteenth-century artists, and it is "difficult to find in the world of art an artist such as Vereshchagin who saw so many countries and peoples and represented in one form or another his impressions of all that he saw."[4]

In addition to his eminent stature as an artist, Vereshchagin was also a historian, ethnographer, geographer, essayist, novelist, journalist, and archaeologist. He was one of the most remarkable and courageous individuals of the nineteenth century. For most of his life, his fearless nature found him in opposition to the Russian state, which he considered an instrument of oppression and violence; in turn, the Russian autocracy believed he was one of the leaders of a conspiracy to overthrow the existing order. Vereshchagin also clashed with military leaders in Russia and Western Europe, who realized the revolutionary implications of his art and forbade children and the military to attend his exhibits.

His physical and creative energies were titanic; he appeared to be in a frenetic rush to compress two or three lifetimes of travel and artistic and literary activity into one, as if he alone were waging a struggle against that curse on humanity: war on a mass scale. In his intrepid, passionate pursuit of fantastic and dangerous risks, his relentless urge to travel and to seek new subjects for artistic treatment, his defiance of death and his struggle against the orthodoxies of his time, Vereshchagin was a typical nineteenth-century Romantic. He wrote numerous articles and more than twenty books in which he buttressed the historical accuracy of his paintings and recounted his travels, his adventures, and his experiences in and observations on war.

Vereshchagin bears comparison with Leo Tolstoy, the Russian novelist and philosopher, in expressing in his works the moral conscience of the age. Like Tolstoy, he believed that war was not only a moral conflict but was also morally repugnant and thus unacceptable.[5] Vereshchagin once remarked about his mission: "Some spread the idea of peace by means of fascinating and powerful words; others present in its defense religious, economic and other arguments; and I advocate the same thing by means of colors."[6] Vereshchagin painted historical and genre themes, landscapes and portraits; he was a brilliant draftsman as well. But the principal historical relevance of his art is war, not the pomp, pageantry, glory, and romantic aura of war, but its true nature—"the bloody details of war," "the abundance of wounds and bandaged limbs,"[7] the agony, pain, suffering, and misery of war, which began to afflict the common masses during the nineteenth and twentieth centuries. Although Vereshchagin is considered Russia's greatest battle painter, with the exception of one or two paintings his work has very little to do with actual battle. He is primarily concerned with the effects of war. Yet, historically, his portrayal of war marks the end of the glamorous forms of that genre.[8] A cardinal feature of his artistic innovation is the serial presentation of paintings, in which three or more works express a story, but each is valid independently. This reflects the literary orientation of his art.

This volume represents the first extensive study in English of Vereshchagin's life and art against the historical, political, economic, military, and social background of his age in its Russian and European contexts. Of all Russian artists of the second half of the nineteenth century, Vereshchagin is eminently germane to our own time, since he dedicated his art and life to the struggle against war, despotism, barbarism, backwardness, and ignorance. This study is primarily an introduction to Vereshchagin's life and art: it covers the salient features of his artistic, literary, and military activity, which are of extraordinarily heroic dimensions. As an artist, Vereshchagin had the distinction of being awarded a major Russian military medal for bravery in action; thereafter, he served as an artist-journalist or war correspondent in the Russian army, often as an aide to a commanding general. He painted in the very heat of war, as cannons and bullets were fired at and around him. I discuss most of the art that made him famous and controversial and caused him much anguish in his opposition to the Russian autocracy and the military. In dealing with his paintings, I have tried to provide the specific historical, political, and social context vital to their understanding. Several pages are devoted to a critical political question: Why has Vereshchagin failed to gain recognition in the Western world since 1904?

Chapter One

VERESHCHAGIN'S EARLY LIFE

Vasily Vasilevich Vereshchagin was born in 1842 in the provincial town of Cherepovets, in northern European Russia, to an established family of the Russian gentry. His father, Vasily, owner of a fairly large estate to which belonged some three hundred fifty serfs, was engaged in the local government as marshal of the gentry. Vereshchagin, in his autobiography, seems somewhat indifferent to his father, who appears to have had little influence on his childhood. Vereshchagin found his amiable, exuberant, flamboyant uncle, to whom he devotes far more attention, a contrast to his languid, dull, orthodox father, who "liked to lie on a sofa for whole days, read and doze." His mother, Anna, however, was an overwhelming presence; although quite superstitious, and frugal, she was intelligent, kind, and affectionate, as Vereshchagin recalled, and liked to read French novels. She managed the household affairs and dominated her serf-servants, who were, in effect, chattels, with whom she never established any human bond or community. She once removed one of Vereshchagin's beloved serfs from the staff because, as she explained to him on inquiry, "I need a servant, and not an adviser."[1]

Vereshchagin's early childhood in provincial Russia was relatively active and happy, and rather rich and varied in human relationships; he forged strong bonds with relatives and maintained them even after he was sent away to school. If he had any grievances, they were against his mother for not sufficiently interpreting and explaining his lessons and for economizing on meals, the best of which she reserved for guests. Frail and shy, he was not the favorite of the couple's twelve children. Vereshchagin's sketch of the family in 1861 indicates that he had one older brother, four younger brothers, and one younger sister; five other siblings had died in childhood. He was an obedient, curious, impressionable, and intelligent child who wanted to be treated like an adult. "I was, the stories went, a sickly, nervous child," he wrote, but there was little basis for this view, and Vereshchagin relates no major or recurring childhood illness. It was not until he entered the Naval Cadet School in 1853 that he suffered a series of ailments.

One of the household nursemaids, a widow who was also named Anna, took the young Vereshchagin under her wing and lavished on him the love and attention that his parents could not adequately provide. She helped develop his fiercely independent character and ego and even protected him from his mother. Although Anna often became angry and disciplined the Vereshchagin children, she seems to have taken Vereshchagin and his brothers—who had their own nursemaid—as her very own and would tear them away from their tutors "at every convenient opportunity." She took the young Vereshchagin for walks along the river Sheksna and to the woods to pick berries and mushrooms, which he loved very much. In his autobiography, Vereshchagin leaves no doubt about his supreme, exclusive love for Anna, who may have symbolized to him all of humanity: "In my memory of that time, the nursemaid Anna remained the most outstanding, the closest and dearest person, already old even then, whom I loved more than anything in the world, more than my father, mother and brothers."[2] Subsequently, Anna would also encourage Vereshchagin's interest in art.

Vereshchagin's involvement in the lives and concerns of the household servants did not make him oblivious to the abominations of serfdom. Although he did not openly express his dislike of the system, perhaps because of his intimate association with the serfs, he took umbrage at his parents' arbitrary, albeit not generally cruel, treatment of them, his mother's indifference to their "labor, devotion and diligence," and, particularly, his parents' arranging of the marriages of their servants, which led to some unhappy, intolerable, violent relationships. His father's attitude regarding such marriages was, "once you get used to it you will like it." In one instance, his father improperly released a servant to twenty-five years of military service for unintentionally crippling Vereshchagin's favorite mare, which had to be destroyed. This was intended as a lesson to other servants to work responsibly.[3] Banishment to military service was a cruel punishment, which carried with it the possibility of death in battle and the probability that the servant could not return to his village to see his family during his military tenure.[4]

Vereshchagin's close association with the servants extended to their children, despite his mother's attempts to shield him from them. She forbade him in general to frequent the servants' quarters, but Vereshchagin "often found the opportunity to sit there while she slept, and especially when she was away. The girls would caress and allow us, me, a boy, various completely instinctive, unconscious liberties." When his mother discovered that her son was being sexually educated in the servants' quarters, she ordered his nurse never to allow him and his brothers in any of their dwellings.[5]

Vereshchagin's awareness of class divisions in his household environment entailed complex psychological and ideological implications for his mental development. It would lead to a conscious need to serve the peasant class as a compassionate exponent of its travails and to an unconscious desire to satisfy his mother's wish that he become a famous, respectable military officer. This dual commitment, quite fruitful and even original in artistic terms, presented an ideological dilemma which he never quite resolved. As a participant, Vereshchagin was impelled to support the wars of the Russian state to the extent that it satisfied his mother's longing that he become an officer, but he would condemn wars for their oppression of the common masses to which he was emotionally wedded. Vereshchagin was consciously aware of his primary mission "as an artist," a phrase that he often used in his correspondence, and he never really saw himself "as an officer," despite his active involvement in war, because that vocation contradicted his mission.

Before his formal education, Vereshchagin, who seems to have been an excellent student, was tutored in mathematics, history, geography, German, and the scriptures. His mother taught him basic arithmetic and French, in which she was fluent. An avid reader, he especially liked the children's stories of the Russian writer Mikhail Chistiakov (1809–85). Vereshchagin's strong interest in art was initiated by the depiction—on his nursemaid's shawl—of a troika of horses pulling a sleigh pursued by wolves. He copied the scene "very quickly and so faithfully that the nursemaid, daddy, mummy and many visitors were surprised and praised me," but here he also laments that no one conceived then the idea of an art education for him. The discovery of artistic forms eventually drew his attention to the English etchings in his tutor's room, the French lithographs in his father's room, and *The Resurrection,* a church icon, which gripped his attention as the ultimate artistic achievement. To further his skills, Vereshchagin began to copy the lithographs and etchings, although he was not allowed to remove them from the walls because his parents feared that he would break the glass frames. That his parents offered no encouragement in this pursuit bewildered Vereshchagin; but it was considered shameful for the son of an established gentry family to pursue art as a vocation.[6]

When Vereshchagin was eight years old, his parents decided on their son's future career by sending him to the Aleksandrovsky Junior Military School in Tsarskoe Selo near St. Petersburg. Although they could afford to have their children educated at home, Vereshchagin points out that the gentry as a whole strongly desired to shift this cost to state expense after the children had reached school age. However difficult it was to abandon "so many dear people"—his nursemaid Anna wept incessantly for fear she would not see her "child" again—Vereshchagin looked forward to this new stage in his life out of a "partly childish carefree attitude and curiosity to see places about which I had heard so much, in addition to a vague, undefined desire to excel, to return as a learned man, a famous, brave officer, perhaps a general!"[7]

To be sure, Vereshchagin never anticipated the actual process of the "inhuman" and "foolhardy" separation from his household and parents until he arrived at the school barracks. When his mother handed him a great many fruit-drops and bid him farewell, Vereshchagin wondered if he would ever see her again. As they reached the baggage room, he clung to her with all his might, grasping her hands and dress never to let go; but the "monsters" forcefully separated him from his mother and pulled him away. "Oh, what a crime it was to leave me there—to desert me!"[8]

At school, Vereshchagin felt that he had been immured in an ant's nest of unfriendly, hostile cadets. The seamier sides of adolescent life were a marked contrast to the tranquil, carefree existence of his household. He was by nature a loner and scorned the conformity, "oppression," and "coercion" that characterized the school's coteries; and, for most of his life, he staunchly maintained that independence. He felt no great longing for his parents, whom he was able to see after a year and, later, during vacation periods. Vereshchagin discovered early that the custom of presenting gifts to many people and offering "bribes to the heads of offices" often facilitated one's stay and studies. He seems to ha.e adjusted easily and quickly to the rather unexacting regimen and eventually came to like the school, which lacked, he observes, "the rudeness, callousness and soldiering" of higher military schools, which "trained not human beings in the broad sense of the word or even good soldiers, but only specialists of the battle-front and square-bashing."[9]

Military officers, headed by a lieutenant general, directed and provided the elementary military aspects of instruction, which included instilling patriotism and reverence for Tsar Nicholas I. Daily duties were performed to the beat of drums. A group of women staff officers, with a hierarchy of their own, supervised and exerted a strong influence on the cadets, and seemed to provide a certain continuity with Vereshchagin's household. They, in turn, were assisted by male duty-attendants, who maintained order during games and other activities and instructed the cadets in marching and in the rifle drill and ceremony.

Vereshchagin studied French, Russian, gymnastics, history, geography, arithmetic, dance, and calligraphy. Thanks to his solid academic preparation at home, he became an outstanding student and rose to the rank of senior sergeant in his company. He was also given classes in drawing, where the Battle of Borodino (1812) was a popular theme; later, Vereshchagin would paint his own series of Napoleon's invasion of Russia and the Russian army's heroic defense at Borodino. At the school he became so adept at drawing portraits that his skill was brought to the attention of a director, but history repeated itself: it occurred to no one there, Vereshchagin regrets, to recognize and develop his artistic talent and to encourage him to pursue a career as an "educated artist." That was not only unthinkable but "madness," because it was not the profession of a nobleman.[10]

In 1853, after completing his studies at the Military School, Vereshchagin enrolled in the Naval Cadet School in St. Petersburg, where he remained until 1860 (Fig. 1). At the beginning of his stay, Vereshchagin suffered several illnesses, which, coupled with his inability to cope with "the dense forest" of mathematical fractions, caused him to fall behind in his studies. He would become, however, the best essayist in his class; and among all nineteenth-century Russian artists, he was probably the most prolific writer. Subsequently, he would suffer from "nervous fever," perhaps a form of neurasthenia, which was considered fatal, and from typhus. Ashamed and humiliated, he considered his whole future in doubt, and felt as if he had fallen from a pedestal.

He found the severe regimen at the new school callous, crude, philistine, and replete with student pranks, cruel tricks, and taunts of which he was often victim: "Gentleness, courtesy, tact were subject to ridicule, but bravado and force were valued and respected to a great extent." He dreaded his company commander who, although he took to Vereshchagin as other teachers did, had a volatile temper. Unlike the former school, where bribes and gifts were offered on a minor scale, corruption permeated the Naval Cadet School, and bribes were the vital, indispensable lubricant of its "normal" operations. Even Vereshchagin's father was not immune; when he would receive a "few lines" from the school about the necessity of a request for his son's vacation, he did not fail "to lubricate" the bureaucratic pens that "creaked of effort." One teacher, more interested in catching his students unprepared in their assignments than in developing their abilities, was not at all squeamish about receiving "gifts" and "offerings" from them. Another company commander accepted gifts from all except the poorest cadets and "victimized to no small extent those who gave him nothing, but on the other hand would not even refuse [the poorest cadets] when they brought him something." Another teacher "set up a whole system of spying," in which cadets who were poor students would inform on their friends to facilitate their own promotions.[11]

Despite the rampant corruption, the professional incompetence of a few teachers, and the intense pressures to excel—with no more than four hours of sleep daily—Vereshchagin, through sheer hard work, application, and tenacity, emerged as the outstanding student of his class. Although he found naval studies and training unrewarding, unpleasant, and ultimately unworthy of pursuit as a career, he was determined to surmount the ordeal of his years at the school, where he felt like an animal

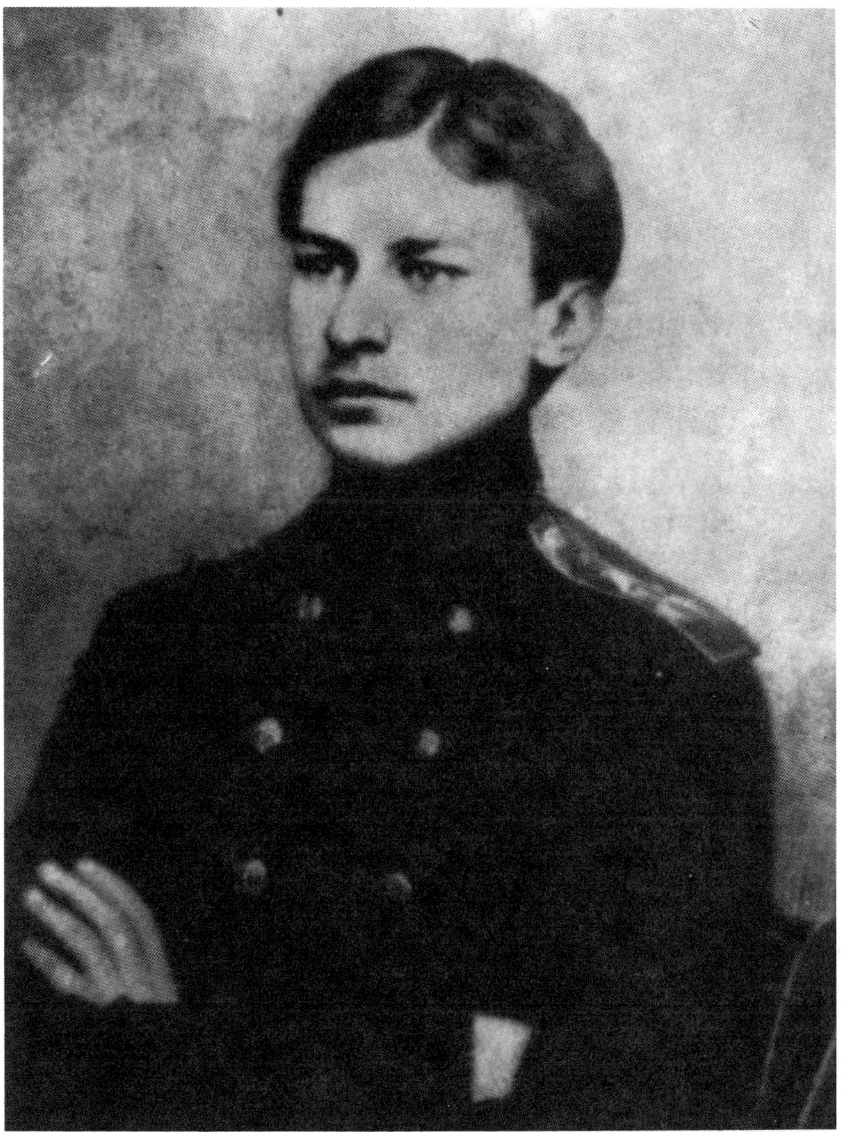

Figure 1. V. V. Vereshchagin at the Naval Cadet School, ca. 1855. From A. Lebedev and A. Solodovnikov, *V. V. Vereshchagin* (Moscow: Iskusstvo, 1988).

driven to compete without really understanding the sense and meaning of what he was learning.[12]

In 1858 and 1859, as part of his naval training, Vereshchagin made two trips to England and France. On both occasions, he became seasick, which led to second thoughts about a career in the Navy. During his first trip, he became "completely engrossed in reading" the works of Alexander I. Herzen (1812–70), the leading Russian social and political thinker of his time, then in exile in London. Herzen's works, although banned in Russia, "enjoyed great authority" there. Vereshchagin remarks that service and commitment to his fellow man were the guiding principles that emerged from his reading. In terms of subsequent events, Herzen's influence was a decisive factor in Vereshchagin's choice of a career as an artist.[13]

Vereshchagin's academic studies included a class in drawing and the instructor immediately recognized his artistic talent and promise. A friendship ensued, and Vereshchagin was invited to the instructor's home to see his works, some of which had required months to complete. Through this relationship, Vereshchagin first recognized the exacting nature of art as a craft—the preparation, care, and time involved in the execution of a painting. It was not, however, until near the end of his studies at the school, when he came to enjoy substantial privileges and more free time, that Vereshchagin began to devote serious attention to developing his artistic talent. He persuaded his father to hire an art tutor whose prediction of Vereshchagin's "rapid success" provided further encouragement and motivation. That this tutor lived in poverty in a room littered with "dust, filth, cigarette stubs, remains of sausage and vodka" hardly deterred Vereshchagin. On the contrary, the tutor's works so impressed him that the disorderly room "seemed somehow a necessary component of the general picture of artistic life."[14]

In 1858, while still a student at the cadet school, Vereshchagin enrolled in a drawing course at the Society for the Encouragement of the Arts, which was a prelude to his study of art at the Imperial Academy of Fine Arts (hereafter Academy of Arts). He soon realized that technical training there was inadequate with regard to drawing figures. He began to make frequent visits to the Hermitage, in St. Petersburg, and became enthralled by the works of Rembrandt, Rubens, and other Classical and

Renaissance artists, particularly Raphael and Poussin, who were the supreme personifications of academic training. During this period, Vereshchagin discovered in art a refuge from the commonplaces and crudities of life and set as his chimerical goal the possession of those works precisely for that purpose.[15] He also noted the high prices that were paid for certain art works. His parents had become accustomed to his interest in art and initially viewed it as merely a passing form of recreation and diversion from his studies, even after he had chosen to take an examination that exempted him from participating in a naval journey around the world. Vereshchagin preferred to remain in St. Petersburg to continue his studies at the drawing school; "aquatic wisdom would serve no useful purpose" in his life.[16]

As it became clear, however, that Vereshchagin intended to renounce his naval career upon receiving his commission and pursue a career in art, his parents, particularly his mother, became disturbed. His father calmly expressed disapproval by refusing to offer any financial support and admonished Vereshchagin to be prepared to endure the "poverty, cold and hunger" of an artist's life. With the added assurance of his inner conviction that he would surmount the life of poverty that befell many artists and that he would attain great success in the world of art, Vereshchagin responded confidently that his life would be "better" than the one his father described. Concerned with her son's future status, prestige, and image, his mother objected vigorously and sought through various means to dissuade him from his "mad" career. She pointed out that "your drawing won't get you into the reception rooms, but in epaulets you will be accepted everywhere." She also enlisted the aid of relatives to assail him for his decision, but to no avail. Interestingly, only an older brother supported Vereshchagin because he, too, wanted to abandon his career as a naval officer.[17]

Vereshchagin's pursuit of a new career in art, partly a revolt of son against father so characteristic of the era, must be understood in historical perspective. During the mid-1850s, a surge of radical thought and public opinion, suppressed by the reactionary reign of Nicholas I (1825–55), could no longer be contained. The intellectual ferment of the period, of what Herzen called "the awakening of Russian society," was "the Russian equivalent of the western European Enlightenment of the eighteenth century."[18] The Russian autocracy under Alexander II was compelled to undertake the most urgent reform by emancipating the serfs in 1861, partly for fear of revolution and partly with a view to modernizing its backward economy along industrial lines. A new generation of militant, radical, atheistic, positivist, and materialistic intellectuals arose to dominate the intellectual scene. "They represented a new type of man who may be defined as an intellectual, politician and conspirator rolled into one, but first and foremost as a man who says 'no' to the existing order."[19] Indeed, Vereshchagin himself would partly assume this role in his art. He would literally challenge generals, tsars, governments, and the orthodoxies of his time. The Russian autocracy, which unsuccessfully attempted to bring him into its fold to tame his rebellious art, considered him a formidable member of the nihilist camp, an agent of the revolutionaries and conspirators. Abroad, he would be suspected of being a secret agent or spy for the Russian government. Other prominent Russian figures who espoused progressive causes were also so described, but the rumor about Vereshchagin persisted.

The leader of the new intelligentsia, Nikolai Chernyshevsky (1829–89), whose moral and political influence is difficult to exaggerate despite the narrowness and dogmatism of his views, had already defined in 1856 the new aesthetic parameters that would shape much of the art for the remainder of the nineteenth century. Chernyshevsky's major task was to subvert the idealism that largely dominated Russian intellectual thought of the 1830s and 1840s. In asserting the superiority of reality to art, Chernyshevsky viewed art not only as a faithful reproduction of "sensible reality," but as directly involved in the major social and political issues of the time through its explanation and assessment of that reality in "progressive" human terms.[20] Many artists, including Vereshchagin, took Chernyshevsky's views to mean that "the goal of art was to understand and explain reality and then apply it for the use of humanity."[21] Vereshchagin acknowledges Chernyshevsky's considerable influence in shaping his aesthetic views and, in fact, would later define "realism" in Chernyshevsky's terms.[22]

Russia's military defeat in the Crimean War in 1855 raised the hopes and expectations of many for major social, legal, economic, political, cultural, and educational reforms. The expected reforms affected the

Academy of Arts in 1859. "The reform-minded public had high expectations that painters, who under Nicholas I had been reduced to the status of bureaucrats . . . would be transformed by means of a well-rounded education into active participants in the renovation of national life and take their place alongside other free professions."[23] The role of the artist had yet to be determined, for it was dependent on the nature and scope of the projected social and political reforms; but Russian art of the latter half of the nineteenth century would ultimately "acquire a special place in social life of equal significance with literature."[24]

To be an active participant in social and political events (albeit without any clear conception of his role) was, Vereshchagin believed, one of the staples of art as a vocation. With this aim in view, he applied for and received in 1860 a two-year stipend to study at the Academy of Arts. As a commissioned naval officer, he was perhaps the most educated student at the academy, a contrast to the "half-literate, raw youths from distant provinces who never managed to overcome their ignorance or to shed their crude manners."[25] He would soon learn to his chagrin that the reforms at the academy had failed to alter its highly bureaucratized character; codes, regulations, and red tape remained substitutes for teaching as well as obstacles to the development of artistic talent. The academy hierarchy, under the control of the Ministry of the Royal Court, stubbornly resisted the efforts of art students to create a specific Russian national art, that is, art as a reflection of Russian reality. According to the academy's pedagogical principles, works of art were a function of laws divorced from the life of society, and the expression, content, and individual interpretation of art were restricted to a set of technical skills. Originality was discouraged as students were taught to imitate Classical, Renaissance, and other artistic models that had no relation to the their immediate concerns. For example, the academy considered genre art "a simple exercise in work from nature," a means of becoming familiar with immediate reality, but of no principal significance as the artist's major objective: the affirmation of his "lofty" skills in his quest for Ideal Beauty in art. It viewed art "as a kind of activity that permits the creation of definite values of independent meaning and determined not by its relation to life, but by the mastery of the artist, his professional habits, knowledge and skill in using the art of the past." Perhaps the most critical shortcoming at the academy was the isolation of students from professors. When students acted unilaterally to create an art club to promote closer ties and discussions with professors, the Ministry of the Royal Court opposed the club, considering it a "definite counterbalance to the Academy."[26] Convinced that no reform was possible, students began to shun their professors. Since student expectations and artistic objectives outlived the academy's resistance to them, discontent, disaffection, and disillusionment mounted and ultimately fourteen students led a rebellion against the academy in 1863.[27]

This revolt marked the emancipation of Russian art from the obsolete criteria—conformity and sterile imitation—of the Academy of Arts. In effect, the students were rebelling against the Russian autocracy and state patronage of the arts. The academy would no longer dictate artistic tastes and serve as the major center of Russian art education. The principal reasons for the revolt were commercial considerations, the popularization of art beyond the two capitals, and the creation of an art reflective of contemporary Russian life. The art espoused by the academy no longer had any currency in the face of changing artistic tastes and a growing demand by the urban middle-class and private market for art work as concrete manifestations of respectability, affluence, cultural attainment, and sophistication. To this extent, the historical parallel with artistic trends and tastes in Western Europe is remarkably similar. There, art had begun to supplant religion among the affluent middle classes and aristocracy. Artists were viewed as "geniuses," as "sages, prophets, teachers, moralists, sources of truth."[28] This view had obtained in Russia, too, but in much weaker form, since the 1830s and 1840s.[29]

The student revolt also marked the dethronement of the old masters of art, and the field of Russian art became wide open; artists could establish their interests and cultivate aesthetic tastes and art patrons. Vereshchagin was quite aware of this during his subsequent art studies in Paris, and would attempt, unsuccessfully, to found an art journal both there and in St. Petersburg. In 1870, the students, now artists, formed the Association of Traveling Art Exhibits and competed against the academy. They came to be known as the Itinerants and dominated Russian art for most of the latter half of the nineteenth century. Their works were considered avant-garde only in content (primarily genre paintings), and their method of realism remained in accordance with academy teachings.

Vereshchagin's own revolt against the academy in 1863 preceded that led by the fourteen students by several months. Although he received a number of awards for his sketches and further encouragement from two competent art instructors, he was disappointed with the slow progress of his artistic development, with the imposition by his instructors of a particular artistic technique which undermined his "faith in the necessity of the *stroke*, purity and harmony of a drawing," with the academy's emphasis on Classical models, and with the poor quality of instruction. He drew many pencil and watercolor sketches in the streets and from nature and developed the habit of drawing from memory. He had yet to attempt oil painting. He remained, however, grateful to the academy for its support of his education and for assisting talented artists. In 1862, in the first of numerous acts of personal protest, Vereshchagin set fire to his sketch, *Ulysses' Slaughter of Penelope's Suitors.* An imitation of a work by the English sculptor John Flaxman (1755–1826), the sketch was much to the academy's liking, but Vereshchagin destroyed it so as never again "to return to such rubbish." By mid-1863, he had "read and heard quite a deal, my mind had developed, and the stupidity of conventional forms and framework had become clear." He abandoned St. Petersburg to develop his artistic skills independently in the idyllic environment of the Caucasus, which had served as a source of creative inspiration for many Russian artists and writers. The summer of 1863 found Vereshchagin in Tiflis, Georgia, where he arrived after living on a diet of bread and water to conserve his meager savings of some one hundred rubles.[30]

In Tiflis, Vereshchagin became acquainted with a well-known Russian artist, Lev F. Lagorio (1827–1905), who soon found work for him as a drawing instructor for the children of a Russian general. Vereshchagin also taught drawing in three schools, which provided him with means of subsistence, and drew various animals to illustrate books for an agricultural organization. This allowed him to travel in the Caucasus, but the flat fee of four hundred rubles he received from the schools was inadequate to cover his expenses. He took utmost advantage of his free time to draw camels, cows, horses, sheep, and other animals in the city and countryside. He worked in such a frenzy—a pattern that he maintained for the rest of his life—that only his "youth and freedom" prevented "this mass of work" from crushing him. He filled three large sketchbooks which he planned to use as the basis for his paintings, but "they were lost or stolen from me."[31]

In the winter of 1864, Vereshchagin inherited one thousand rubles from the estate of his uncle. This enabled him to travel to Paris to study at the Ecole des Beaux-Arts, the French equivalent of the Russian Academy of Arts. Among the instructors there was the versatile artist and sculptor, Jean Léon Gérôme (1824–1904), one of the most popular Neo-Classicists and Orientalists of the 1850s and 1860s. A masterly use and balance of color and tone and a command of fine detail and solid technique were the staples of Gérôme's art.[32] As a rule, foreigners were not allowed to attend the school, but Gérôme accepted Vereshchagin as a probationary art student solely on the basis of his Caucasus drawings. Possibly, Vereshchagin's heavily detailed works were influenced by his study under Gérôme, whose studio he visited frequently.

Since Gérôme's artistic success stemmed partly from the popularity of his Turkish and Egyptian genre works, Vereshchagin perhaps saw his own potential artistic success in terms of depicting the diverse primitive, exotic nationalities and nomadic tribes of the Caucasus. In general, the Oriental trend was an effort to fertilize the arts "by exotic influences" and by a return to the very sources of Western civilization, to new images of Western roots.[33]

As in the Russian academy, Vereshchagin discovered, however, that he was in another academic mold and was unable to develop artistic autonomy, although he did acquire some experience painting in oil, a medium it would take many years for him to master. The various artistic approaches, styles, and techniques of his multiple art instructors inhibited the attainment of technical command, distinctive style, and the fluent transition from drawing to painting. Thus, his early works lack integration, color harmony, and psychological depth and are, in general, dry, static, schematic, and somewhat hyperbolized.

Vereshchagin ultimately became a master of sketches and character studies because of his abundant experience in the Caucasus and Central Asia. As an artist, he was like a historian: in his sketches and studies he selected and collated the facts of human existence and types, nature, and general phenomena for artistic assessment in his paintings. For example, Vereshchagin drew his series of Central Asia paintings from direct observation and actual combat; his sketches and studies were derived from accounts of others and from documentary sources. Vereshchagin's sketches and studies, many of which are unsigned and undated, are, in effect, a diary of his travels and observations. His paintings are ideological reflections on or explorations of the social, religious, natural, and historical phenomena that shape human nature, ethnic types, and existence; he appears to be attempting to discover the roots of the bewildering and disturbing cultural contradiction between the grandeur, beauty, and diversity of human creativity and the poverty, cruelty, and barbarity of human life. Quite often Vereshchagin juxtaposed this contradiction in his art: he explored the direction and content of "progress" and the objective historical and human factors which determine it. Most likely, his enthusiastic reading of Henry T. Buckle's *History of Civilization in England* (London, 1857) profoundly influenced his art, despite the staggering complexities that Buckle's ideas posed for artistic expression; but Vereshchagin at least hoped that his own exposure of human barbarity, fanaticism, and suffering would contribute to human progress.

Buckle's work is a seminal, eloquent, but untenable study, which enjoyed enormous international popularity and was in full accord with the strong positivist current in Russian and West European thought. He sought to make history a scientific study. Buckle maintained that geographical, environmental, and climatic factors played a key role in human and social development and that the accumulation of knowledge would eventually lead to the concrete, fundamental laws that determine the rational, progressive course of human perfectibility. He believed that the historian's function was not to compile and narrate the facts of history but to explain and interpret them in terms of fixed laws and principles governing human development:

> The unfortunate peculiarity of the history of man is, that although its separate parts have been examined with considerable ability, hardly anyone has attempted to combine them into a whole, and ascertain the way in which they are connected with each other. In all other

> great fields of inquiry, the necessity of generalization is universally admitted, and noble efforts are being made to rise from particular facts in order to discover the laws by which those facts are governed. So far, however, is this from being the usual course of historians, that among them a strange idea prevails, that their business is merely to relate events, which they may occasionally enliven by such moral and political reflections as seem likely to be useful . . . in the whole literature of Europe there are not more than three or four really original works which contain a systematic attempt to investigate the history of man according to those exhaustive methods which in other branches of knowledge have proved successful, and by which alone empirical observations can be raised to scientific truths.[34]

Vereshchagin's emphasis on the fixation of historical, objective fact largely explains the documentary, photographic, narrative orientation of his paintings, but his works almost invariably have another dimension. Hence the tension between accurate presentation of historical reality and artistic imagination in many of his paintings. Many of his works also display a significant measure of formal experimentation and novelty that were largely lacking in the art of the Itinerants.

In Paris, Vereshchagin learned to draw multiple figures and to portray perspective and elements of the natural environment. Gérôme, although a versatile artist *qua* artist, hoped as a teacher to make Vereshchagin a Neo-Classical artist and advised him to copy from Classical works at the Louvre. To Vereshchagin, such works were merely an idealization of reality, and, in another act of rebellion, he stubbornly rejected Gérôme's advice. When Vereshchagin received financial assistance from his father, he "broke loose from Paris as if from a dungeon and took up drawing freely with a certain frenzy."[35]

In March 1865, Vereshchagin returned to the Caucasus to travel, to observe, and to draw sketches of numerous ethnic types and the customs, traditions, religious holidays, and rituals of the Shiite Moslems and other sects. The exotic, unique folk customs and the fanatical, barbaric character of the religious practices of the Caucasian nationalities were largely unknown to the Western world and attracted increasing attention there during the 1850s. Vereshchagin perceived a potential market for his sketches, many of which would later be used as illustrations in historical studies of Central Asia.[36] After traveling for six months, Vereshchagin returned to Paris with a view to creating a journal for the publication of the "mass of drawings" he had created. Although he received permission to found his journal in November 1865, he could not raise financial backing to realize it.

At the end of 1866, Vereshchagin resumed his studies under Gérôme and Alexandre Bidá (1813–1895). They were highly impressed by his drawings, some of which were later published (1868) in a French journal. In the spring of 1867, Vereshchagin, his meager resources exhausted, joined his family at the estate of his uncle in Liubets. That summer, while walking along the Sheksna River near the estate, the loud, harrowing groans and sighs of gangs of boathaulers gripped his attention. Vereshchagin was struck by their large numbers, their sheer brute strength, and their wretched existence. After the emancipation of the Russian serfs in 1861, the number of boathaulers grew as "unemployed and unemployable house servants were joined by an army of jobless peasants from villages, also hard hit by the emancipation. The demand for labour in factories and industry was growing, but not fast enough to absorb the flood of new labour."[37] After talking with some of the boathaulers, Vereshchagin considered creating a painting about them; this would mark his first assault on Russia's social conditions and historical backwardness. The suggestion in Vereshchagin's work (*Boathaulers* [1866; Pl. 1]) that Russian peasants had exchanged one form of slavery for a more invidious form, or that the Russian peasantry was still in bondage but now homeless and no longer tied to the land, is difficult to avoid. A painting on the same subject (Pl. 2) would bring fame to the Russian artist Ilia Repin (1844–1930) in 1873.

Vereshchagin made a number of fine studies of boathaulers as tragic pathetic laborers in tattered clothing chained to their work. Three studies are worthy of brief note. In his best psychological study, Vereshchagin depicts one figure struggling to move forward as, with head raised, he grips the straps around his chest in a desperate effort to find relief from their crushing hold. Although physically stronger, the second figure, has a grim, hopeless expression; his folded arms around his chest indicate he is resigned to his fate. The last figure, sweating, and hat in hand, is simply exhausted from his task but makes every effort to press on. Only this figure appeared in the final sketch of the painting; he is clearly identifiable in the left foreground (see Pl. 1).[38]

Although the studies showed great promise for a major painting and were valuable to Vereshchagin as psychological portraits, they had little or no relation to the final sketch because they were incompatible—ideologically and structurally—with the painting's horizontal format. Unlike Repin, Vereshchagin did not wish to individualize or to draw psychological portraits of the boathaulers and make them objects of sympathy and admiration; he wanted to document objectively the *mass* character of boathauling and the collective effort of the boathaulers as they rhythmically sway from side to side in relation to the water current.[39] Above all, Vereshchagin sought to compare the boathaulers to long teams of harnessed cattle—hauling in unison, impoverished, degraded, enslaved, and exhausted by their oppressive work. Factually, Vereshchagin's work is accurate, but it lacks the luminous color and artistic allure of Repin's painting (see Pl. 2), a lateral view of eleven figures in similar tattered clothing whose individuality can evoke the viewer's sympathy and admiration. Interestingly, Repin's separate studies of boathaulers are quite similar to those of Vereshchagin.[40] The social protest in Repin's work is implicit; in Vereshchagin's it is explicit. Thus, Repin distorted the reality of boathauling by sacrificing historical accuracy for human appeal and calculated ambiguity; nevertheless his study remains a great work and has become a classic of nineteenth-century Russian art. Vereshchagin, however, never completed his work, ostensibly because he lacked the funds and had to devote his time to earning money after a rift with his parents. In its final, unfinished form, Vereshchagin's work is dry, pale, static, and lacks nuance; he was unable to make the effective, harmonious transition from his sketches and studies to painting in oil. On the other hand, the grim content of the work also shaped its pallid form. Nonetheless, *Boathaulers* is valuable as a historical document.

When Vereshchagin read that Repin was the first Russian artist to deal with boathaulers, he wrote to a friend:

> Repin has completely failed to understand the *essence* of the boathaulers; 5–6 ill-assorted people, even if typical, do not convey the

> idea of a *regiment* of boathaulers who are stamping their feet in the sand under the sun because of one barge. In my sketch there were 3–4 such regiments. First, I conceived my 'Boathaulers' long before Repin. Second, in my 'Boathaulers,' no less than 200–250 men were hauling each barge—whole regiments of people. *This is the whole crux of the matter.* In France, Germany, Egypt and Spain, barges are hauled by a tow-rope, but *thousands* of people haul them only here, in the nineteenth century.[41]

Vereshchagin's humanist mission would eventually find full expression in his Turkestan series of paintings; it was a mission that would take him to almost every continent to expose relentlessly, and at frequent risk to his own life, the intellectual and moral stagnation, the suffering, misery, cruelty, barbarism, and fanaticism of human life, and the tragic reality of war not only in their Russian but in their universal manifestations. Vereshchagin would ultimately emerge as a singular phenomenon in Russian and world art.

Chapter Two

THE ART AND ADVENTURE OF TURKESTAN AND INDIA

In late July 1867, a penniless and aimless Vereshchagin learned through the academy of an unusual opportunity for him as an artist to serve as an orderly for General Konstantin P. Kaufman. That this was a conscious attempt by the academy to win Vereshchagin back either to itself or to military service cannot be wholly disregarded. Kaufman was to become General of the Russian military forces in Turkestan (currently the countries of Turkmenia, Uzbekistan, Tadzhikistan, Kirgizia, and Kazakhstan), the new Governor-General of Turkestan in the Russian colonial conquest of Central Asia. This was the age of colonial empire and annexation of strategically important territories in Russia's quest for status as a world power.[1] Tsarist expansion into Central Asia alarmed Great Britain, who became suspicious of the Russian threat to India, with the potential of a military conflict. Vereshchagin was an apt choice for the position because he defended Russia's conquest of Central Asia as a "civilizing mission." For him, its benefits outweighed and rendered hollow the protests of the European powers about Russia's aggressive designs and the realignment in the balance of powers. Vereshchagin was convinced that any firsthand experience of Asiatic barbarism would change the minds of "myopic politicians" whose views of it were shaped by the fictional works of "sentimental travelers."[2]

In Turkestan, the Russian government sought to establish a rich cotton base for the growing textile industry and to develop consumer markets,[3] as well as to thwart England's penetration of the region. Kaufman's mission was to encourage the population's acceptance of Russian occupation and institutions and to establish administrative, political, economic, and social order in the newly conquered region, whose feuding khanates, particularly the Emir of Bukhara, resisted Russian rule. "The Western portion of Turkestan, which became Russian, had been ruled by rival khans from Bukhara and Kokand. The cultural and religious tradition of Islam provided the sole unifying element, but this affected the nomadic population very little. Turkestan, though blessed with ample resources and an industrious population, suffered from alternating despotism and anarchy."[4]

Vereshchagin met with Kaufman to discuss the conditions of his work and favorably impressed the general with his educational background and the Caucasus sketches. They reached an agreement that assured Vereshchagin artistic autonomy and freedom of movement in Central Asia. He would serve without military rank and uniform and, for administrative purposes, would receive the salary of an ensign. Throughout his life, Vereshchagin tried to avoid any official connection with the Russian government, apparently for fear that it might subject any art he exhibited in Russia or abroad to academy review and hence to an approval of content.[5] As circumstances developed, Vereshchagin would receive a salary from the Russian military until 1874. He did not foresee the conflicting loyalties—between his own vision of artistic truth and his patriotism—that would arise; later he sought to extricate himself from the dilemma, but at great personal sacrifice: the destruction of three of his finest paintings.

As a roaming civilian, Vereshchagin was vulnerable to the very real danger of sudden attack from Central Asian tribes; hundreds of Russians had been kidnapped and enslaved in the region. He always carried a revolver and was accompanied by an armed underling or personal servant. In practice, Vereshchagin became an attaché as well as an observer of administrative operations. His connection with the military apparently created suspicion abroad that he was a Russian agent in the guise of an artist and traveler. Presumably, his task was to use his works to acquaint the Russian military as a whole with various aspects of life in Turkestan, and, ultimately, to glorify the Russian military in its conquest of Central

Asia. He viewed the trip as a means of acquiring additional artistic training and of unlocking, at state expense, another unknown culture. Later he would write books and numerous newspaper and journal articles about his experiences in Turkestan. Vereshchagin also had another purpose, as he later recalled: "I went to Turkestan by chance, and till now I don't know whether it was the right thing to do. Probably, it was. I went there, however, because I wanted to learn of the real nature of war, of which I had read and heard, and to which I was so near in the Caucasus."[6]

In August 1867, he set out on the long journey to Turkestan, where his work and military experiences would prove to be a turning point in his artistic development and world view. As in the Caucasus, he quickly became deeply immersed in and absorbed by the little-known, strikingly diverse civilization rich in history; he cultivated a rapport with the local inhabitants in order to conquer their fear of being sketched. His account of his activities in Samarkand—once the magnificent capital of the dreaded Mongol conqueror, Tamerlane (1336–1405)—is typical of his daily routine: "I rode about the town and outside of it everyday, inspecting the mosques, bazaars and schools, especially the older mosques, among which some remarkable specimens still remained. There was so much material for study and sketching that it was difficult to decide which I should begin with; the scenery, buildings, costumes, faces and manners, were new, original and interesting."[7]

In Turkestan, Vereshchagin's art became technically more mature and vital. It began to breathe a harmony of color and tone, spatial depth and perspective. His output, especially in Tashkent, was prolific, entailing more than 250 sketches and 30 paintings. There may be classified into four basic categories: (1) studies of the basic religious and cultural features of Asiatic society and its ethos, which entailed rampant, organized, "professional" begging, as well as cruelty, debauchery, slavery, and the subjugation of women; (2) sketches or portraits of characteristic types of the region's diverse nationalities; (3) studies of the ruins of ancient monuments which reflected magnificent architecture and a high culture; and (4) military battles between the Russian and Moslem armies. Some of these works will be discussed below.

Vereshchagin was struck by the contrast between, on the one hand, the beauty of the Turkestan landscape, the fierce, resolute, proud character of the people, the graceful architectural forms, the exquisitely colored costumes, the natural bond between man and nature, and, on the other, the fanaticism, poverty, cruelty, and barbarism that permeated that life. This paradox emerges graphically in the Turkestan series.

By May 1868, after some eight months in Turkestan, Vereshchagin had yet to witness military battle. While Kaufman's army advanced toward Samarkand, Vereshchagin remained behind to work in a village and learned that the Emir of Bukhara planned to wage there a "holy war" against the Russian army. Vereshchagin could not resist the urge to witness the war. Joining a small detachment of men, he "immediately abandoned the village" and sought to join Kaufman in Samarkand; when he approached the city in early May, Vereshchagin was horrified by the carnage, especially the numerous scattered headless corpses of soldiers and horses that had yet to be cleared from the battlefield. Kaufman had already captured Samarkand and had liberated some ten thousand slaves of the ruling Moslem hierarchy.[8]

As Kaufman prepared to leave Samarkand with most of his forces to engage the Emir of Bukhara elsewhere, the soldiers of another khanate arrived in Samarkand and united with the local population to storm and recapture the Russian fortress. Vereshchagin witnessed the religious frenzy that the mullahs were capable of arousing in the local population. He brought this to Kaufman's attention, but the general assigned no significance to it prior to his departure and left a detachment of some five hundred soldiers, along with two hundred civilians (Russian administrative personnel, merchants, Jews, Hindus, Persians, and Tatars), to garrison the fortress. On June 2, tens of thousands of Moslem forces began to encircle the Russian fortress.[9]

On the following morning, the pandemonium and gunfire of the raging battle found Vereshchagin drinking tea in the fortress; as soon as he realized that his own head was at stake, he rushed to the fortress wall, seized a rifle from a dead Russian soldier, and took part in the ensuing six-day battle to repel the attack. He offered his services as a "common volunteer" and refused to serve as an officer. During the battle, six couriers were beheaded as they rode to apprise Kaufman of the attack and of the dwindling Russian forces and their lack of supplies; after some four days of battle, one courier finally broke through. After the second day, one hundred and fifty Russian solders and probably thousands of Moslems were lost. Moslem efforts to penetrate the fortress by explosives and stones were repelled by hand grenades. The Russians withstood the attacks and undertook an offensive, raiding and setting fire to the enemy's dwellings, the shops of a large bazaar near the fortress, and the mosque that served as a Moslem stronghold. Despite the enormous disparity in forces, the superior training, weapons, and discipline of the Russian troops ultimately prevailed over the massive, frenzied onslaughts of the Moslems. When the Moslem soldiers learned of Kaufman's victory over the Emir of Bukhara, they realized their cause was hopeless and the frequency and severity of their attacks decreased. Kaufman returned to Samarkand on June 7 and later plundered the city in retaliation.[10]

In the defense of the fortress, Vereshchagin was always in the forefront of battle, where his courage and leadership proved to be a genuine inspiration to the Russian soldiers; he was the first to be awarded the Cross of St. George for outstanding bravery. In one instance, a stone flung into the fortress struck his leg and drew considerable blood, but he concealed the injury because he was ashamed to show others that he had been wounded by a stone. Vereshchagin engaged in hand-to-hand combat in several raids beyond the fortress. Twice he was outnumbered, but his cries for help saved him from "certain death." In two separate instances, gunshots dislodged his hat and his rifle during combat. Perhaps at this point the "charm in danger," as Tolstoy described it in "Sevastopol in December," had firmly and permanently gripped Vereshchagin:

> At the moment when you know that a missile is flying at you, you will surely realize that this shot is going to kill you. But the feeling of self-love sustains you, and no one will notice the knife that is piercing your heart. But when the shot has flown by without having touched you, you revive, and a certain joyous, inexpressibly pleasant feeling overwhelms you, but only momentarily, so that you discover a special kind of charm in danger in this game of life and death. You want a cannonball or a bomb to strike closer and closer to you.[11]

In the course of the battle, Vereshchagin took part in pursuit of a detachment of Moslem troops who were beheading dead Russian soldiers on the field; later, he participated in the process of identifying the corpses by their physiques and the documents they carried. After several days of battle, the accumulation of putrefying dead soldiers and horses near the fortress walls emitted an unbearable stench and posed a serious health hazard to the Russian soldiers. Most of the men refused to touch the bloated corpses, but Vereshchagin and a few others performed the grim, nauseating task of loading them on bullock carts for removal.[12] Vereshchagin had at last witnessed and experienced the "real nature of war"; it was not the glamour, pomp, glory, and ceremony that he had imagined.

After Kaufman reestablished Russian control of Samarkand, he warmly thanked Vereshchagin for his exemplary role in the defense of the fortress. Some Russian soldiers believed that "if not for Vereshchagin, Samarkand would have been lost." Vereshchagin, however, "considered it his obligation to tell Kaufman that the general opinion of the soldiers was that he [Kaufman] had *left without securing the fortress.*" One member of general staff advised Kaufman to execute Vereshchagin for his scandalous insinuation. Vereshchagin's remark, however, did not affect his friendship with Kaufman. He emphatically rejected Kaufman's offer of a military decoration; but the general, on his own initiative, recommended Vereshchagin for the award of the Cross of St. George, which he received from an independent commission. Later, however, the Russian government awarded him the Cross of St. Stanislav, which he refused to accept.[13]

In late 1868, Vereshchagin brought all of his Turkestan works to Paris, which was, along with Munich, a major center of the art world at the time. One can only speculate that he went to Paris with a view to creating an exhibition; but either his contacts there were inadequate or his works were not considered of sufficient interest or merit to justify one. He was, however, able to publish some of his sketches in two French journals. The early stages of an artist's career are marked by the constant need for promotion, recognition by his peers, and money to undertake further work until a financial base is established; it was these factors that compelled Vereshchagin to cultivate influential contacts in Russia. Fortunately, however, he received his share of the family estate from his father, who did not want his children to wait until his death to divide his holdings. Vereshchagin sold a large piece of this property, which provided enough money to enable him to complete his paintings in Paris.[14]

When Vereshchagin learned that General Kaufman would be in St. Petersburg in early 1869, he returned to Russia and arranged, with Kaufman's active support, a month-long exhibition of his paintings and his sketches of ethnographic types along with zoological and mineralogical specimens and a wide range of artifacts he collected in Turkestan. Vereshchagin's works arrested the most attention and interest. Of the three paintings that he exhibited, one—*The Opium Eaters* (1868; see Fig. 4)—he would later give to Kaufman, who in turn would present it to a grand princess, and two—*After Victory* (1868; see Fig. 2) and *After Defeat* (1868; see Fig. 3)—were presented to General Alexander Geins of the military staff in Turkestan. Geins, who became Vereshchagin's business manager in 1874, would later give them to Tsar Alexander II, who put them on permanent display in his study. Three smaller works were sold privately.[15]

The principal purpose of the exhibition was to acquaint the Russian public with the little-known civilization and region of Central Asia. There can be little doubt that the exhibition heightened Kaufman's military reputation and reflected a major territorial conquest by the Russian tsar. This marked Vereshchagin's first official Russian exhibition; the press reacted in uniformly favorable terms, thus establishing his "wide popularity." The reviews emphasized Vereshchagin's vivid and faithful portrayal of the various nationalities of Turkestan and the technical features of his works, but they failed to realize the significance of *After Victory* and *After Defeat,* the forerunners of Vereshchagin's daring onslaught on and denunciation of war. Tsar Alexander II and his wife visited the exhibition on opening day. He was so impressed by those two paintings that he asked Kaufman to introduce him to the artist, but Vereshchagin declined and instructed Kaufman to tell the tsar that he was ill. Perhaps he was reluctant to observe the custom of kissing the tsar's hands and shoulders, or perhaps he did not want to be urged to return to the Academy of Arts, which consciously sought to attract disaffected artists after the student revolt in 1863. Two years later, the tsar sought to commission, through the academy, an extensive series of paintings, but Vereshchagin realized he could not fulfill the terms within the stipulated time of less than five years, and no specific agreement was reached.[16]

The three paintings noted above invite brief discussion. Two are scenes of the battle of the Samarkand fortress; the third depicts a depressing feature of life in Turkestan, the widespread use of opium. The battle-scene paintings are contrasting studies in reactions to death in combat. *After Victory* (Fig. 2) emphasizes the barbarism that follows death in war: two Moslem soldiers have been touring the battlefield, searching for dead Russian soldiers to behead. Here, after such atrocity, a soldier and his partner, who holds a sack to contain the gory collection, contemplate their trophy with keen interest, for it will bring them a reward, usually in the form of clothing. A small flock of ravens in the background—a staple of Vereshchagin's battle paintings—feeds on the remains of the bodies. The painting is competently and effectively executed and evinces great technical control of color, tone, and harmony. *After Defeat* (Fig. 3) is inseparable from *After Victory,* although it is better integrated and far more subtle in conception, design, and execution. At first glance, it seems to be a simple battle scene, but deeper examination reveals the extent to which Vereshchagin had succeeded in embodying his ideas in art. In contrast to *After Victory,* this painting stresses the callous attitude of Russian soldiers toward death. Two piles of dead Moslem soldiers, shot as they attempted to penetrate the fortress, lie randomly alongside its internal wall. The white cap in the left foreground probably belongs to the Russian who lies dead behind the soldier nonchalantly lighting his pipe in the immediate foreground. In the left background three Russian soldiers stand deep in discussion, entirely indifferent to the horror around them; they seem to be taking pause before the next attack on the fortress. Death is so prevalent that it becomes a commonplace of life. The fortress walls tower over the living and the dead, perhaps suggesting man's capability of descending to lower forms of human life. In their moral and singular insight into its deadening nature, both paintings express Vereshchagin's penetrating reflections on war. War not only suspends morality and civilized behavior but also life for both the vanquished and the victors. War entails a double death: the unfortunate die physically, while the survivors, in their total lack of humanity for the fate of their fellow man, suffer another form of death.

The Opium Eaters (Fig. 4) based on Vereshchagin's observations in Central Asia, is a brilliant psychological study in human degradation. Seeking escape from their misery, six outcasts in tattered clothing sit in a

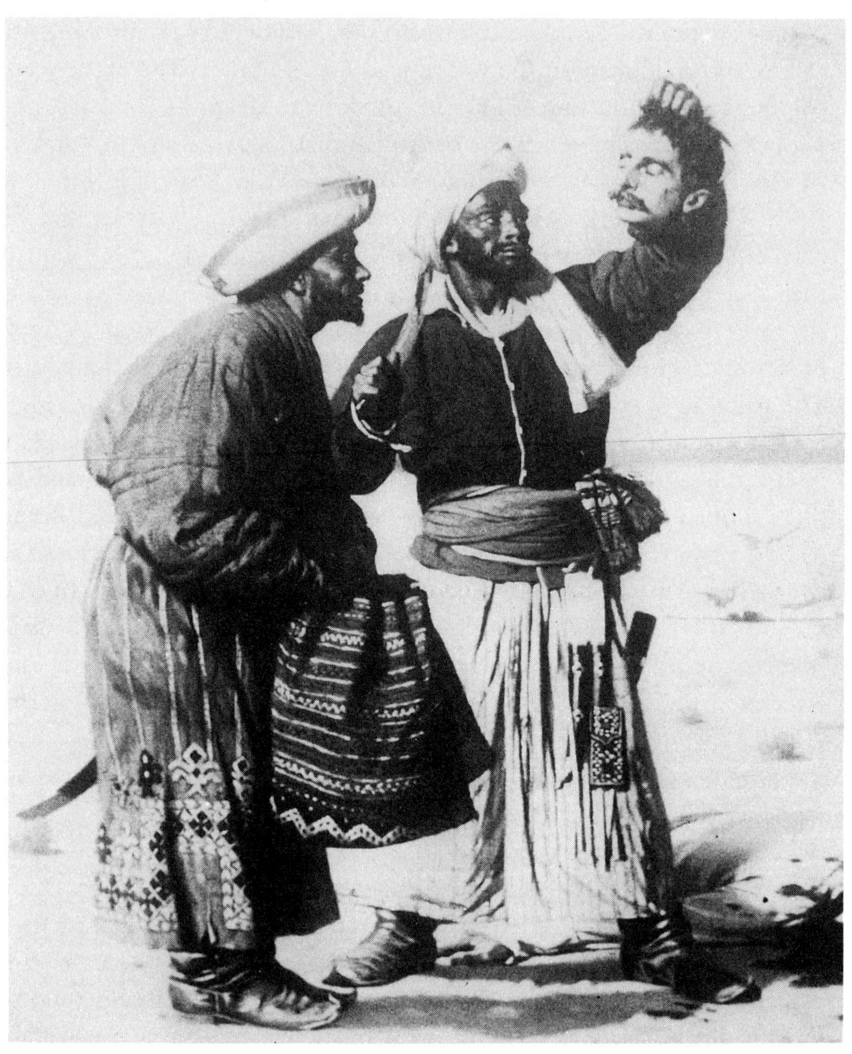

Figure 2. *After Victory.* 1868. 46.5 × 32.5 cm. By permission of the Russian Museum, St. Petersburg.

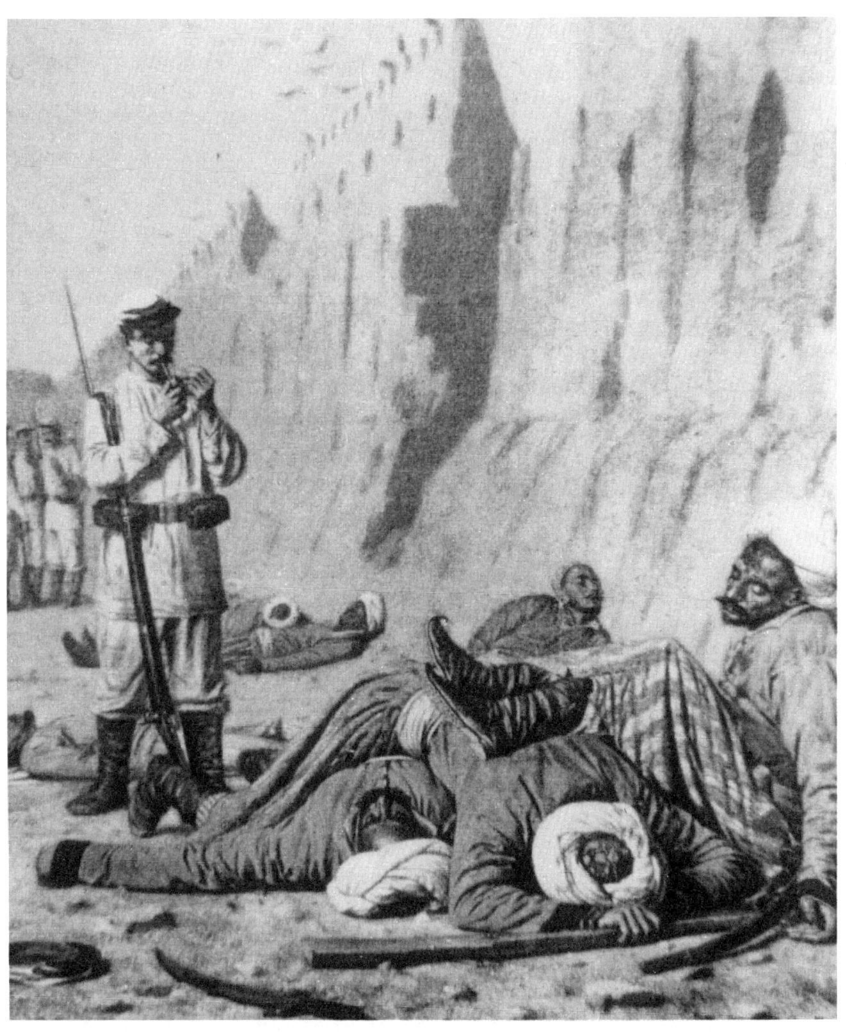

Figure 3. *After Defeat*. 1868. By permission of the Russian Museum, St. Petersburg.

street den, experiencing the effects of opium. Two have already reached oblivion as they bury their heads in their folded arms. With his eyes partly open, the figure at the extreme left sinks into a stupor, awaiting the final stage with his arms prepared to receive his slumping head. The figure on the extreme right is in the early stages of stupefaction; his hands rest on his knees, and his expression reflects a certain comfort, a relief from his tragically helpless life. In the center the oldest of the group peers outside the den, and seems as yet only slightly affected by the drug. To his left, sits the youngest figure, whose eyes and lips express the sweet, dreamy stage of oblivion. In 1871, Vereshchagin submitted the three above-mentioned paintings for the International Art Exhibit in London. One newspaper called Vereshchagin "a great talent," "the Russian Gérôme," and described his two battle paintings as "sensational" and "extraordinarily executed."[17]

Vereshchagin's contacts with the Russian military created an opportunity for him to return to Turkestan in 1869 for additional artistic work; he held the civilian rank of "collegiate registrar" and was under the jurisdiction of General G. A. Kolpakovsky, governor-general of the Semireche region of Turkestan. The journey led through Siberia, where Vereshchagin witnessed the harsh, cruel conditions endured by Russian political exiles and criminals in Russian prison camps. There is no evidence that he painted Russian prison life, and it is doubtful that he would have been allowed to. With Tashkent as his base of operations, he traveled to Kokand, Samarkand, and other areas during his stay in Turkestan from 1869 to 1870.

In the summer of 1869, Vereshchagin was, for the first time, in the Semireche region (of what is now Kirghiziia and Kazakhstan) near the Chinese border. Here he resumed his artistic activity, sketching homes, temples, and the local inhabitants. He also crossed the Chinese border to visit various locales, particularly Chuguchak, a city of striking architectural monuments. There he painted two splendid works (*Ruins in Chuguchak* [1869] and *Ruins of the Theater in Chuguchak* [1869]) of a magnificent monument and theater which had recently been destroyed in a religious uprising of the Taranchis (Uygurs) and Dungans (Chinese Muslims) against the Chinese rulers.

The region near the Chinese border posed a double danger to the Rus-

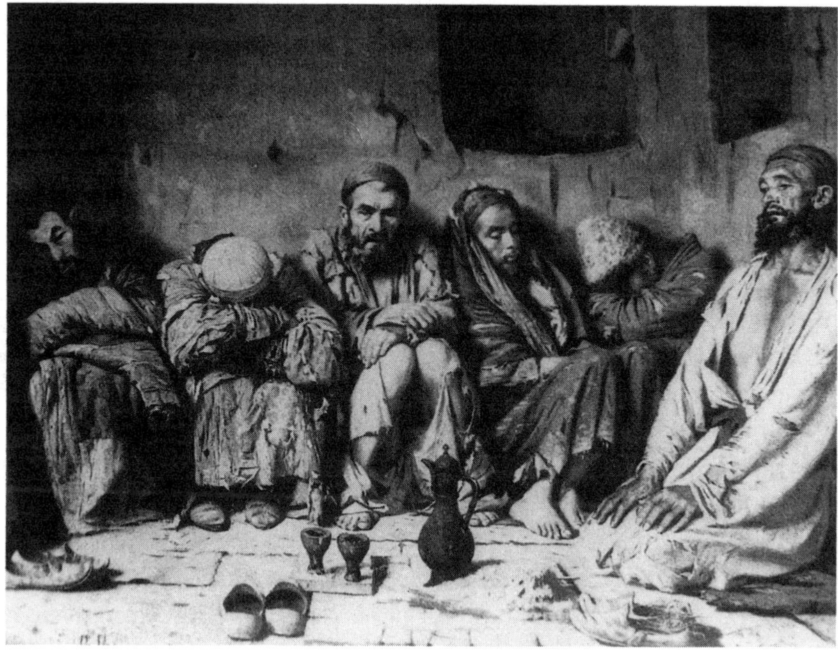

Figure 4. *The Opium Eaters.* 1868. Oil on canvas. 40 × 47 cm. Museum of the Arts of the Uzbek Republic, Tashkent.

sian settlement: the frequent clashes between feuding tribes, khanates, and Chinese nomads; and the numerous wild animals, especially tigers.

The border clashes affected Russian territories inhabited by the Kirghiz and Kazakh population. The Chinese Sultan of Kuldja often incited the local population to plunder and murder Russian soldiers and administrative personnel and to steal livestock from the Kirghiz, Kazakh, and Taranchi settlers in Russian territories. In response to these sporadic strikes, a small detachment of Russian soldiers—about one hundred cavalry of Siberian Cossacks and sixty infantry soldiers—was formed after receiving an order to stage a counter-raid across the Chinese border in late 1869. Its purpose was to capture the livestock of the nomadic Chinese population and thus discourage it from further raids in Russian territory. Although still recovering from a bout of fever, Vereshchagin joined the detachment to observe Chinese life, dwellings, and monuments and to discover new subjects for his art. Two later paintings—*Surprise Attack*

(1871; see Fig. 8), and *Encircled! They Are Pursuing* (1872; see Fig. 9)—were based directly on his experiences in the raid.

The troops reached a Chinese village and rounded up several thousand head of livestock, but during the raid, "the spirit of destruction gripped" the Russian cavalry. They plundered homes and looted trivial belongings; what they could not bring back they destroyed. As the detachment returned to the Russian border, it encountered a large number of Chinese soldiers and members of the local population utterly enraged by the loss of their livestock and belongings. They began to surround the Russian cavalry and infantry to prevent them from herding the animals across the border. The recovery of their livestock, and not necessarily the extermination of the Russian soldiers, was the primary objective of the Chinese. In the panic and fury of the fray, a Russian platoon was put on the defensive for fear of being slaughtered, a fate one Cossack suffered before their eyes. Outnumbered, one group of Russians retreated in panic. Vereshchagin, on horseback, rushed to stop them and was struck in the head by a lance, but it slid off the smooth fur of his cap. As the battle progressed, he and several soldiers became separated from the detachment and were attacked. In his defensive maneuvers, Vereshchagin was unseated from his horse as it stumbled over the body of the commander, who had been knocked unconscious. Vereshchagin managed to hold the bridle in one hand and, with revolver in the other, repelled the soldiers, who were armed with sabres and lances. Believing that Vereshchagin's revolver was inexhaustible after four rounds of fire, his pursuers took flight. Vereshchagin's self-defense also saved the life of the unconscious commander. Ultimately, the Russians survived the attack and returned to their own territory with their large bounty.[18] Vereshchagin had once again become a hero to the Russian military.

After he returned to St. Petersburg in 1870, he received a letter from General Kaufman offering him a three-year subsidy to settle in Munich and bring to fulfillment his Turkestan experiences and artistic production; this resulted in an album published in London in 1873 and in St. Petersburg in 1874. According to Kaufman's letter, the purpose of Vereshchagin's work in Munich was "to acquaint the civilized world with the life of a little-known people and to enrich learning with materials important for the study of the region."[19] That Vereshchagin's art would be used to justify the Russian conquest of Central Asia is implicit in the letter, or at least that was what Kaufman expected from a military hero. Working in Munich appealed to Vereshchagin because he had repeatedly failed to make any progress in Paris. West European recognition of his art would be the standard of achievement and would enhance the success of his exhibitions in Russia. He thus sought to establish new contacts with prominent artists in the German art capital, especially with Alexander E. Kotzebue (1815–99), an academic historical and battle painter who received commissions from the Russian autocracy; with Jozef Brandt (1841–1915), an outstanding Polish historical and animal painter, and with Theodor Horschelt (1829–71), a battle and animal painter whose studio he rented shortly after Horschelt's death. That space was not entirely suitable for his work, and Vereshchagin rented an additional studio with full exposure to sunlight for the creation of his landscape and other paintings. Probably the greatest attraction in Munich was a German woman, Elisabeth Marie Fischer, whom he had met previously and whom he married shortly after he settled there. She served as Vereshchagin's secretary, aide, and companion on many expeditions and journeys to the Himalayas and India until the late 1880s, when they were divorced on grounds of incompatibility.[20]

Vereshchagin spent two years in Munich, intensively working and reflecting on his artistic production in preparation for forthcoming exhibitions. During that period, Pavel M. Tretiakov, a Moscow industrialist and art patron, visited Vereshchagin's studio and expressed an interest in buying the Turkestan paintings. He would later purchase many of Vereshchagin's paintings, extend loans to him, and correspond with him about acquiring his works.

In April 1873, Vereshchagin held his first one-man exhibition—of the Turkestan works—in the Crystal Palace in London. The exhibition coincided with alarm in the British press and Parliament over Russia's rapid conquest of Central Asia. The press agreed "on the expediency of maintaining an expectant and vigilant policy," including the suggestion that Britain establish "certain military positions which might be useful in the contingency of war." Despite the pledges of the Russian government that its presence in Central Asia posed no threat to British interests in Persia and Afghanistan, whose ruler, the Emir of Kabul, was a British ally, for the

British it was "rather an intellectual pastime than a political proceeding to inquire whether the possible civilization of barbarous tribes compensates for the unwelcome vicinity to India of a formidable rival." If, however, the assurances of the Russian government were genuine, its conquest of Central Asia, like the British conquest of India, was legitimate, since both were a "part of the scheme of Providence for civilizing and enriching the East; and therefore a scheme in which overweening ambition, or mere love of conquest and supremacy, can have no place." There was another potential source of conflict between the two countries: Russia's capture of new markets and sources of supply threatened the supremacy of British economic interests.[21]

Vereshchagin's exhibition became directly and perhaps uniquely involved in the political tensions between Britain and Russia and would partly fulfill his commitment to, or confirm the expectation of, the Russian military to allay strong British suspicions of Russian military intentions in Central Asia. One of the conditions he set for the large exhibition was that none of his works—13 paintings, 81 studies, 133 sketches—was for sale, probably because he planned to exhibit them together in Russia or because of the tsar's or Tretiakov's interest in them. In the introduction to the exhibition catalogue, Vereshchagin crafted a subtle statement of Russian foreign policy: "The barbarism of the Central Asian population is so apparent, its economic and social situation is so low that the sooner European civilization, from one side or another, penetrates that region the better. If these faithful sketches help to dispel the doubts of the English public concerning their real friends and neighbors in Central Asia, the difficulties of the journey and the exhibit will be more than rewarded."[22] The implication is clear: Russian colonization was analogous to, or identical with, that of the British, and thus Russia posed no danger to the "tranquility of India" and other countries.[23]

The British press devoted rather extensive coverage to the exhibition. It was highly laudatory of the "artistic value rather than missionary purpose of his exhibition which makes us advise our readers to go and see it." Vereshchagin impressed the British public by adding eighteen works to the show during its tenure from April to the summer of 1873. His exhibition also eased some of the explicit doubts about Russia's motives in Central Asia: "The public mind is still sufficiently strong in regard of all that concerns the confines of Russian and British ascendancy in the East to make of the present a timely moment for M. Wereschagin's exhibition." Vereshchagin's works had introduced the English public to "an absolutely new world. They are not like anything that has ever before been seen in England; they stand alone in their beauty and barbarism." This same reviewer commented on the numerous sketches of the Central Asian nationalities: "Mr. Wereschagin is a draughtsman of as much spirit and insight as fidelity; and in these heads he has given the ethnographer and physiognomist a set of documents such as within their range are probably without parallel." His works also evinced a "certain savagery" and the tangible influence of Gérôme and the Munich school. Vereshchagin, however, painted in his own manner and would, "if we mistake not, make for himself a name in Europe." The excessive, appalling brutality and cruelty of the battle paintings, however "eminently picturesque," also reflected "a certain rude vigour which is not Bavarian, but semi-barbaric and Russian."[24] Although most of the reviews stressed the amplitude of Asiatic barbarism, none dealt with the "real nature" of war. If Vereshchagin hoped to instill revulsion against it, he accomplished little; but he did establish himself in Europe as an artist of unmistakable talent and promise.

The barbarism that so repelled the English spectators is vividly portrayed in *Presenting the Trophies* (1872; Fig.5) and its sequel, *Rejoicing* (1872; Pl. 3). In the former, a small group of Moslem warriors has placed a collection of blackened Russian heads between two pillars for inspection by the Emir of Bukhara and his retinue; for their grisly offering, the soldiers will be rewarded with robes. The scene is the courtyard of a magnificent palace, its exquisitely carved columns and ceilings brilliantly captured in all their colors and minute details. The famous throne of Tamerlane is visible between the second and third pillars. The mullahs maintain a critical distance as if afraid to come too close to the gruesome collection of trophies that is so incongruous in relation to the surroundings; they passively look on as the emir inspects a head, which he has randomly rolled off the pile like a ball with his left foot. The stench of the blackened heads forces one mullah to cover his nose. Once again the heights of human creativity and imagination, as expressed in the structural splendor and

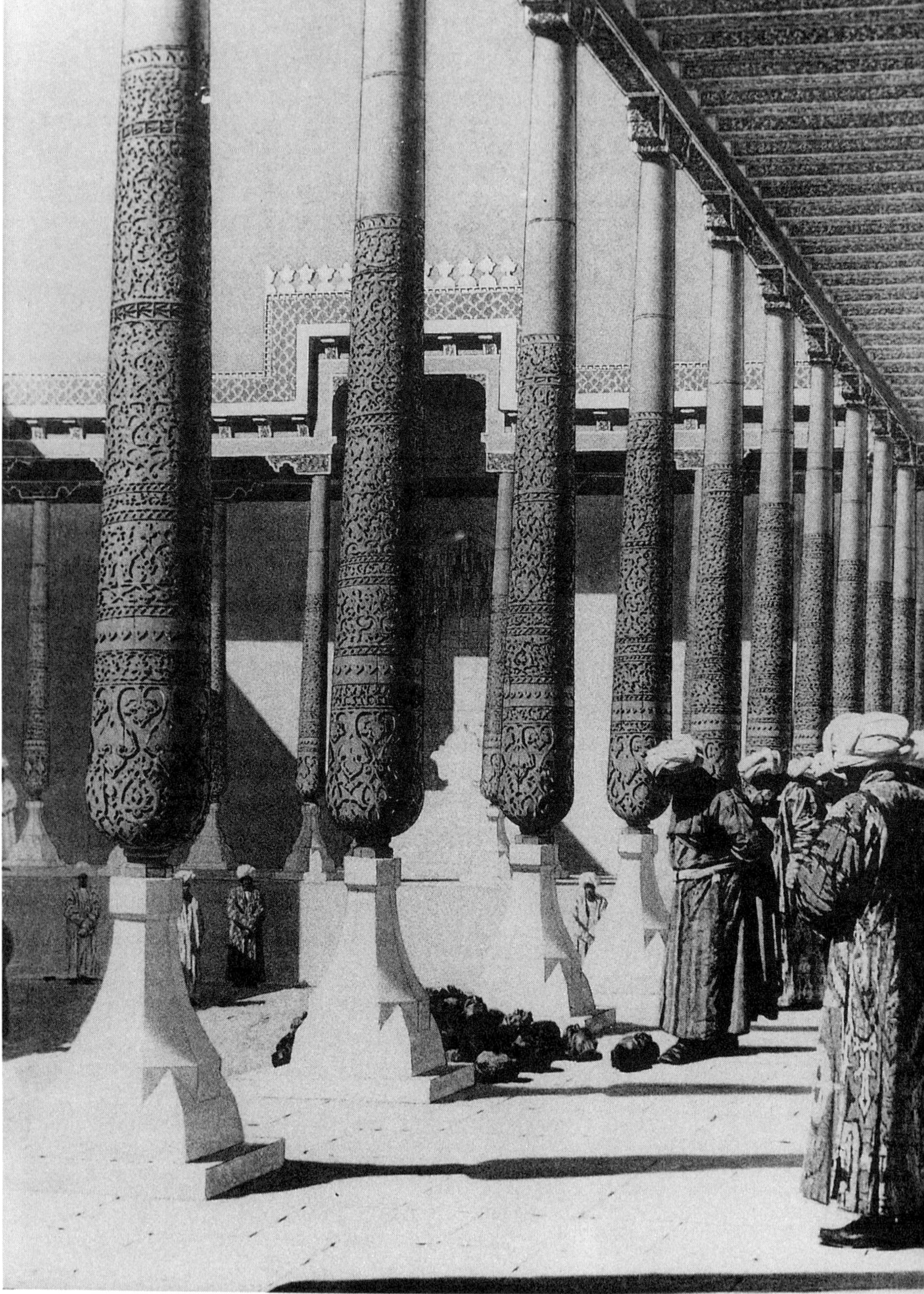

grace of the palace architecture, are contrasted to the depths of human barbarism.

Rejoicing takes place in Registan, the central square of Samarkand, and depicts the people giving thanks in front of the decaying Shir-Dar Mosque with its minarets, melon-shaped domes, and geometrically patterned facade. Flanking tigers on the upper facade of the mosque perhaps reflect Chinese influence. In the center of the painting, one mullah grips a pole, one of the ten on which a Russian head is mounted; he seizes the attention of the crowd, whipping it into a frenzy for a holy war against the infidel Russians. The figure on a gray horse in the right foreground may be a warrior chief. Levels of the Moslem social hierachy are portrayed in planes of ascending importance; several mendicant dervishes sit and stand in the foreground with their collection boxes and observe the ritual. The well-balanced, integrated painting cogently conveys the diverse colors of the Orient; extraordinary spatial depth lends it a mass character. These two works, as well as many others that portray abject poverty, the institutionalized forms of begging, and human degradation, are very convincing.

One other painting, *The Selling of the Child Slave* (1872; Fig. 6), is worthy of note for its depiction of the darker corners of Central Asian life and for Vereshchagin's technical mastery of chiaroscuro. The servant of a wealthy old man has opened the door to admit a flood of sunlight that illuminates the scene. The old man wears an opulent yellow robe and a thick, twisted beaklike turban that gives him the appearance of a predatory bird. Facing him is the principal object of the transaction, a handsome young boy, of probably five or six, who has been stripped of his clothing for the old man's scrutiny. The tragically helpless boy, whose nakedness contrasts with the heavy garments of the old man and the slave dealer, unwittingly participates in the examination. With arms slightly outstretched, he looks curiously at the old man, who plays with a string of beads while he awaits the slave dealer's reply to his offer. The old man fixes lustful eyes on the boy's beautiful body, but he is niggardly and has not offered the slave dealer enough. The dealer, in green, brown and blue

Figure 5. *Presenting the Trophies.* 1872. Oil on canvas. 240 × 171 cm. Tretiakov Gallery, Moscow.

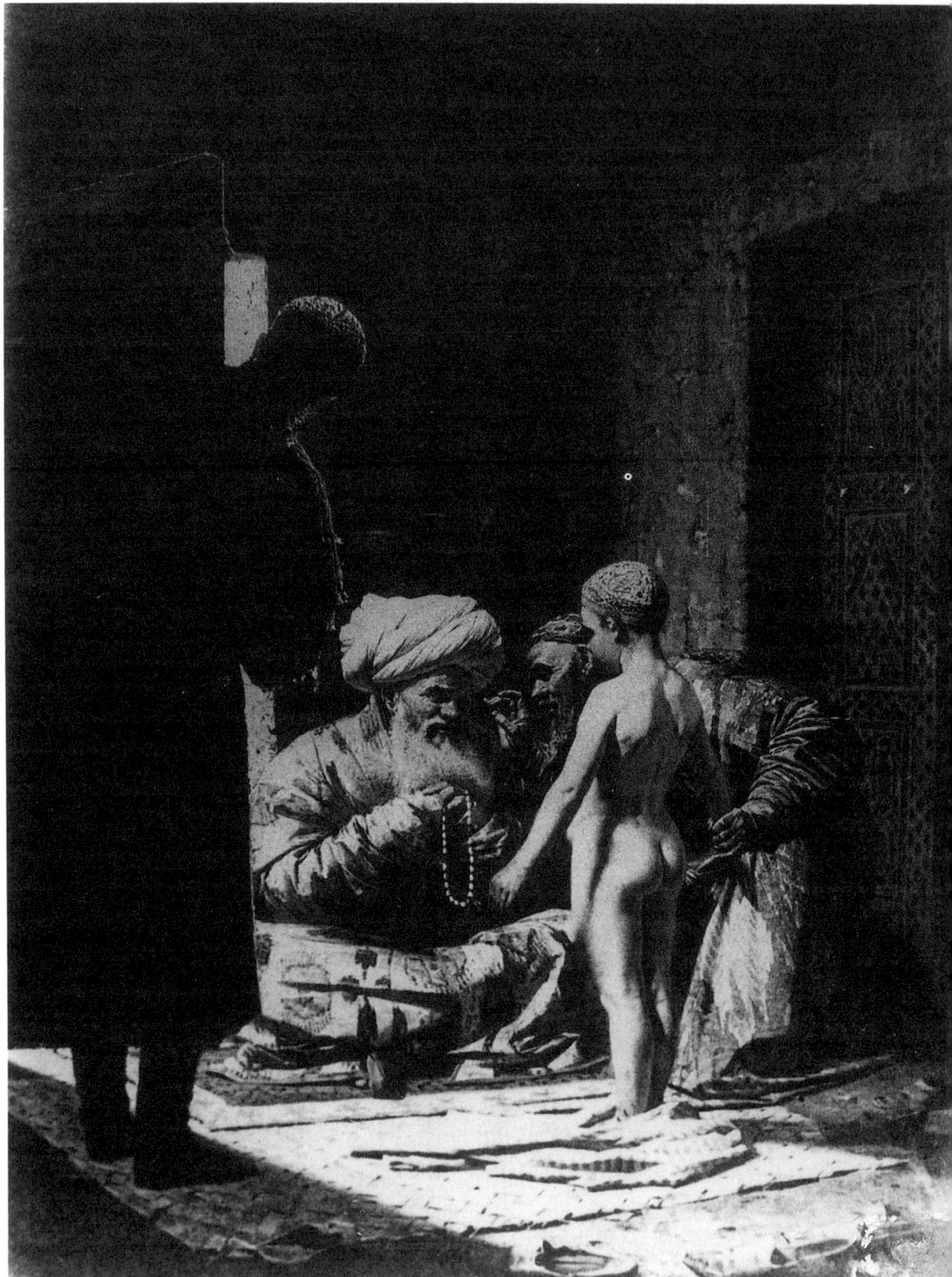

robes, sits between the old man and the child and is a tough bargainer. He seems to understand the old man's weakness—lust will triumph over his miserliness—as he whispers to him, perhaps emphasizing the quality and purity of his product. His firm grasp of the boy's right hand suggests that he will not part with him easily. He gestures with his right hand, bringing it within range of the old man's left eye without interrupting his lascivious gaze: the old man will have to pay somewhat more to consummate the deal.

Perhaps the most imaginative and penetrating work in the Turkestan series is *Doors of Tamerlane* (1872–73; Pl. 4). Tamerlane (1336–1405), the infamous medieval Oriental conqueror who attempted to restore the empire of Genghis Khan, left pyramids of human skulls as monuments to his numerous conquests. In the painting, Vereshchagin attempted to expose what he perceived to be the primary reason for the lack of human progress in Asia: the utterly blind devotion of the population to the despotic, arbitrary will of its rulers. Two heavily armed warriors in magnificent embroidered robes flank the richly carved imperial doors to the ruler's palace. They are not so much guarding the entrance as they are absurdly and tensely staring at it, prepared and eager at any moment to commit destruction at Tamerlane's bidding should he emerge. The doors are not merely symbols of Tamerlane's awesome military might and glory, but they also represent the Asiatic mind, which cannot conquer and transcend its own closed doors regarding the role of authority.

Warfare paintings are central to the Turkestan series, and two are directly germane to Vereshchagin's battle experiences in the defense of the Samarkand fortress. *By the Fortress Wall. Let Them Enter* (1871; Pl. 5) depicts a long row of Russian soldiers, waiting stealthily behind a fortress structure and ready with their rifles and sabres to engage the Moslems, whose voices and battle cries penetrate the fortress wall. The Russian commander, with sabre bared, is in the immediate foreground. Vereshchagin—who is crouching to his left—proposes that the charge be given to engage the enemy at the break in the wall before they enter the fortress. The commander rejects the suggestion with his left hand and

Figure 6. *The Selling of the Child Slave*. 1872. Oil on canvas. 123 × 92 cm. Tretiakov Gallery. Moscow.

whispers, "Sh, sh, let them enter." The painting is notable for its harmonious colors—the white uniforms of the soldiers against the trees and light blue sky—and subtle shades of sunlight on the fortress and the troops. The tension and anxiety of the moment—the sense of the enemy's presence—are captured in the effectively rendered pose and facial expressions of the men in the foreground, and particularly of the soldier who stands behind the drummer, gripping his left shoulder. The sequel to this painting, *By the Fortress Wall. They Have Entered* (1871; Fig. 7), is a contrast to the order, anticipation, and tension of battle readiness depicted in the former; it portrays the terrible disarray—death and suffering—that followed the assault on the fortress. The unity of death has replaced the unity of life for both the vanquished and victor. In the background a row of newly dead Russian soldiers are being carried away on stretchers for mass burial. In the immediate foreground lie the dead and wounded Moslems who penetrated the fortress wall; they will be the last to be carted away. A wounded man lies in the foreground; his right hand is raised, perhaps in a futile attempt to gain the attention of the three Russian soldiers on the ridge of the fortress wall above. One stands guard near the Russian flag, while the other two relax, casually smoking their pipes, in utter indifference to the dead and wounded immediately below. As Tolstoy observed in "Sevastopol in August," the survivors of war are guided by "the instinct of self-preservation and the desire to escape as speedily as possible from that dread place of death."[25]

During the first days of the defense of the Samarkand fortress, a Russian soldier hit by a bullet in the chest made an indelible impression on Vereshchagin, who reconstructed the event in *The Fatally Wounded Soldier* (1873; Pl. 6). The work, perhaps an original concept in battle paintings—which usually depict the fatally wounded simply lying dead on the battlefield—is an extraordinarily realistic and objective rendition of the process of suffering and death. The wounded man breaks from the ranks of those fiercely defending the fortress behind him, and swiftly reeling from unbearable pain, drops his rifle, grips his chest with both hands and lunges ahead with all his remaining strength to take his final few steps before he collapses. These instinctive steps mark his very last efforts to defy death, although he knows that his end has come. His mouth, face, and neck, distorted by pain, express the anguish that precedes his death;

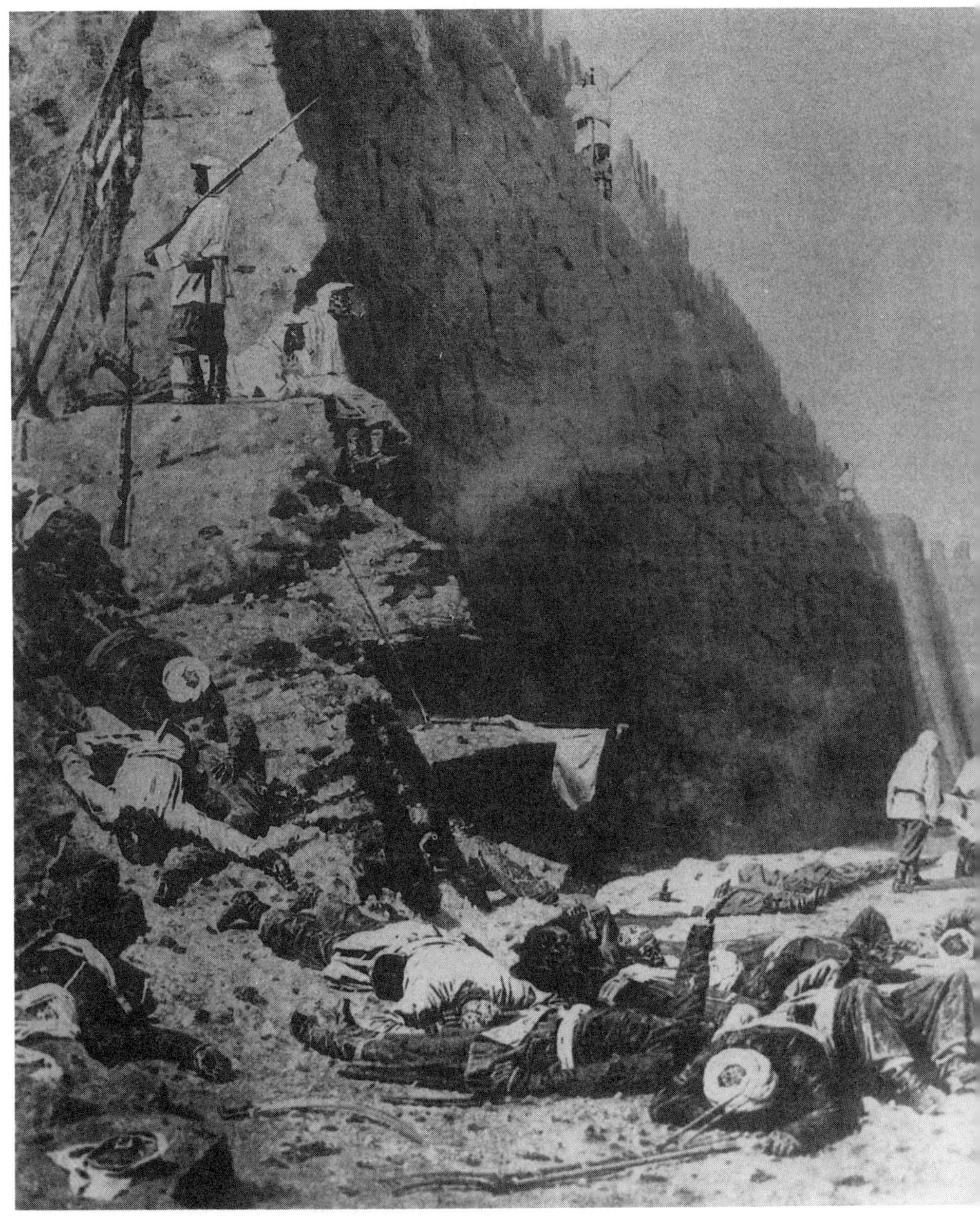

Figure 7. *By the Fortress Wall. They Have Entered*. 1871. Oil on canvas. Destroyed.

his eyes are fixed on the ground that awaits his final rest. A light-blue dusty screen heightens the drama of battle action in the background and, more importantly, isolates the soldier, allowing the viewer to focus on the psychological and physical scope of his tragic death.

Vereshchagin's participation in the Chinese border clash served as the basis of two paintings, *Surprise Attack* (1871; Fig. 8) and *Surrounded! They're Pursuing* (1872; Fig. 9), which he believed were most characteristic of a battle scene. On the frame of *Surprise Attack*, Vereshchagin inscribed: "We will perish. We will not disgrace the Russian land. We are not ashamed to be killed." The two paintings are remarkably similar in idea to Leo Tolstoy's own experiences of the Crimean War as recounted in the Sevastopol stories of the 1850s: they glorify the extraordinary courage, determination, and patriotism of the ordinary Russian soldier, and they condemn war. Vereshchagin could say, as Tolstoy did in the conclusion of "Sevastopol in May," that truth was the hero of his paintings. *Surprise Attack* concerns a detachment of Russian soldiers who are camped in a valley and are under secret observation by Moslem scouts. The Russians come under sudden attack by a horde of Moslem warriors on horseback. Five Russian soldiers have been cut down by sabres, and, in the right foreground, another is being struck. In the right center, two cover their heads with their arms in frightened anticipation of a strike. Six unarmed soldiers flee to take cover in a square of men hastily assembled for defense against the onslaught. Hopelessly outnumbered, they close ranks, heroically to resist to the last the onrushing Moslems. The Russian leader, with sabre drawn, looks out bravely and defiantly at the enemy, prepared to trade blows with the Moslems. Presumably, the leader's position is similar to that of Vereshchagin when he was under attack by Chinese warriors. In *Surrounded! They're Pursuing*, the courageous Russian detail has miraculously withstood the onslaught and has forced the Moslems to retreat at a considerable distance, where they will perhaps regroup. Despite its survival, the detachment seems to be in a more precarious defensive position: it has suffered casualties and, surrounded by the enemy, will not be able to resist another attack. Some ten soldiers encircle what remains of the square line of defense. One still shoots at the enemy; another, with rifle pointed upward, stands after firing it; another is on his knees reloading a rifle; to his left a wounded man crawls to obtain

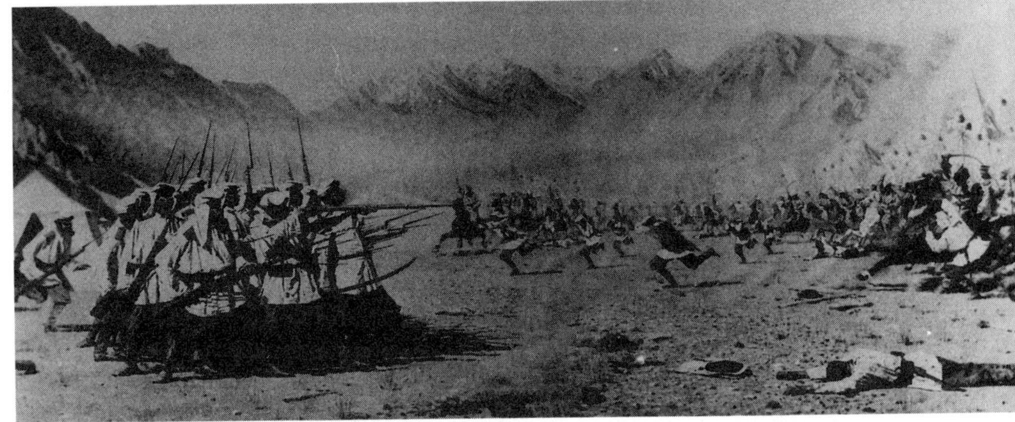

Figure 8. *Surprise Attack*. 1871. Oil on canvas. 82 × 206 cm. Tretiakov Gallery, Moscow.

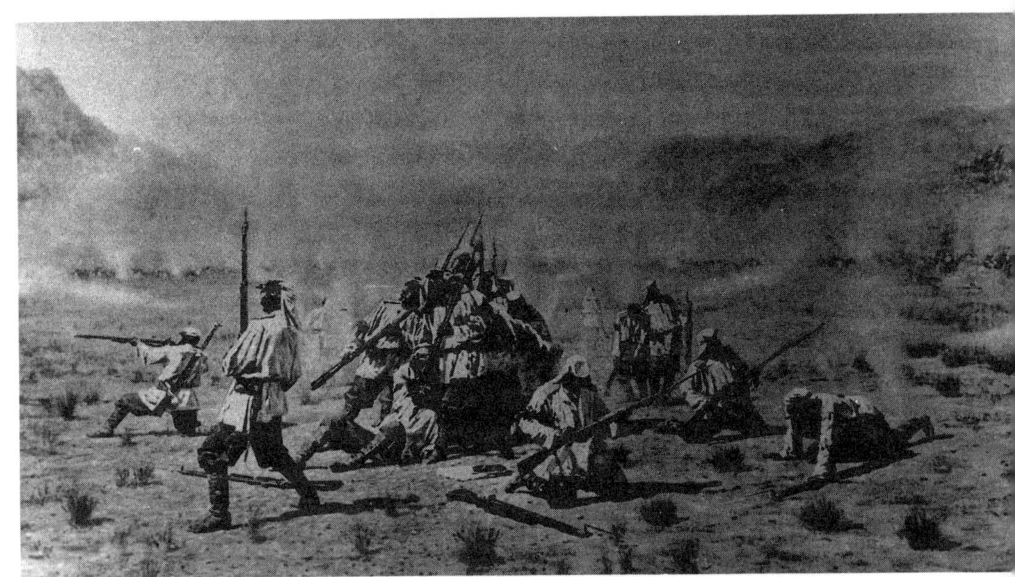

Figure 9. *Surrounded! They're Pursuing*. 1872. Destroyed.

another loaded rifle and then resume his battle position. The soldier behind him appears to be seeking a target. Another helps a wounded comrade return to the square, which has now become the second line of defense. In the background are several soldiers in various battle positions. The former square line of defense has diminished in numbers. Its wounded commander, supported and kept abreast of the course of events by the soldier at his side, still seems able to direct the defense. The various poses and positions of the men are vivid and realistic. Veiled by the dust raised by their own retreat, the Moslem warriors are barely visible in the background, but the positions of the Russian soldiers around the square realistically convey a sense of action, courage, and urgency as the desperate but heroic survivors prepare to take their last stand against another attack.

Two other paintings invite brief discussion for their significance in the Turkestan series. *The Forgotten Soldier* (1871; Fig. 10) created such a storm of controversy that eventually Vereshchagin felt compelled to destroy it. This portrays a little-known dimension of war, an artistic creation of a potential occurrence. Against a background of river, plain, and mountains a Russian soldier lies dead on a slight slope, having escaped notice when the dead were collected and buried after battle. Two eagles as well as a flock of ravens have come to devour him. One raven perched on his blood-stained chest seems to protest the unwelcome appearance of the eagles that will displace him from his discovery. A grave is visible in the extreme right background.

The essential idea that flows from the Turkestan series as a whole is embodied in *Apotheosis of War* (1871; Pl. 7), a work which perhaps confirms the Japanese proverb that "a general's victory rests on soldiers' bones."[26] With a sense of irony, Vereshchagin dedicated the work "to all great conquerors, past, present and future. This picture is not the creation of the artist's imagination—it is historically correct. Tamerlane and many other heroes raised such monuments on their battlefields, leaving the bones to be cleansed and whitened by the sun and rain, by wolves, jackals, and birds of prey."[27] The painting may be based on Tamerlane's conquest of the large city of Isfahan in central Persia in 1387. When the population rebelled against Tamerlane, he crushed the revolt by plundering the city and slaughtering seventy thousand people. A large pile of

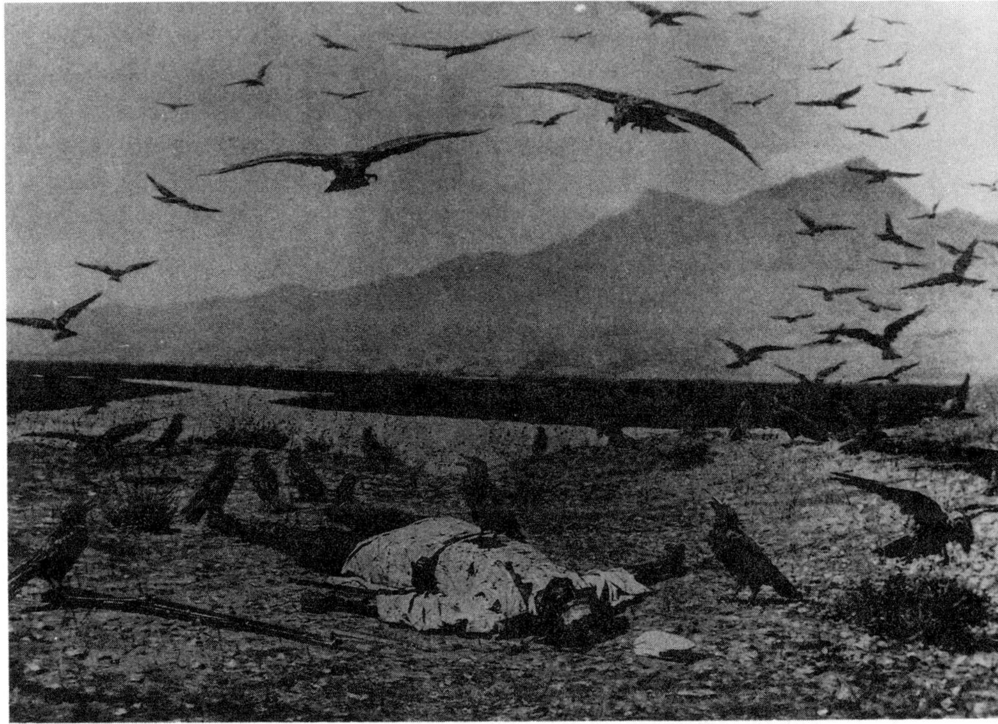

Figure 10. *The Forgotten Soldier.* 1871. Oil on canvas. Destroyed.

their skulls—collected as a monument to his victory—was left beyond the city. The ruling khanates continued this practice to Vereshchagin's times, and many of his studies of ruined Central Asian monuments also include small pyramids of skulls.

Apotheosis of War is notable for its starkness; nevertheless, its gruesome subject conveys the devastating results of war and human barbarism. That it can be interpreted as the aftermath of a nuclear or Nazi holocaust gives it a contemporary perspective. A pyramid of human skulls, some of which bear the marks of sabre blows, directly confronts and repels the viewer in all its horror. The sun-bleached skulls have become a permanent, integral feature of the landscape, as blending naturally into it. Ravens persist in their futile efforts to feed on the skeletal remains. In the background, a once-blossoming landscape, formerly filled with gardens and other evidence of human creativity, has been reduced to a wasteland, and, in the right background, the great city lies in ruins. A pale blue sky, shaded with white and brown, and the mountains successfully convey the interaction of light, air, and color. The work breathes an appeal for noble, constructive human endeavors and ends. Yet, in the context of the Turkestan collection, the painting poses a paradox: Vereshchagin disparaged barbarism and condemned war, but he justified war as a necessary evil—as part of the white man's burden—to eradicate barbarism. His support of war and of Russia's civilizing mission issued from his beliefs in the inevitability of historical progress through reason and science and in Russian cultural superiority to uncivilized peoples.

After the London exhibition Vereshchagin looked forward to exhibiting the Turkestan series in St. Petersburg and enlisted the support of his friend, Major General A. K. Geins, a military specialist on Turkestan and subsequently Vereshchagin's business manager, and of Vladimir V. Stasov (1824–1906), an art and music critic who vigorously advocated a native Russian art and critical realism. Stasov was also the ideological mentor of the Itinerants, who had revolted against the academy in 1863. Vereshchagin met Stasov in February 1874, after which a friendship and extensive correspondence followed until the beginning of the twentieth century. Stasov tried to fulfill in art criticism the highly significant role that the Russian literary critic Vissarion Belinsky (1811–48) played in Russian literature. Stasov's role in promoting and defending Vereshchagin's art in Russia cannot be overemphasized. He was the artist's invaluable colleague and aide, although they often had disagreements of various kinds over which they temporarily ceased to correspond with each other. Further, Stasov would often act on Vereshchagin's behalf during the latter's travels abroad.[28]

In December 1873, before he had made plans for the St. Petersburg exhibition, Vereshchagin sought permission to sever his military connection for "domestic reasons." He perhaps naively believed that his resignation would finally resolve the conflicting loyalties that had developed in his association with the Russian military and that his art would somehow be immune from its criticism after his resignation. The Russian military support implied a commitment to a favorable presentation of its conquest of Central Asia. In war, victory, not truth, is the overriding concern of generals. Vereshchagin no doubt defended that conquest and victory intellectually, but the demands of his art could not. He was probably aware of the ideological implications some of his paintings had for the military. Curiously, his request was not granted immediately, but he was given a leave of absence; the decision to accept his resignation was not reached until May 1874, when he was in Bombay, India.[29]

The exhibition, consisting of about 250 pieces, was held in the halls of the Ministry of Foreign Affairs; the lighting was very poor and lamps were required to illuminate the works. Vereshchagin received an unspecified honorarium for his exhibition. Admission was free, except on certain days, and the proceeds from those fees and the sale of some thirty thousand catalogues—which cost pennies and were subsidized by Vereshchagin—were designated for the construction of an elementary school in Novgorod and for the improvement of secular teaching. Vereshchagin planned to add five thousand rubles to that sum, hoping to set an example for others. One visitor to the exhibit remarked on the crowds that attended: "The exhibit attracted so many people that reinforced police detail and gendarmerie were called to duty, many times during which they were forced to lock the doors of the exhibit and to admit people in groups, for very long lines had formed at the entrance from morning to the very closing of the exhibit."[30]

If Vereshchagin's London exhibition was quite successful, the St. Petersburg show was an "unprecedented success," a "colossal phenomenon," as Ivan Kramskoy (1837–87)—the leader of the Itinerants—put it.[31] The Russian press was highly laudatory of the exhibition, but there was some criticism that Vereshchagin had brought disgrace to the Russian military and had slandered Russian soldiers by depicting their disarray and confusion in battle. The Russian writer Vsevolod M. Garshin (1855–88) and the composer Modest P. Mussorgsky (1839–81) were so moved that they dedicated a long poem and a ballad to Vereshchagin on *The Forgotten Soldier*. No doubt, Tsar Alexander II, his family, retinue, and General Kaufman and other members of the Russian military attended the exhibition during the opening days, eager to observe the results of Vereshchagin's three years of work and how it reflected the might, glory, and victory of the Russian army in Central Asia. Before the exhibition, Vereshchagin had asked Kaufman to inquire of the tsar's interest in acquiring the entire Turkestan series for one hundred thousand rubles. Tretiakov and another art collector, Dmitry P. Botkin, also expressed an interest in purchasing the entire Turkestan collection. Botkin apparently intended, however, to make a profit by buying the collection and then selling part of it to Tretiakov. Vereshchagin found this unacceptable and never negotiated with Botkin. Before his journey to India, Vereshchagin had refused a handsome offer for individual paintings in the Turkestan series.

Vereshchagin could not give Tretiakov a "positive response" until he knew if the Tsar wanted to acquire the works. In dealing with Tretiakov, to whom he preferred to sell the Turkestan series, Vereshchagin attached four conditions to the acquisition: that the series remain indivisible, that it be accessible to public exhibit in Russia, that it not be sent abroad, and that Vereshchagin retain exclusive right of photography.[32]

Kaufman introduced Vereshchagin to the tsar, whose personal examination of the exhibition was the moment of truth. On this occasion, perhaps Vereshchagin felt that his resignation from the military accorded him a large measure of independence in meeting the tsar. Although his family and retinue were ambivalent about the works, the tsar initially appeared to be delighted with the paintings as a whole. Since Kaufman was a strong supporter of Vereshchagin's art, the tsar was probably influenced by his comments and opinions on certain paintings. Kaufman, after he had seen the paintings, understood that at least four of them were fraught with dangerous consequences both at home and abroad, since they raised questions and even doubts about the Russian "civilizing mission" in and the conquest of Central Asia at such human cost to the Russians and the apparent military weakness of the Russian army in relation to the primitive Moslem forces. Russian soldiers viewing *The Forgotten Soldier* (see Fig. 10) perhaps wondered whether they, too, would suffer the same fate. As one observer put it: "What a grave state responsibility lay on the head of one man. A young lad who has seen these truthful battle scenes will hardly remain enthusiastic about military heroism and imagine war something like only bouquets of glory, decorations and such like."[33] That Russia's presence in Central Asia led to a pyramid of skulls and a wasteland was surely a justifiable conclusion to be drawn from *Apotheosis of War* (see Pl. 7). The Russian intelligentsia, dedicated to the destruction of the Russian autocracy, and the populist movement, dedicated to educating the Russian peasants about the evils of the system, could only draw ammunition from the exhibit.

On opening day, Vereshchagin followed Kaufman and the tsar and his retinue as they examined the paintings; the tsar asked Vereshchagin about the historical background of *Apotheosis of War*. When they stood before *The Forgotten Soldier*, the tsar "made a discontented grimace and with an expression of extreme displeasure in his voice" stated: "In my army such incidents cannot and could not happen."[34] As Vereshchagin recalled, Kaufman castigated him for fantastic renditions and inventions, for giving too much rein to his imagination, and forced Vereshchagin reluctantly to admit that he had never actually witnessed the scene of the forgotten soldier.[35] Vereshchagin had debased and dishonored the Russian soldier. Thereafter, the Russian censor forbade for twenty years any reproduction of *The Forgotten Soldier* in the press. Although Kaufman informed Vereshchagin that the tsar could not purchase "such a slander on the Russian army," it was rumored that the tsar would buy the entire Turkestan series as well as offer Vereshchagin an annual pension. This strongly suggested a position in the academy, in which Vereshchagin had no interest. The Russian military and bureaucracy questioned Vereshchagin's patriotism and mounted similar criticism against *Surprise Attack* (see Fig. 8) and *Surrounded! They're Pursuing* (see Fig. 9), which depicted Russian soldiers not in victory but in humiliation and ignominious defeat. On that same evening, Vereshchagin suffered an attack of nerves, became pale and almost unrecognizable, and wept; he had burned three of the paintings that had come under assault (*The Forgotten Soldier*; *Surrounded! They're Pursuing*; and *By the Fortress Wall. They Have Entered*). Subsequently, rumor spread in Russia and abroad that Vereshchagin had destroyed his works because they were not to the liking of the tsar and military circles. Destroying the paintings was the price he had to pay for his association with the Russian military and throne; it was probably his only alternative as he "became frightened of what would follow when they" tried to "muzzle" him with money and thus compromise his artistic integrity.[36] He found the rumor-ridden capital unbearable and, even before the exhibit ended in April, he and his wife, accompanied by attendants, servants, and loads of supplies and gifts, departed for India. Negotiations for the sale of the Turkestan paintings were left to Geins.

Interestingly, another exhibition of his paintings was held in Paris, primarily to raise funds, and was greeted with extraordinary enthusiasm.[37] After he realized the tsar's indecision about purchasing the works, Vereshchagin pursued Tretiakov's strong interest in them, but the two could not agree on the price. Vereshchagin could not wait for the tsar's final decision because he needed money to support his trip to India. In Vereshchagin's absence, Geins finalized the sale with Tretiakov on May 1, 1874, for ninety thousand rubles (payable in three yearly installments after an initial payment of forty thousand rubles). Tretiakov expanded his gallery to accommodate the collection after an art institution and society had refused it because of lack of space; eventually, he donated the works to the city of Moscow.

With Vereshchagin gone, the Russian government was rightly concerned about how civilians and military circles elsewhere would perceive Russian military might and readiness should Vereshchagin exhibit the Turkestan series abroad (as he later did in photographs). In an effort to counter that possibility, in late April 1874 the Russian Academy of Arts decided to confer on Vereshchagin a professorship for his "fame and particular works in his artistic pursuit"—the highest and most coveted position to which a Russian artist could aspire, since it accorded both prestige and wealth in the form of government and private commissions. The academy hoped to accomplish three objectives by its offer: to prevent Vereshchagin from exhibiting his Turkestan series abroad; to strike a blow against the growing influence and success of the Itinerants, with whom Vereshchagin had allied himself in early 1874; and to recover its predominant position in the art life of the country. When he learned in Bombay of the professorship, Vereshchagin wrote to Stasov to have him submit his reply not to the academy, which would have laid the matter to rest, but to a newspaper on September 11, 1874, for public notices: "I have been informed that the Imperial Academy of Arts has made me a professor. I regard all ranks and distinction in art as absolutely harmful and flatly reject the title."[38] The statement is as much a painful reflection of Vereshchagin's consequential connection with the military—"all ranks"—as it is a rejection of the academy's offer.

Stung and infuriated by Vereshchagin's tactless public insult and repudiation, the academy decided to retaliate. To be sure, it could have ignored Vereshchagin's refusal, but its hierarchy was also consumed by petty jealousy of the formidable success of his exhibition. As Tretiakov pointed out, Vereshchagin had suddenly emerged out of nowhere with a mass of paintings and had achieved both "fame and capital" through one exhibit, while other artists at the academy, however diligently and conscientiously they tried, were unable to produce anything of substance, and "behave deferentially with their superiors and wait for an academic and professorial rank like manna from heaven."[39]

About two weeks later, the academy hierarchy prompted one of its mediocre artists, the academician Nikanor Tiutriumov, to launch a slanderous attack on Vereshchagin; the allegations rallied the academy's critics—including Stasov and eleven Itinerant artists—to Vereshchagin's defense and effectively repudiated it. Tiutriumov asserted that Vereshchagin was quite adept at making "money, money and money" and at self-promotion by allowing free admission to the exhibition, selling catalogues at nominal cost, and destroying "two" paintings. His unprecedented rejection of the professorship, Tiutriumov continued, emanated from a desire to gain a reputation for originality and to separate himself from the family of Russian artists. More importantly, the exhibited paintings were not the exclusive creation of his own hand, since it was physically impossible for any artist to create so many paintings in four or five years. Rather, Vereshchagin produced "the whole mass" of works in collaboration with other artists in Munich and merely signed his name to them. Tiutriumov based this allegation on the fact that Vereshchagin had admitted no one into his Munich studio. Pangs of conscience, his attacker asserted, thus played an additional role in Vereshchagin's rejection of the professorship. The use of lights during his exhibit was intended not so much to illuminate but to conceal various artistic deficiencies in the paintings, which would have impaired their salability. The academy, however, chose to ignore those deficiencies and offered him the professorship in view of the "enormous mass of paintings" (!) and the difficulties that he endured in his journey to Central Asia.[40] What Tiutriumov could not mention, of course, was that if Vereshchagin were motivated by greed, he would certainly have accepted the professorship because it would have accorded him a considerable measure of wealth.

Stasov took up the cudgels for Vereshchagin three days later. He regarded Tiutriumov's allegations as tantamount to malicious slander and subject to civil action. He demanded that Tiutriumov substantiate his charges, especially that Vereshchagin collaborated with other artists.

Tiutriumov could not meet the challenge and admitted that his account was based solely on rumors. Stasov also wrote to the Munich Association of Artists to request an inquiry into Vereshchagin's work and associations during his three-year stay in Germany. In addition to Stasov, it behooved eleven Itinerant artists to defend Vereshchagin because in January 1874 he had participated in their exhibit and had applied for membership in their association, but never actually joined. For the Itinerants, a more scandalous charge against a Russian artist had yet to appear in the Russian press. In a subtle taunt to the academy, they claimed that Tiutriumov had no right to speak on behalf of all Russian artists. The Itinerants rejected Tiutriumov's unfounded allegations and observed that Vereshchagin could "remain in the family of the Russian artists with honor, whatever the academic Tiutriumov thinks of him."[41]

The most damaging rebuttal to the academy came from still another quarter. One writer pointed out that the free admission, the low cost of the catalogues, and the donation to education demonstrated that greed was not the principal motive behind Vereshchagin's exhibition. The academy's grant of the professorship on the basis of a mass of paintings and difficulties in travel not only insulted Vereshchagin but also clearly demonstrated that fundamental assessment of artistic talent was beyond its purview. In a taunting allusion to Tiutriumov, the writer noted that the academy often awarded the title of academician to artists who "lacked the most elementary knowledge ... of colors and coloring," and was offering a professorship to Vereshchagin for his trying journey. In terms of that criterion, it was quite conceivable for the academy to award any sailor a professorship merely for making several trips around the world.[42]

The results of the investigation by the Munich Association of Arts, which included the testimony of Vereshchagin's servant, disclosed that "in all art circles, the fact of slandering such an eminent artist as Vereshchagin aroused very strong indignation; and, without a single exception, all the numerous artists who know the works of Vereshchagin by photograph expressed the utmost confidence that the high originality of these paintings on the subject of the war in Tashkent decisively exclude the work of any other hand except that of the master himself."[43] This ended the bitter polemic; ironically, the academy itself had enhanced Vereshchagin's reputation in the eyes of the public. But the government took steps to prevent further discussion of the incident in the press; it temporarily suspended the newspaper that had published Vereshchagin's "indecent letter" and forbade publication of any public expression of sympathy for him and any material derogatory of the academy.[44]

The St. Petersburg exhibition had brought Vereshchagin temporary financial security, but also a great deal of personal anxiety and frustration in the first year of his very costly journey to India. In his haste to escape the capital and the harrowing experience of destroying his paintings, he left the management of his affairs exclusively in the hands of General Geins. He eventually learned that the general's lack of competence matched his lack of scruples. Geins had given many of Vereshchagin's paintings to his "fashionable friends" from the nobility and military on the pretext of influencing the tsar to purchase the Turkestan series, but his real intention was to advance his own military career. Geins never informed Vereshchagin of the terms of the sale of the Turkestan collection to Tretiakov, where it would be housed, the contribution of the proceeds from admission fees to the District Council of Novgorod for the construction of an elementary school for girls, and payment for a plot of land which Vereshchagin had purchased to build a large indoor and outdoor revolving studio in Paris. Geins assured Vereshchagin that he would publish an album of the Turkestan series with his own introduction and explanatory texts; but during Vereshchagin's absence he planned to include the works of other artists and, ostensibly, to serve as their agent. Despite large expenditures for engraving, the album was never published.[45] Moreover, Geins failed to reply to four of Vereshchagin's letters.[46] In April 1874, Vereshchagin wrote to Tretiakov that it would be a "misfortune" if Geins did not send him money for his India trip, the planning of which he could not complete without funds from the sale of the paintings to Tretiakov.[47] Suffering from constant anxiety—"literally day and night"—and gnawing doubts about the completion of his journey, Vereshchagin was compelled to ask Stasov to take charge of his affairs. In September and November 1874, he also asked Tretiakov to send 12,500 francs to Paris for the plot of land, to destroy the promissory notes payable to Geins for the purchase of the Turkestan paintings, and to send him 2,000 British pounds.[48] In December 1874, Vereshchagin requested that Stasov relieve Geins of his duties as business manager, take into his own custody paintings and other materials, and send him 15,000 rubles.[49] It was only in March 1875 that Geins finally sent Vereshchagin a telegram and an unspecified sum of money.

Vereshchagin's experience with Geins raises one vital question: why did Geins, whom he considered a close friend, largely fail to keep Vereshchagin informed and to fulfill his instructions? Possibly, Geins' role in the sale of Vereshchagin's paintings to Tretiakov angered Alexander II, who foresaw no competitor in his interest to acquire them, and thus ordered Geins to sever his connection with Vereshchagin.

In artistic terms, Vereshchagin's trip to explore the exotic culture of India was fruitful and quite similar to his travels in the Caucasus and Central Asia in terms of collecting materials for a future set of paintings. He planned to create on his return to Paris in 1876 a series, *The Indian Poem*, that would be "not only of English-Indian but of universal significance."[50] The Russo-Turkish War of 1877–78, however, interrupted his work on them. Among the paintings that resulted from the trip are a rear view of *The Taj Mahal Mausoleum in Agra* (1874–76; Pl. 8) by the Yamuna River and *The Main Temple of a Monastery in Tassiding (Sikkim)* (1875). Vereshchagin masterfully presents the striking grace and beauty of the architectural forms of these two monuments with compelling authority and authenticity.

Compared to his other destinations, travel in India, however, was much more difficult and stressful because of extremes of cold and hot weather; dangerous animals; tormenting insects, which deprived Vereshchagin and his wife of sleep; the dense terrain; and jungles, mountain passes, rivers, and steep gorges which required traveling by foot, horseback, ponies, bulls, boats, and trains. Vereshchagin often had to hire new attendants at various points to carry newly acquired supplies, gifts, and Indian artifacts. In the tropical regions, he contracted malaria, which subsequently affected his general health. During the trip, he learned that the English suspected him of being a spy for the Russian military and believed that his sketches of mountain passages and streams were the results of a reconnaissance mission for Russian military penetration of the region. The English authorities wanted assurances from the Russian government to the contrary. Vereshchagin obtained letters from the Russian Ministry of Foreign Affairs in St. Petersburg and from the Russian ambassador to

England, stating that he had no formal connection with the Russian government. He also asked Stasov to place a short piece in a Russian newspaper, maintaining that Vereshchagin's "independence as both man and artist precludes any possibility of similar suspicions."[51]

In January 1874, Vereshchagin and his wife, despite warnings of grave danger, climbed 15,000 feet to the summit of Djongri, a peak of the Kanchenjunga Mountain in the Himalayas; they were attempting to reach the shelter of a shepherd's summer hut from where he would sketch the chain of snowy mountains. A snowstorm eventually made the ascent of the slippery and already snow-covered mountain more taxing. The weary entourage, skeptical of the safety of ascending during the storm, began to lag far behind with food and supplies. Only the Vereshchagins, a hunter, and a servant reached the peak. They suffered from extreme cold and hunger but quenched their thirst by blending snow with a bottle of sherry wine. The hunter, his matches wet from the snow, managed to light a fire with his rifle. The flames, however, "roasted" one side of their bodies while the other side became covered with a thick layer of ice. On continuing the ascent to the hut, Vereshchagin's wife collapsed and fainted—probably from fatigue and lack of oxygen at high altitude—but recovered quickly. In dire need of food and supplies, Vereshchagin had to pay his reluctant servant to locate the entourage; but when neither servant nor entourage appeared, Vereshchagin himself went in search of the party. After a brief descent, he became too exhausted to continue. Two servants ascending the mountain to join the couple probably saved Vereshchagin from freezing to death when they discovered him in the snow and carried him back to his wife. He suffered painful headaches and his face remained severely inflamed for several days after his rescue. The Vereshchagins finally reached the shepherd's hut, where they found provisions and shelter from the elements. Despite his "violent headache" and swollen face, Vereshchagin managed to create several quick sketches, although he had to be physically supported by two servants at each side. He promised to return to the mountain summit "in a completely vigorous condition, and ... shall study these changing shadows and these effects of light which are only visible at such a height as this." Three days later, after they had descended the mountain, the Vereshchagins found their entourage waiting for them in the town.[52]

Chapter Three

VERESHCHAGIN AND THE RUSSO-TURKISH WAR, 1877–1878

When Vereshchagin returned to Paris in late March 1876, he found himself the victim of a swindle involving the purchase of land and the construction of two art studios. He had entrusted the management of his affairs to supposed friends, who had altered the building contract after he had signed it; the additional items doubled the original cost of construction. Vereshchagin initiated litigation against the French architects and builders who had cheated him, but he lost the case. After he received the remaining payments from the sale of the Turkestan series, Vereshchagin had exhausted all his funds. When the studios were ostensibly finished, he faced added costs for improving the generally shoddy construction, particularly of the ceilings, which were on the verge of collapse. In desperate need of money, he wrote to Tretiakov in September 1876 for a loan of ten thousand rubles, assuring him that the Indian paintings on which he was working were more than sufficient collateral.[1]

In June 1876, a few months after Vereshchagin returned to Paris, Serbia and Montenegro, encouraged by Russian Slavophiles, declared war on Turkey in an effort to achieve independence from centuries of oppressive Turkish domination. Fully backing the war, the Russians provided financial and medical support. In July 1876, Vereshchagin donated one hundred francs to the Serbian cause. Artists, writers, poets, doctors, nurses, and thousands of others joined the Serbian army as volunteers.

Ivan Turgenev, the Russian novelist, stated that if he had been younger (he was then sixty), he would have joined the Serbian army.[2] In *Anna Karenina*, Tolstoy, who first reacted skeptically to the war and then sympathized with it, provides a telling and generally accurate account, however ambivalent, of the overwhelming impact of the Serbian cause on Russian society as a whole:

> In the circle to which Sergey Ivanovich belonged, they spoke and wrote at the time about nothing else but the Slavic question and the Serbian war. All that the idle crowd usually does to kill time was done on behalf of the Slavs. Balls, concerts, speeches, fashion shows, beer, cafes—all this testified to the sympathy with the Slavs.
>
> From much that was written and spoken on this question, Sergey Ivanovich did not agree on specific details. He saw that the Slavic question had become one of those fashionable diversions which always replace one another and offer society an object of involvement. He saw, too, that many people with selfish and vain purposes were involved in the matter. He recognized that newspapers published much that was superfluous and exaggerated with the sole aim of drawing attention and of outshouting others. He saw that in this general animation of society that those who leaped forward and shouted louder than others were those who had failed and who had suffered injury: generals without armies, ministers without ministries, journalists without the opportunity to publish, party leaders without adherents. He saw that much in this was frivolous and absurd; but he saw and recognized an unquestionable growing enthusiasm that united all classes with which one could not but sympathize. The slaughter of people of common Christian faith and the Slavic brethren evoked sympathy for the sufferers and indignation against the oppressors. And the heroic deeds of the Serbs and Montenegrins struggling for a great cause generated in the whole people the desire to help their brothers not in word, but in deed.
>
> In this, however, there was another phenomenon that delighted Sergey Ivanovich. That was the manifestation of public opinion. The national soul had definitely expressed itself, as Sergey Ivanovich would say. And the more he became involved in this cause, the clearer it

seemed to him that it was a cause destined to acquire vast dimensions and to create an epoch in Russian history.[3]

M. G. Cherniaev, the Russian general who commanded the Serbian forces, saw the war in terms of an abstract "holy" idea of Slavic solidarity. The war put the Russian government "in an embarrassing position between pro-Slav Russian public opinion, which urged intervention, and the Powers (England, Austria-Hungary, France, Germany), who insisted on neutrality. For the Serbs, the decision for war represented a desperate gamble that would succeed only if Russia were involved. Serbia's military forces were clearly inferior to those of Turkey, and during the four months of war Serbian leaders intermittently sought a truce."[4] Although Russia prepared for war, her hesitation to enter it stemmed from fear of conflict with England, who was suspicious of Russia's expansion into the Balkans and its threat to British interests in Constantinople. Cherniaev, however, was unworthy of his mission and failed to bring unity and order to the Serbian and Montenegrin forces and the undisciplined and inexperienced Russian volunteers. The war ended in a stalemate, and an armistice was concluded in October 1876. Turkey, however, promised to introduce internal reforms in Serbia and Montenegro and to ease the plight of the Christian minorities in the Ottoman Empire.

During the Serbo-Turkish war, Vereshchagin, among other Russians, expected Russia imminently to come to the aid of the Serbs and Montenegrins. In October 1876, in anticipation of hostilities and the mobilization of Russian forces, and motivated by patriotism, Vereshchagin requested to join the staff of the Russian army as a volunteer; quite surprisingly, as it turned out, his request was approved by General A. Gall, of the general quarters of the commander-in-chief of the Russian army, and Grand Duke Nicholas, who accepted Vereshchagin's request "with pleasure" but offered no salary. Vereshchagin also had the opportunity, if he so desired, of dining daily with Grand Duke Nicholas. Stasov informed Vereshchagin that the approval was based on his bravery in defense of the Samarkand fortress. Two other artists, Evgeny Makarov (1842–84), a portraitist, and Nikolai Krasovsky (b. 1840), a battle painter for the Russian royal court, were invited to become salaried members of the Grand Duke's staff.[5]

After the armistice, however, the failure of Turkey—who relied on British support and possible intervention—to introduce long-awaited reforms precluded a diplomatic solution, and Russia finally declared war on Turkey in April 1877. Before the declaration was made, Rumania agreed to allow Russia to use its railways to transport troops and supplies to the arena of conflict; the success of the Russian campaign depended, to a large degree, on access to these rail lines. The Russian military soon discovered, however, that "the routes taken by existing tracks and differences in gauges between Russian and Rumanian railways impeded the flow of troops and materials—inadequacies which were not exposed as vital to the campaign until Russian forces were held up from July to December at Plevna."[6] The resolution of this technical problem ultimately contributed to the Russian victory.

Russia's entry into the war against the decaying Ottoman empire entailed numerous domestic and foreign policy advantages and opportunities. By mobilizing Russian nationalist fervor in support of the Slavic cause, Russia's victory over Turkey would perpetuate the unity of all Russian classes, heighten the prestige of the autocracy, and erode domestic political dissent and opposition; internationally, the liberation and unification of the Slavs—a long cherished hope—would at last be realized, making Russia a decisive contender in European politics on equal terms with England, Austria, France, and Germany. Slavic unity was perhaps what Tolstoy meant by the "epoch-making" dimension of the war. For the Russians, this was not ostensibly a war of conquest or of national defense; it was a war to dutifully liberate their oppressed, enslaved Slavic brethren—the Serbs, Montenegrins, Bulgarians (and Rumanians)—and to free Christian minorities from Moslem rule. To be sure, Russia did consider in its victory over Turkey the possibility of extending its frontiers to the Mediterranean, or at least of expanding them in the Balkans, Asia Minor, and, conceivably, the Persian Gulf. That may be precisely why the government at first refused military aid from Serbia. When, however, Russian forces suffered their third defeat at Plevna in September 1877, the military realized that it could not conquer the Turkish army without the help of Serbia, whose entry into the war encountered British opposition.

While in Paris, Vereshchagin, who undoubtedly sympathized with the

Slavic cause in the Balkans, was also possessed by that "charm in danger," that exhilarating defiance of death, that recurring urge to escape from the intrinsic isolation of imaginative work into the thick of human action, or, as he simply put it, by "a great desire to see with my own eyes a regular European war," and to "observe, feel and study people."[7] He was assigned, without salary or military uniform, to the main staff of generals Dmitry Skobelev, Commander of the Caucasian Cossack Brigade, with whom he had become friends in 1868 in Turkestan, and Iosif Gurko, Commander of the Russian Advance-Guards, who led the winter offensive in the Balkans and captured Adrianople in January 1878. In the course of the war, Vereshchagin would temporarily join the staffs of other Russian generals who engaged the Turkish army. One cannot determine what the Russian army expected of him; he was highly regarded and respected as a war hero, and because he had apparently changed his outlook by destroying three of his Turkestan paintings, perhaps the military hoped for his positive portrayal of Russian victory.

In any case, he was attached to General Skobelev's staff. Vereshchagin kept minutes of several minor military discussions and sketched the general terrain and the positions and fortifications of the Russian and Turkish forces for various commanders, but this appears to be the extent of his artistic services to the Russian military. Under Generals Skobelev and Alexander Strukov, however, he performed a broad range of tasks. If there was a single factor about Vereshchagin that overwhelmed his contemporaries, it was his commanding presence (Fig. 11):

> He was tall, lean, somewhat round-shouldered, with a pale, oblong face full of intelligence and energy, with a large, open, fine forehead that seemed chiselled from ivory. He had deep, small, hawk-like eyes that were close to the bridge of his nose; and from beneath his thick eye-brows there was a boldly drawn hooked nose and a long beard already touched with gray streaks. He was refined in the simplicity of his behavior, modestly dressed, with the Cross of St. George in the buttonhole of his frock-coat—that was Vereshchagin, who by his external appearance alone immediately commanded amazing confidence and admiration.[8]

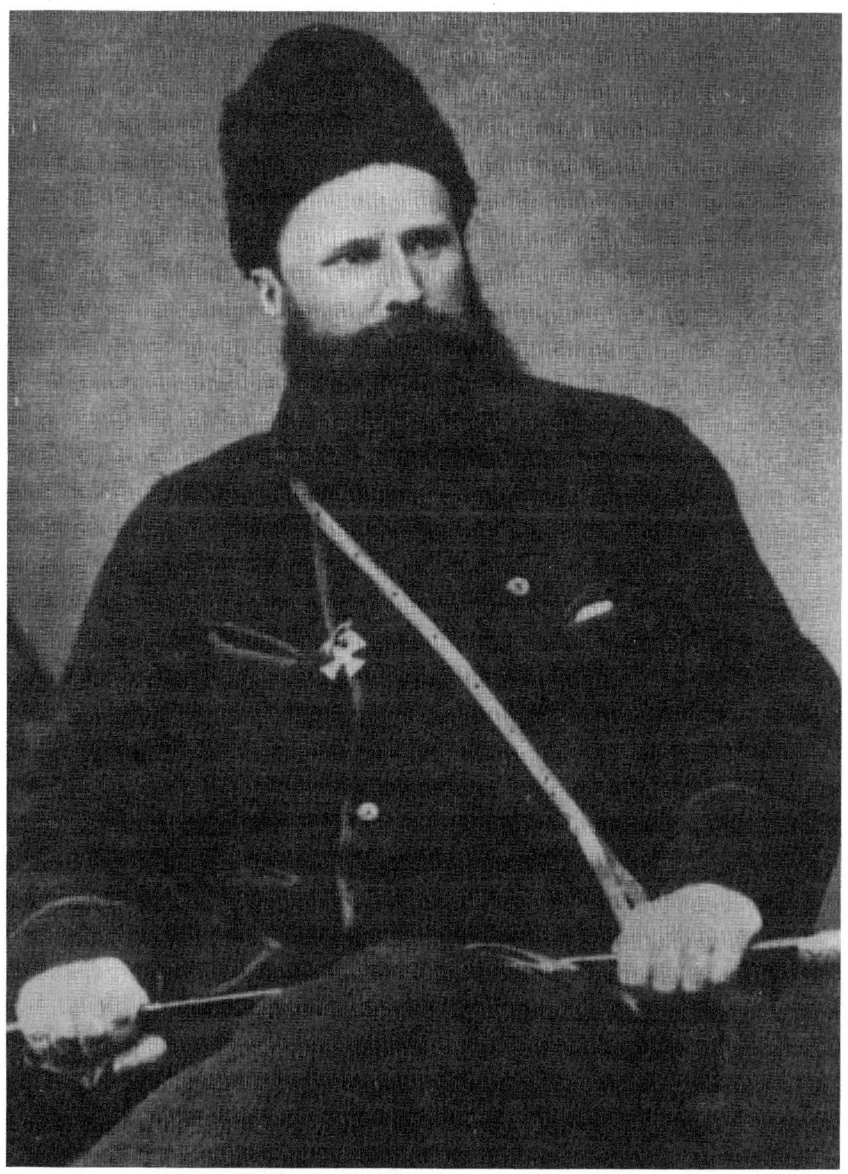

Figure 11. V. V. Vereshchagin during Russo-Turkish War, 1877–78. From A. Lebedev and A. Solodovnikov, *V. V. Vereshchagin* (Moscow: Iskusstvo, 1988).

Several days after Russia declared war against Turkey, Vereshchagin left Paris to join Skobelev's detachment in Kishinev, Rumania. His two younger brothers, Alexander, a career officer who rose to the rank of general, and Sergey, an amateur artist, also served in the army, the latter as a volunteer. During his journey, Vereshchagin had to return to Paris to replace damaged art materials. Three weeks later, he was ready for action in the Bulgarian city of Giurgevo, situated on the left bank of the Danube River, which marked the Turkish frontier. From across the Danube, Turkish forces were bombarding the town and an array of merchant vessels, which they mistakenly believed would be used to transport Russian troops across the river. The Russian army had to free the Danube of Turkish gunboats before it could engage enemy troops. In his feverish haste to witness the explosion of bombs in water and their effect on nearby buildings, Vereshchagin boarded a vessel that was under direct bombardment. Shell fire struck the ship's bow and hull and "turned everything between decks upside down"; Vereshchagin was not injured, but he believed that the very next round of fire would mark his doom. He relates that it "was most interesting to see how the bombs fell into the water and made fountains rise high into the air. . . . I did not get many compliments for having made my observations from the ship. Some simply refused to believe that I had placed myself in the middle of the target; others called it useless bravado; it did not occur to anyone that these very observations were the object of my stay. If I had a paint-box with me, I should have painted some explosions." When asked why a talented artist was risking death when he could have remained home, Vereshchagin replied: "If they had been shooting at my home, I would have made off. I would have done so because it's not my wish at all to be killed in a useless way, but I just couldn't miss the chance to see at close range the color effect, and, to tell the truth, I really haven't seen anything like it in my life."[9]

Shortly thereafter, a friend of Vereshchagin, a staff member at Russian military headquarters, granted him permission to join a torpedo-mining squad in Mali-Idjos in northern Serbia, the Russian naval guard base. In June, Vereshchagin and Lieutenant Nikolai Skrydlov, a former classmate at the St. Petersburg Naval Academy, took part in several night missions to lay buoys in the Danube as guides for Russian torpedo boats to chart their courses in setting mines. Earlier, Skrydlov had shown Vereshchagin a staff document critical of the "backward state of the preparations" of the Russian army, which ultimately proved to be accurate despite the military reforms of 1874. The next expedition against Turkish boats involved laying torpedoes in daylight and attacking an armored vessel. After the mines were set, a large Turkish steam launch caught sight of the flotilla of Russian torpedo boats concealed between the river bank and a small island; it opened fire without inflicting damage. For a short while, the launch turned away to seek help from a torpedo boat and then reappeared in pursuit. Skrydlov quickly directed his boat, *The Joke*, to engage the launch as it approached on the left; the other Russian boats lagged behind, some because of apparent engine failure. Turkish soldiers on the banks waded into the river to open fire at close range. A hail of bullets created confusion on the boat, and a cannon shot staggered it. On board, Vereshchagin thought his end was near. The boat shook under relentless fire, began to take on water, and became a defenseless target; the crew took cover. The Turkish launch was almost alongside the boat. Two bullets struck Skrydlov's legs as he manned the bridge. The boat's engineer prayed as he waited for Skrydlov to give the command to fire. In panic, the helmsman maneuvered the boat to the right, veering it away from the steamer. The wounded Skrydlov seized the helm to reposition the boat and attempted to fire, but gunfire had severed the conducting wire of the launcher and the torpedo failed to project. Without adequate engine power, the boat took on additional water and was helpless. Vereshchagin, ready and eager for action as he manned the stern torpedo, realized the boat was doomed and attempted to stand on the gunwale, when he suddenly felt a "violent crash under me and a blow on my hip—such a blow as might have come from an axe." A bullet had ricocheted and struck his hip muscle. The boat drifted toward the bank and again came under fire. Vereshchagin tried in vain to respond with his rifle. The boat continued to drift until it reached a row of merchant vessels anchored in a narrow strip of water between an island and the bank. The Turkish torpedo boat, which had observed the clash, now joined to deliver the fatal blow; but with one last surge of engine power, the Russian boat found refuge near a small island where the steamer could not follow, and the enemy retreated. After securing the hull, the Russian party returned to base.[10] Vereshchagin and Skrydlov had become the first Russian casualties of the war and the first heroes as well.

Vereshchagin's hip wound at first seemed minor, but it gradually became infected and required treatment in a Bucharest hospital, where the increasing pain was relieved by morphine injections. Efforts to remove the embedded particles of clothing which caused the infection were unsuccessful; gangrene set in, combined with an attack of malaria. As fever sapped his strength and occasionally led to unconsciousness, Vereshchagin lost hope of recovery and dictated his will.[11]

An operation, however, saved his life; he spent eight weeks convalescing in an infirmary. His wound prevented him from participating in military action for the remainder of the war, and his activities were limited to observing and sketching major battles and related events and to conferring with General Skobelev, among others.[12]

While Vereshchagin recuperated in July and most of August 1877, the war continued. Russian troops were superior in number, training, and discipline, though clearly inferior in weaponry; the Turkish army's American Winchester repeating-rifles and Peabody rifles had twice the firing range of the Russian single-shot rifles.[13] By mid-July, Russian forces had made rapid and significant inroads into Turkish-held territory. Under the command of Grand Duke Nicholas, brother of the tsar, the Russian army had crossed the Danube and had seized a strategic point in the Balkan Mountains, the Shipka Pass. In late July, however, the Turkish army mounted a counter-offensive, and the Russians, despite a preponderance of forces, suffered bewildering setbacks and heavy casualties, especially in two attempts to capture Plevna in northern Bulgaria. By September, Rumanian troops (and in December those of Serbia, which required large subsidies for equipment and mobilization) had joined the Russian forces.

In late August 1877, before his wound had fully healed, Vereshchagin, apprised of the Russian army's second defeat at Plevna, and against the advice of physicians, left in a phaeton to observe a new assault on that city; he rejoined General Skobelev, under whom his two brothers served. When he reached the battlefront, Vereshchagin witnessed the third attempt to capture Plevna. The Russian high command designated August 30, the name-day (i.e., the day of that saint after whom a person is named) of Tsar Alexander II, for the massive assault of 115,000 Russian and Rumanian soldiers with 532 field guns against 34,000 Turkish soldiers with 108 field guns. On the rainy morning of the multilateral assault, the tsar and his retinue had breakfasted and sipped champagne on a small slope near Plevna, confident of a decisive victory in honor of the tsar. In *Alexander II at Plevna on August 30, 1877* (1878–79; Fig.12), Vereshchagin recreates the scene, for which he would later be accused of undermining the tsar's prestige in the eyes of the Russian people. The painting originally contained a small pyramid of champagne bottles which Vereshchagin removed before his exhibition in St. Petersburg. At the extreme right, the tsar sits listlessly on a folding stool, as if it were a throne; he is surrounded by his military staff in full dress, who strain to observe through their field glasses the effects of the artillery attack on the Turkish redoubts. Grand Duke Nicholas sits immediately behind the tsar, possibly relating the course of events, although very little is visible through thick puffs of gun smoke and overcast sky. The horizontal format of the painting accentuates the isolation of the tsar and his retinue from the theater of action; they play no role in the battle, although it is they who are ultimately responsible for the impending Russian defeat. The bombardment, ineptly organized and coordinated with infantry penetration to seize key positions, could not smash Turkish defenses and merely resulted in the seizure of a redoubt outside Plevna. General Skobelev's forces, however, after capturing Turkish fortifications, came closest to the gates of Plevna and might have captured it with timely and substantial reinforcements from the Russian central command but were compelled to retreat under heavy Turkish fire. Vereshchagin's younger brothers were casualties of the Russian defeat: Sergey, who had previously survived five wounds, was killed, and Alexander was wounded. When Vereshchagin was told that many Russian soldiers in Turkish-held territory were lying wounded with raised hands, the thought that his brother was still alive haunted him. According to one witness, Vereshchagin later closely examined the faces and bodies of the soldiers on the battlefield in an attempt to identify his brother, but to no avail; it was impossible to recover Sergey's body in the "horrible mass" of bloated and decaying corpses. He attempted to draw a general picture of the human slaughter, but, overwhelmed by compassion, he could see nothing beyond the constant flow of his own tears and could not continue.[14] One officer who

Figure 12. *Alexander II at Plevna on August 30, 1877.* 1878–79. Oil on canvas. 60 × 202 cm. Tretiakov Gallery, Moscow.

had seen Sergey's body in the battlefield later told Vereshchagin that Sergey's face was "horribly disfigured and covered with blood."[15] The Russian and Rumanian forces lost almost twenty thousand men, and five thousand Turkish were dead. In December, a reshuffle of the Russian high command led to a victory in Plevna.

After this third and worst defeat at Plevna, Vereshchagin decided to wait for Russian troop reinforcements and observe another assault on Turkish positions. He wrote to his wife that he wanted to remain in the Balkans because he feared that he would not see another war in his lifetime. He surveyed the battlefield, drew sketches of the casualties, and visited the overcrowded, understaffed hospitals, where he observed the amputation of arms, hands, legs. He listened to "hopelessly crippled" and wounded Russian soldiers protesting the war's needless torment and destruction of the Russian people. He was pressed into service and "forced" to hold one patient during surgery and to hand instruments to the surgeon. This episode finds artistic expression in *After the Attack. Dressing Station at Plevna* (1881; Fig. 13). Here, in five Russian medical tents that had accommodations and staff for five hundred soldiers, eight thousand men were treated. In front of the tents a mass of wounded Russian soldiers wait patiently to receive medical attention before they return to Russia. In the extreme lower left wounded Turkish soldiers also await medical treatment. Striking in its realism and balance, the painting renders in rich detail an extraordinary diversity of figural poses against the

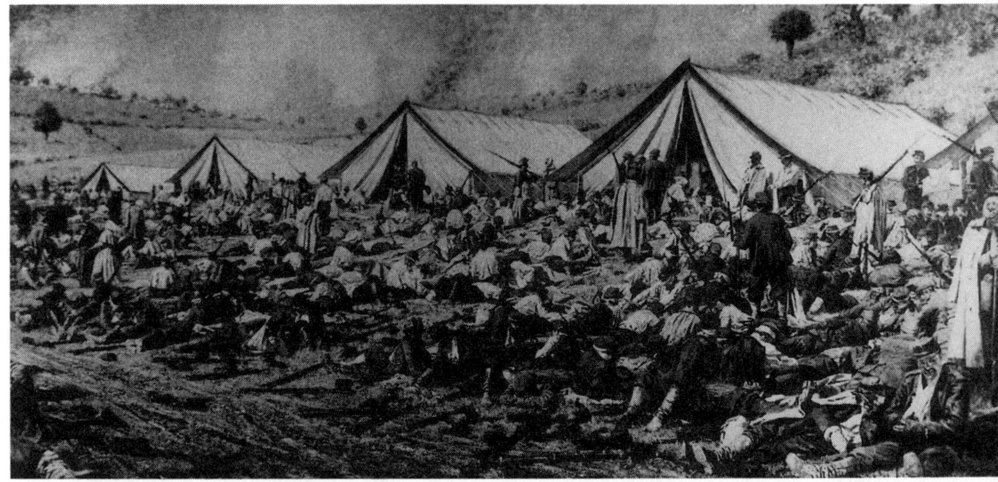

Figure 13. *After the Attack. Dressing Station at Plevna.* 1881. Oil on canvas. 183 × 402 cm. Tretiakov Gallery, Moscow.

dramatic background of burning Bulgarian villages. In constrast to the mass of others, the individual is represented by the soldier in the extreme right foreground, his face swathed in a blood-stained bandage, who stands supported by a cane. The prelude to *After the Attack. Dressing Station at Plevna* is *Before the Attack. At Plevna* (1881; Fig.14); it recalls *By the Fortress Wall. Let Them Enter* (see Pl. 5), which portrayed Russian officers—including Vereshchagin—leading the troops. *Before the Attack. At Plevna* shows how radically Vereshchagin's estimate of the competence of the Russian military command had changed in light of his Balkan experiences. The poses are far less schematic and the formation of the soldiers in relation to the officers is reversed. Their positions and facial expressions echo a passage from Tolstoy's "The Wood-Felling" (1856):

> The spirit of the Russian soldier is unlike the bravery of the Southern nations, for quickly kindled and cooling enthusiasm. It is as difficult to set him on fire as it is to compel him to lose courage. He does not need effects, speeches, warlike shouts, songs, and drums. On the contrary, he needs calmness, order, and the absence of all that is forced. In the Russian, the real Russian soldier, you will never observe boast-

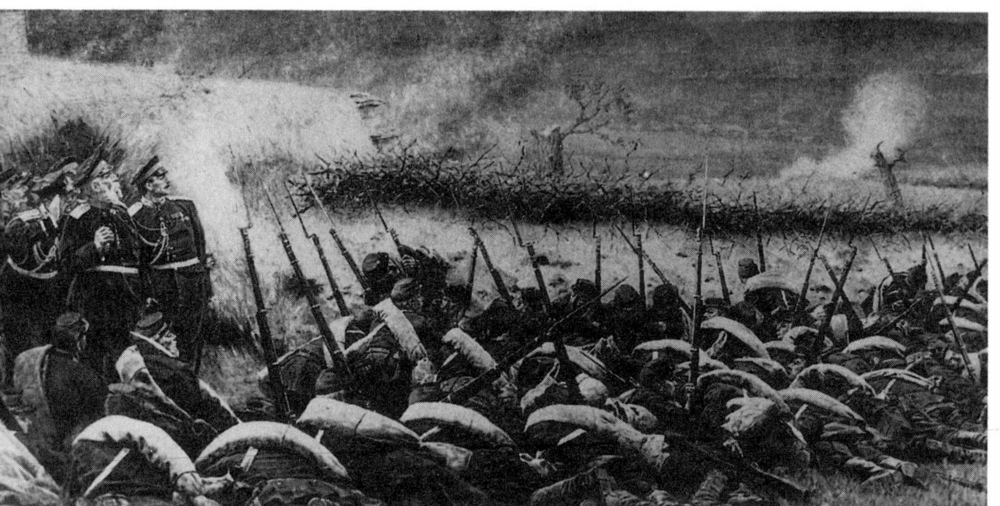

Figure 14. *Before the Attack. At Plevna.* 1881. Oil on canvas. 60 × 202 cm. Tretiakov Gallery, Moscow.

> ing, bravado, the tendency to get demoralized or excited in the face of danger. On the contrary, modesty, simplicity, and the capacity to see in danger something quite different from danger—these are the distinctive traits of his character.[16]

In Vereshchagin's work, about forty infantry soldiers calmly await the order to storm the muddy terrain of Plevna. When Grand Duke Nicholas was preparing for the assault on Plevna, Vereshchagin heard him express grave doubt about whether his troops could advance "in such mire," but since it was the Tsar's name-day, the attack proceeded, with disastrous consequences. In the painting, the bearded general seems rather skeptical of the effectiveness of the military bombardment of the Turkish positions and receives, as did the Russian commander from Vereshchagin in *By the Fortress Wall. Let Them Enter* (see Pl. 5), the advice of an aide immediately behind him. *Before the Attack* is of military significance because it partially explains the Russian defeat at Plevna by demonstrating that the military assault on Turkish positions was negligible without a corresponding advance of the infantry to engage the Turkish forces, who merely shifted positions to avoid Russian artillery fire. When, however, the infantry finally moved to engage Turkish soldiers, it had to cross, as shown in the painting, a difficult and muddy terrain, and thus became an easy target for the enemy, who inflicted heavy casualties.

Vereshchagin also witnessed how the war had uprooted the Bulgarian population, whose property was plundered in the Turkish retreat and who required food, shelter, clothing, and medical care in the winter of 1877 after unspeakable Turkish atrocities. He saw the bodies of numerous Russian soldiers whose clothing had been stripped and whose ears, noses, heads, and genitals had been severed by Turkish troops. Vereshchagin re-creates this episode in *The Conquerors* (1878–79; Pl. 9), in which six Turkish soldiers dominate the center foreground, unify the picture, and shape the action of the remaining troops in the background. The figure in the center has stripped a Russian officer of his uniform and, with the aid of two companions, has donned it—however tight the fit—for amusement of his fellow soldiers, all of whom seem insensitive to the slaughter that they have committed. One Turkish soldier in a tan coat salutes the "officer," while the soldier sitting at the extreme left participates in the gaiety by slipping his foot into a boot removed from the dead Russian to his left. The figure in the right foreground has tucked a pair of Russian boots under his left arm and has flung an officer's coat over his right shoulder. The rest of the Turkish troops are scouring the battlefield to strip Russian bodies of their boots and uniforms; some are leaving with their bounty, while others are coming to join the search. The heads and decapitated bodies of Russian soldiers lie scattered in the field.

After the Russian victory in December, Vereshchagin observed the bodies of thousands of Turkish prisoners of war who had frozen to death because of inadequate clothing and lack of food. In their march from Plevna to the Danube, many of the half-frozen Turkish soldiers cried and begged to be allowed to warm themselves in homes; although most were ordered to keep marching, some were permitted to run briefly into sheds, where enterprising Cossacks sold them bread. The result of such cruelty is given artistic treatment in *The Road of the Prisoners of War (The Road to Plevna)* [1878–79; Fig. 15]. As Vereshchagin recalled:

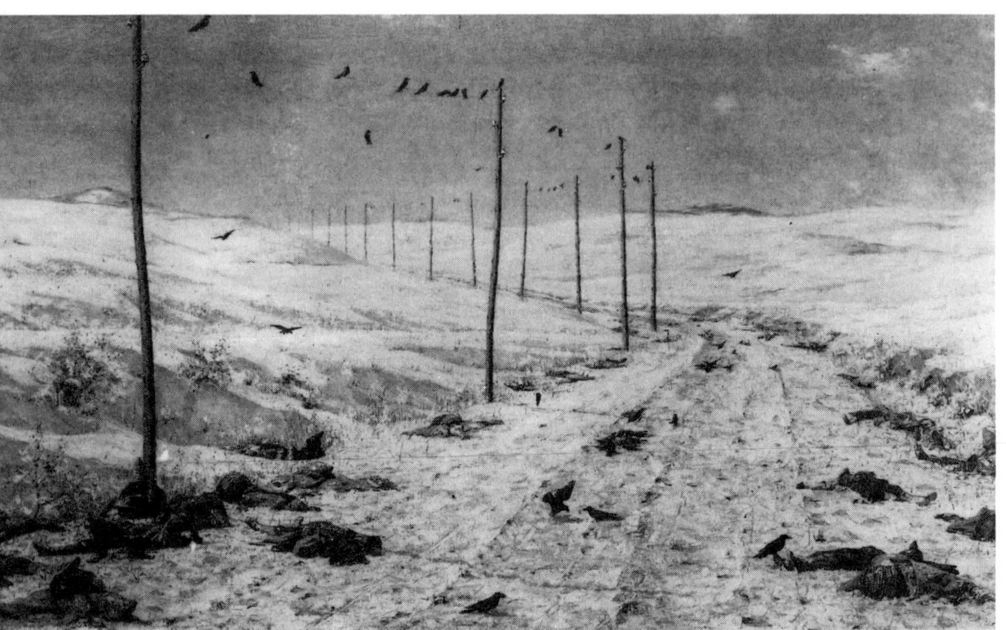

Figure 15. *The Road of the Prisoners of War (The Road to Plevna).* 1878–79. Oil on canvas. 182 × 281 cm. By permission of the Brooklyn Museum, New York.

The road from Plevna to the Danube for a distance of thirty to forty miles was literally strewn with the bodies of frozen and wounded Turks. The frost set in so suddenly, and with such severity, that the brave defenders of Plevna in their stiff-frozen overcoats were too weak to resist it, and by ones and twos fell on the road, and were frozen to death. With the assistance of a Cossack companion I tried to raise some of these fallen and set them on their feet, but they fell down again, so completely enfeebled were they, though evidently anxious to follow their comrades. Sitting and lying in the snow they moved hands and feet as though they longed to be moving, but were powerless. The next day their movements became less, and they lay on the snow by the hundreds, prostrate on their backs, moving lips and fingers as they gradually and slowly froze to death. (Having heard that this kind of death was one of the least painful, I closely examined the faces of the corpses lying in every imaginable position along the road,

> and convinced myself that every face bore the impress of deep suffering. This form of death then is evidently also not painless.) I recollect two Turks in particular—an old man and quite a youth, seated by the side of the road, warming themselves by a diminutive fire of a few sticks. When I stopped my horse near them in the morning, the youth tried to speak with me, but burst into tears, and I could only understand, 'Oh, Effendi, Effendi!' I answered, pointing to heaven, 'Allah, Allah!' The older man was silent, and looked gloomily down. On returning to Plevna in the evening I sought out the place where I had left them; the little fire had long burnt itself out, the young Turk lay prostrate and apparently dead, while his companion sat motionless beside him bent almost double. He, too, was probably also dead. The first few days there was nobody to remove the dead and dying, so that passing carts and gun-carriages crushed their bodies into the snow and rendered it impossible to extricate them without spoiling the road.[17]

Later, Vereshchagin would accuse General F. Radetsky of negligence at Shipka: instead of carefully inspecting the Russian batteries, trenches, and dug-outs during a blizzard and bitter cold weather (temperatures ranged from –12 to –20 degrees F) that gripped the Balkans from December 5 to 17, Radetsky engaged in his favorite pastime of playing cards, while thousands of his troops suffered frostbite and froze to death. One Russian officer reports that in six regiments ninety officers and almost nine thousand soldiers fell ill, and thousands of frost-bitten feet and hands were amputated. He does not indicate how many soldiers died, but he does claim that Russian officers did take active measures to prevent soldiers from freezing to death.[18] General Radetsky's report to the Russian military command was "All is quiet at Shipka," which is precisely the sarcastic title of Vereshchagin's triptych, which echoes *The Forgotten Soldier* (see Fig. 10) but has the naturalistic, scientific character of *The Fatally Wounded Soldier* (see Pl. 6), in which death is studied as a process. In the first painting *All Is Quiet at Shipka* (1878–79; Fig. 16), a hooded Russian sentry, dutifully standing with rifle, tries to keep warm amidst a developing blizzard. In the second piece, he turns away, shielding his face to resist the intensifying blizzard that begins to devour him. In the third piece, the storm completely overwhelms him, and he perishes. This work,

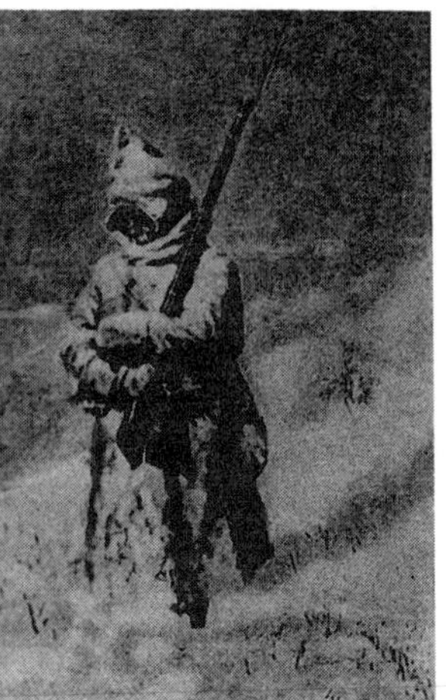
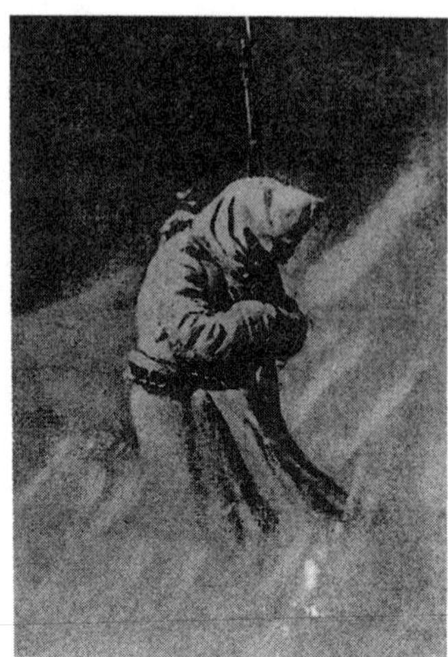
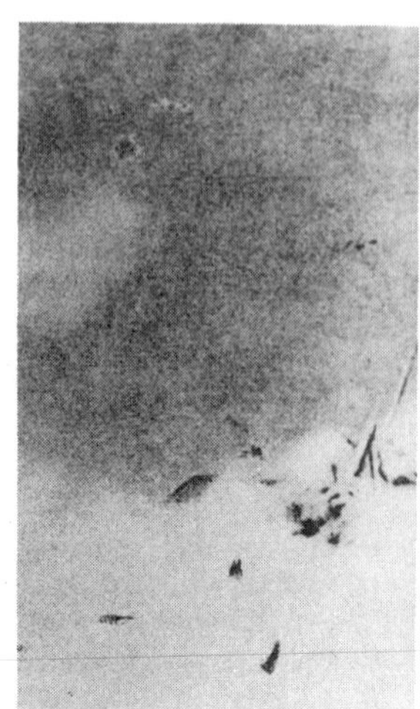

Figure 16. *All Is Quiet at Shipka.* 1878–79. Oil on canvas. Whereabouts unknown.

as well as *The Defeated. Funeral Service* (1877–79; Fig. 17), received the greatest attention wherever they were exhibited. *The Defeated. Funeral Service* is based on an exercise in military maneuvers in Telish in northern Bulgaria, during which Russian forces were to feign an attack on a Turkish fortress but instead were ordered to attack without adequate preparation; as a result, half the regiment was killed and massacred. When, two days later, Russian troops captured the fortress, they gathered the headless, naked bodies of their fellow soldiers for mass burial; in the extreme left foreground of the work a priest and a Russian soldier conduct a funeral service. V. Nemirovich-Danchenko (1844–1936), a Russian writer and journalist who served as a correspondent in the Russo-Turkish War and who often saw and wrote about Vereshchagin in the Balkans, comments on this painting when it was exhibited in St. Petersburg in 1880:

> When I stood before this canvas which portrayed a field overgrown with dry grass and covered with thousands of corpses of disfigured, naked soldiers, I repeated to myself: 'True, profoundly true. . . .' Here are the victims of mistakes and ambition. This is the fate of these people who finally, nevertheless, came to the aid of everyone and

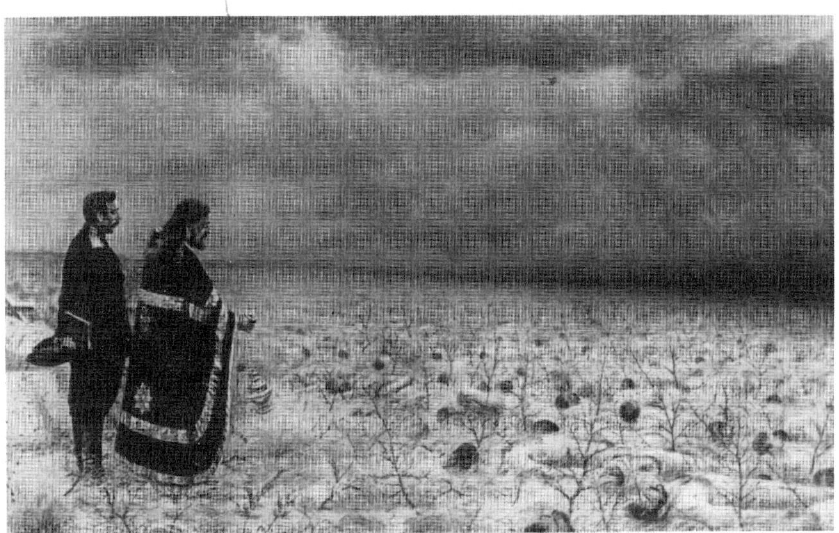

Figure 17. *The Defeated. Funeral Service.* 1877–79. 179 × 300 cm. Tretiakov Gallery, Moscow.

> everything. . . . This was a great sin-offering. Vereshchagin truly understood it—and that explains the animosity with which some attacked him, and the delight which others expressed. The crowd did not take delight and expressed no animosity. It stood deeply staggered before the painting and was dominated by reverential silence which grips one at a grave, when the coffin of a friend or brother is being lowered.[19]

The Russian military and royal court intended to ban *The Defeated. Funeral Service* from exhibition in St. Petersburg in 1880, but decided instead to assail it as a false representation of the war. A member of the royal court protested to Vereshchagin that the work was "historically inaccurate," to which Vereshchagin countered, "historically accurate, your highness." And, during the course of the exhibit, the Russian priest who actually performed the service publicly confirmed the accuracy of the painting.[20]

By the end of December 1877, Vereshchagin had created, at great risk to his life, about forty major sketches and studies, some of which depicted the winter advance of General Gurko's army of seventy thousand guards through the Balkans. Vereshchagin drew other pieces in the heat of battle, when he would sit on his folding stool as if he were working in his studio; this rare and peculiar setting seemed to combine the solitude of creative activity and vital involvement.

Before he joined General Skobelev's campaign, Vershchagin enclosed his work pieces—including two bundles of Turkish military uniforms that he had removed from dead soldiers—in a strapped, waterproof bundle and entrusted them to a recent acquaintance, Doctor M. Stukovenko, the director of the Russian military hospitals at Plevna, for safekeeping and deposit at Vereshchagin's apartment in Sistovo, Bulgaria. When Stukovenko arrived in Sistovo, he suffered an attack of typhoid fever and gave the bundles to a Russian staff-captain, N. Kirilin, who claimed that he gave them to the chief of police of Sistovo, Colonel Podgursky, for delivery to Vereshchagin's apartment. When General Strukov inquired in Sistovo about the delivery, Podgursky denied receiving the bundles. Apparently, Stukovenko gave Vereshchagin's materials to Kirilin in early February 1878, almost six weeks after he had taken custody of them.

Vereshchagin, unaware of these events and waiting to receive his work pieces and Turkish uniforms as he began work on the Balkan war paintings, later (early July 1878) asked Stasov to write a public request for Stukovenko to send him the sorely needed pieces. When he eventually learned they were missing, Vereshchagin noted that their loss precluded "many marvelous paintings" of the winter offensive. "They remained in my mind, but it was impossible to present them on canvas without the studies." The Red Cross and Generals Strukov's and Skobelev's soldiers, who temporarily remained in Bulgaria after the war, conducted an intensive search in the latter half of 1878 in Sistovo and Gabrovo, but without success. Subsequent searches also proved fruitless.[21] That the sketches and studies were never recovered suggests that they were discarded or, more likely, that they were burned after they were associated with the Turkish uniforms.

Another episode concerns Vereshchagin's desire for revenge against two Turkish irregulars, soldier-bandits (bashi-bazouks) notorious for their extreme cruelty; they were captured after they had slaughtered Bulgarian "infant children from the wombs of their mothers." The bandits were tightly bound back-to-back and cast on the ground. A crowd of angry Bulgarian children and women gathered and began to curse, spit, and throw clods of dirt and stones at them as the Russian soldiers looked on. Vereshchagin asked General Strukov, one of Skobelev's aides, to hang the two bandits, because he had never witnessed such an execution, "was much interested in the process," and wanted to sketch it. The request shocked Strukov, who questioned Vereshchagin about his uncharacteristic thirst for blood. Not wanting their deaths on his conscience, Strukov rejected the request and left the decision to Skobelev. Vereshchagin was confident that Skobelev would immediately comply. A day later, a large crowd surrounded the two bandits and brutally beat them as they sat on the ground pleading for mercy. Vereshchagin points out that "It would have been more merciful to have hung them. They were lying on the ground swollen and quite blue from being bound up. . . . Their turbans and fezzes had been knocked off their heads, and the faces were battered and blood-stained by stones and clumps that the throng kept continually throwing at them." When Skobelev arrived, he agreed to hang the bandits after a court martial; but Strukov pleaded with him not to kill them for his sake. They were released, and Vereshchagin sketched them for a subsequent painting, *Two Hawks (Bashi-Bazouks)* [1878–79; Pl. 10].[22]

In late December 1877, Vereshchagin was near Sheinovo, a Bulgarian village south of the Shipka Pass in the Balkan Mountains, and serving as secretary, aide, observer, adviser, confidant, messenger, draughtsman, and companion for General Skobelev. The Russian forces were preparing a three-pronged winter offensive to break a major Turkish defense hold; this was to be followed by a steady advance to Adrianople to engage the Turkish forces of Suleiman Pasha. Vereshchagin, still limping and using a cane, wore a "half-military, half-civilian costume," consisting of a large cossack hat, a short Rumanian fur coat with long hair, huge boots, and a sword hung over his shoulder: "The officer's Cross of the Order of St. George was the only thing which a little counterbalanced the excessive picturesqueness of this costume." He observed the difficult passage of Russian troops over the snow-covered mountains and the "decisive battle which now seemed inevitable." The Turkish forces advanced and opened fire on Skobelev's troops and on the Turkish block-house in which Vereshchagin was sketching the Tunja Valley. Vereshchagin relates how he was affected: "The first [shell] buried itself in the wall; the second flew on to the roof and covered me with sand and all kinds of things, although I was sitting on the other side of the house; the third monster struck and pierced the roof close to me with an outrageous noise, and threw such a mass of earth and rubbish upon me that I went away without finishing my picture; the colors of my palette had received such a strong mixture of foreign particles that I was obliged to throw them away."[23] Vereshchagin remarks that Skobelev's forces could not return artillery fire because they lacked guns and could not penetrate Turkish positions because of heavy snow. The Turkish army resisted Skobelev's first assault, which lacked reserve support; but the second attack, combined with the forces of General N. Sviatopolk-Mirsky, turned the tide, driving the Turkish forces from their positions and leading to the surrender of their commander and his army of twenty-two thousand men. There were five thousand Russian and one thousand Turkish casualties. After the battle, Vereshchagin surveyed the dead on the field and discovered a Russian soldier who had been shot at very close range and whose face still expressed great pain:

> One body attracted my attention; the face, which was young, showed him to have been what one calls raw youth. He was a volunteer. The body lay apart from the rest, and arms and feet stretched out, the eyes open. His boots—that most important article of clothing in a campaign—had been taken off, his pockets turned out, and a large number of letters lay about—the enemies who robbed him were not likely to care for those letters. But they had left him also the golden cross round his neck. I took up the letters and glanced at them to discover the name of the fallen youth. He was the son of a noble family [Iankov] in the south of Russia. All the tenderness of a mother was expressed in these letters: she blessed him over and over again, besought him to spare himself, told him of packages sent off with his favourite syrup, etc.[24]

Vereshchagin buried Iankov, placed a cross on his grave, and sent, through Stasov, the letters to Iankov's mother. He surveyed the Turkish casualties, collecting their uniforms, weapons, and other artifacts for his future paintings of the war.[25]

The swift Russian offensive and the capture of Adrianople on January 21, 1878, marked the final Turkish defeat and resulted in a highly complex set of maneuvers for an armistice. Russian troops were ready to enter Turkish territory, but faced a dangerous dilemma: if they advanced to Constantinople and the Turkish Straits, they "undoubtedly would have provoked war with England and Austria-Hungary."[26]

When Vereshchagin learned in Adrianople of the impending armistice, he burst into the headquarters of Grand Duke Nicholas, who was left with the task of negotiating a mere armistice for the Russian government. Vereshchagin expressed to the grand duke the absurdity of an armistice, considering the heavy Russian casualties and the Turkish massacres of the Bulgarian population. According to Vereshchagin, as he argued with the grand duke, in that light the war should never have been started because it established or affirmed nothing, although he never really defined what it should have accomplished. The grand duke, who at first personally favored an armistice, suddenly became eager to seize the Turkish Straits and Constantinople and, as he wrote to his brother on January 21, "there finish the holy cause you have assumed."[27] Vereshchagin wanted the grand duke to confirm that an armistice had been reached, to which the grand duke replied that it was not he who was responsible for the decision, but his brother, the tsar. Vereshchagin told the grand duke to evade the tsar's orders and to cut the telegraphic lines with St. Petersburg, which he himself would do if so ordered.[28] In fact, that was precisely what the grand duke did so as not to be deprived of the glory of victory by A. Gorchakov and N. Ignatev of the Russian Foreign Ministry, who "were intently jealous at not taking part in the peacemaking and wanted to hold everything up till one or other could play the chief role."[29] The grand duke, "worried lest the Foreign Ministry induce his brother to halt the advance . . . cut telegraphic communications with St. Petersburg and advocated seizure of Constantinople and the Straits."[30]

There is another version of this incident:

> On 19 January, in the morning, some hours before the Turkish plenipotentiaries reached his [the grand duke's] headquarters, he received a decisive telegram from Gorchakov informing him of the Tsar's desire that he should delay the communication to the Turks of

> the bases of peace by asking first for their proposals and referring them to St. Petersburg, thus giving time for some agreement with the Austrians to be reached: in any case, operations were not to be stopped. This telegram threw the commander-in-chief off such balance as he still possessed. In his access [*sic*] of anger he so far lost control of his senses as to order the telegraph lines connecting him with St. Petersburg to be cut.[31]

According to yet another version: "Russian forces were instructed to advance to the capital of Turkey until Turkish plenipotentiaries accept conditions of peace, but not to occupy it."[32] Whether the grand duke cut the lines before or after Vereshchagin's suggestion cannot be determined. In Vereshchagin's account, the grand duke made no mention of whether he had already cut the lines or would cut them. Since Gorchakov's message did not entail a command and thus allowed considerable latitude, on January 24 the grand duke chose to press on with "operations" and moved the Russian army to the vicinity of Constantinople. On January 20, the Turkish government accepted Russian conditions of peace and signed an armistice the next day, knowing that Russia would not be able to dictate its terms without the ultimate approval of England and Austria-Hungary. In early February, England sent her fleet to the Sea of Marmora to forestall the Russian capture of Constantinople, which, after the impressive victories of generals Gurko and Skobelev, was "the prize of all prizes" in the conquest of Turkey and the elimination of its rule in Europe, which may have been the real Russian objective.[33] In March 1879, the Treaty of San Stefano between Russia and Turkey failed to satisfy England and Austria-Hungary, who altered it in their favor into the Treaty of Berlin—chaired by Chancellor Bismarck—in July 1878. But the treaty did not provide any lasting solutions to the problems in Turkey (e.g., the persecution of Christian minorities) and the Balkans. Serbia, Montenegro, and Rumania gained full independence, and Bulgaria received limited autonomy under the political and military jurisdiction of the Turkish sultan, but the Slavic countries were disappointed with their new territorial boundaries. "For the Balkan peoples, then, the Berlin Treaty meant not peace with honor but rather frustration of national aspirations and future wars. The direct and logical outcome of the Berlin settlement was the Serbia-Bulgarian War of 1885, the Bosnian crisis of 1908, the two Balkan wars of 1912–1913, and the murder of Archduke Francis Ferdinand in 1914."[34] Austria occupied Bosnia and Herzegovina merely through her neutrality in the war. While Turkey was "defeated" and lost most of her European possessions, Russia acquired minor territories in Eastern Asia at the staggering human cost of about 150,000 casualties. Diplomatically, the Russian government had been humiliated in the Treaty of Berlin, and thereafter it experienced bitter disillusionment, profound domestic tensions (terrorist attacks, peasant revolts, the threat of political collapse), economic dislocation, and financial disaster that absorbed its energies until the assassination of Tsar Alexander in 1881; this was followed by a period of extreme repression during the reign of Alexander III.[35]

This was the turbulent setting in which Vereshchagin exhibited his Balkan war paintings in February 1880. The irony of the Russo-Turkish War is that Russia suffered the most and gained the least, while England and Austria, without any human losses, had emerged as the ultimate victors through timely military tactics and astute diplomacy. In seeking the status of a world power, Russia lacked a military-industrial complex; its economic and technological backwardness could not sustain its military ambitions, particularly when those ambitions threatened the balance of power, which England jealously maintained to its economic and military advantage.

Vereshchagin remained with generals Skobelev and Strukov until after the signing of the Treaty of San Stefano in February 1878. Through his aide-de-camp, Grand Duke Nicholas asked Vereshchagin, despite his vocal disagreement with Russian generals and his criticism of the conduct of the war, if he would accept an award for his "military services." Vereshchagin declined; and when he was officially informed that he would receive a golden sword for personal valor, he laughed, expressed his gratitude, and left for Paris before it could be presented to him.[36]

When he returned to Paris in late February 1878, Vereshchagin's first tasks were to repair the roof of his studio and to obtain loans from his brother and Stasov in St. Petersburg. He then began work on the Indian paintings that the Russo-Turkish War had interrupted. He traveled to London for additional items of clothing for his studies and there met the

Prince of Wales, who sought unsuccessfully to commission a number of paintings on India. Vereshchagin's artistic conception of the Balkan war paintings gradually took shape, but he encountered technical problems: "With every feeble impulse to embody an idea I face technical obstacles and difficulties which muddle what I have conceived if it is not well defined." Surely, the loss of the major sketches and studies also contributed to Vereshchagin's difficulties and partly eviscerated the Balkan war series, which, on completion in 1883, consisted of twenty-five works and fifty studies, and became essentially a chronicle of artistic "documents" of specific stages which Vereshchagin witnessed either before or after battle; many of these have been recounted above. Moreover, the depiction of a major Russian victory at Plevna in December 1878 is missing from his collection because he did not observe the conflict. The French writer Emile Zola (1840–1902), with whom Vereshchagin has much in common, might have called the Balkan paintings objective, scientific studies by a naturalist observer who consciously seeks to change society; it is probably that naturalist orientation in Vereshchagin's works which satisfied the positivism of the period for the facts of life and made his art so popular. That positivism was linked to a strong belief in evolutionary "progress," which Charles Darwin had established as a fundamental tenet of existence and survival. In terms of nineteenth-century international relations, Darwin's theory of natural selection was extended to war in the struggle for affluence and in the assertion of racial and national superiority. Victory in war was the measure of a nation's ability to survive and prosper.

The Balkan war paintings are more natural and fluent in execution than the Turkestan collection; what they lack in imaginative power is compensated for by a striking and compelling realism that consciously aims to shock the viewer.

The materials that Vereshchagin had brought with him to Paris—with the exception of clothing, weapons, and other artifacts—consisted of rough, random sketches of battlefields, troop positions, soldiers at rest and in motion, dressing stations, ethnic types, dead and wounded soldiers, Turkish atrocities, and mass graves. These sketches, many of which were on scraps of paper, even cigarette paper, proved inadequate; now resigned to the loss of his working pieces in Bulgaria, Vereshchagin made two trips to Plevna and Shipka in December–January 1879 and in October 1880 to sketch additional areas and military sites. On Vereshchagin's first return, General Skobelev granted his request—made through Vereshchagin's brother—for three soldiers and two horses to accompany him, plus allowances for the group and for care of the horses. In October, Grand Duke Nicholas expressed an interest in acquiring Vereshchagin's paintings, as did Tretiakov and D. Botkin, both of whom visited Vereshchagin at his studio. The grand duke's interest may be related to Stasov's unilateral request to the tsar's court to extend financial aid to Vereshchagin as a down payment on his Russo-Turkish War series; the court denied the request. When Vereshchagin learned of Stasov's action, he became angry him and he admonished Stasov, "Please don't do that again without my knowledge." Later, however, Grand Prince Alexander, who became Tsar Alexander III in 1881, also expressed interest in the paintings. In March 1879, Vereshchagin sent Stasov—the first of the projected series—*The Road of the Prisoners of War* (see Fig. 15), to explore the court's interest in purchasing it for seven thousand rubles. Stasov first asked Tretiakov of his interest in the work, but the latter made no commitment. The painting portrayed the road from the Danube to Plevna scattered with Turkish soldiers who had frozen to death because of inadequate clothing and food. The work is an indictment—as most of the series would be—of both the Turkish military for failing to provide their own soldiers with sufficient food and winter clothing and the Russian military for allowing them to freeze to death as prisoners of war. The painting so displeased certain courtiers that the grand prince did not even want to see it and waited, as did Tretiakov and Botkin, until Vereshchagin had completed the series. In November 1879, during the grand prince's visit to Paris, Vereshchagin refused to visit him or to allow him to view the war paintings simply because the prince had refused to see *The Road of the Prisoners of War.* After this episode, Grand Duke Vladimir, the President of the Academy of Arts, began to severely criticize Vereshchagin for the "*impossible* subjects" of his paintings. When this comment reached Vereshchagin's attention, he noted that it did "not recommend [the grand duke's] ability to distinguish obedient icon-daubers from independent artists." Later, Vereshchagin sold the painting in Europe; its present whereabouts is unknown. Vereshchagin remarked to Stasov that "They are all waiting for the time when they can acquire the paintings at a cheap price. They themselves will be at fault if, *to my regret*, the paintings miss them." In early April, however, aware that the grand prince had made no commitment for the Russo-Turkish collection, Tretiakov offered Vereshchagin seventy-five thousand rubles in five annual installments for the unfinished collection, which would be based, in his view, on the "sacrifices of the Russian people, the brilliant heroic deeds of the Russian soldier and of several individual personalities [i.e., generals]." For Vereshchagin, Tretiakov was in effect dictating for the content, size, and cost of the collection, and his offer was unacceptable.[37] In May, Vereshchagin wrote a firm but polite letter to Tretiakov:

> As for your letter to Vladimir Stasov about my painting which you saw, obviously you and I disagree *a little* in assessing my works and *a great deal* in their orientation. As an artist, what I am faced with is *war*, and I *bash* it with as much strength as I have; whether my blows are effective—that is another question, a question of my talent, but I bash it with all my might and without mercy. You, however, obviously, are concerned not so much generally with the *universal idea of war* as you are with particulars. For example, in this instance with the sacrifices of the Russian people, brilliant heroic deeds of Russian soldiers and some individual figures, etc. hence even the painting that you saw seems to you worthy of being only 'an introduction to the future collection.' But I consider the painting one of the most vital of all that I have created.[38]

In a conciliatory conclusion, Vereshchagin regretted that his paintings were "not coming into such good hands as yours." Some three weeks later, in another letter to Tretiakov, from whom he had recently borrowed 10,000 rubles plus interest, Vereshchagin explained that the offer of 75,000 for the collection, in view of his mounting financial debt and his limited physical ability to paint only four large works annually, could not support a modest standard of living: "Just consider, what am I, an artist who has already used up much strength and health for the development of my talent, going to live on?" Vereshchagin understood Tretiakov's natural desire to purchase the series as cheaply as possible, but if

Tretiakov did not express at the moment a serious interest in buying them, the prices would probably be higher later, from 50,000 to 100,000 rubles for each of the large paintings. If unable to sell the paintings collectively in five years, Vereshchagin intended to give them to a dealer to be sold in pairs or individually. For Tretiakov, *The Road of the Prisoners of War* did not specifically deal with the *Russian* heroic dimension of the war, and his view of the future orientation of the Balkan war series did not preclude "complete freedom" for Vereshchagin, since he noted to Stasov that "all that Vereshchagin finds necessary to do should be done." Tretiakov was not tempted by Vereshchagin's bait to purchase the series collectively rather than separately later, and he would not change his original offer despite the prospect of higher prices in the future.[39]

In the spring of 1879, the Prince of Wales invited Vereshchagin to hold an exhibition in London (Kensington Museum) of his Indian works and about 7 from the Russo-Turkish War series—180 pieces in all. The exhibition was very well received in the British press despite the fact that British suspicions of the formidable Russian threat to its interests had changed to outright dislike, if not hatred of Russia. Rumors arose that the prince planned to buy *The Procession of Elephants* (1875–79); but the English press dissuaded him from purchasing a painting from a Russian artist.[40] Several newspapers refused to cover the exhibition, and the *Times* reportedly did not publish its art critic's favorable review. No doubt, the Indian paintings attracted the most interest, but the Balkan war series, as the reviewer of *The Daily Telegraph* pointed out, also "significantly heightened the interest" in the exhibition and in Vereshchagin, "whose genius and energy alone have gained him powerful and influential friends in England and in his own country." He added: "One must see the whole collection for two reasons: Its Indian part, which includes, by the way, a memoir of the journey of the Prince of Wales, full of interesting and significant details. The other part, the war paintings, provided each with a lesson more striking than all that the peaceful traveler was ever capable of bringing home and conveying to the heart of the people." Another critic from *The Chelsea News* (Chelsea was the art center of London) observed that the paintings "demonstrate the enormous energy, the great individuality combined with extraordinary mastery and, in many instances, with paramount coloring." He suggested that young artists see the exhibit in order to draw "a lesson more useful than all the dry instructions" of the members of the Royal Academy of Arts. Critics from *The Daily Chronicle* noted: "It is not often that one experiences at art exhibits such genuine joy as in seeing Vereshchagin's collection. Both the vivid accomplishment of the scenes which he depicts and their artistic qualities are just as extraordinary as they are instructive and interesting."[41]

From London, Vereshchagin brought his exhibition to a French art club in Paris in December 1879. It was an admission-free display of three hundred works from his Indian and Balkan war collections and photographs of his Turkestan series; although Vereshchagin could have sold those off like "loaves of bread," none were for sale because he looked forward to selling them in Russia. As the two-week exhibition came to a close, Vereshchagin noted that its success was growing like a "snow-ball; literally the whole city is interested in it, people are flocking to see it." This was the first one-man show by of a Russian artist in Paris, and it proved to be a stupendous success, "a revelation," the opening of "new horizons," "an event," one that would "mark an epoch."[42] The exhibition elevated Vereshchagin to the front ranks of European artists and established his international reputation as the most well-known Russian artist of his time.

A good measure of the success of Vereshchagin's first show in Paris was surely due to Turgenev's efforts to publicize it and arrange private viewings for his numerous friends—intellectuals, writers, artists, journalists—and to write to many French newspapers and journals about it. In these letters, he characterized Vereshchagin as "unquestionably the most interesting figure of the Russian art world at the present time." Elsewhere, he wrote that "Vereshchagin is undoubtedly the most original Russian artist of all that Russia has produced, and for that reason alone he deserves the attention of the Parisian public."[43] Turgenev was already quite familiar with and an admirer of Vereshchagin's paintings when he saw the Turkestan exhibit in 1874 and the London exhibit of 1879, but he did not meet the artist until shortly before the Paris exhibition, when the two struck up a warm friendship. Turgenev made at least two visits to Vereshchagin's studio, during which his help was solicited in connection with the exhibit.

Of the thirty French reviews of the exhibition, only one was negative.

French artists found it difficult to believe that Vereshchagin could have created so many paintings in less than five years.[44] One critic remarked that "this is a rare exhibit which is destined to acquire the significance of an event in the life of Paris." Another pointed out that "we do not want to say that Vereshchagin's talent has risen to dizzying heights where no comparison is conceivable. We are saying that this is a solid talent, very powerful and deeply original." Another critic saw the secret of Vereshchagin's fascination in his artistic independence.[45] Still others noted the influence of Gérôme and such academic battle painters as Horace Vernet (1789–1863), Edouard Détaille (1848–1912), Alphonse de Neuville (1836–85), and, particularly, Ernest Meissonier (1815–91), although there is very little battle action as such in Vereshchagin's paintings. Rather, the novelty of his exhibit was the range and diversity of his talent, from his depiction of the colorful splendors of Indian architecture to the unknown or forgotten aspect of war—its suffering, pain, and death on a mass scale. It was the latter dimension that attracted the greatest attention. As the well-known French journalist Jules Valles put it:

> With his palette and brush, Vereshchagin brings humanity more good than Napoleon caused it evil with his great army. His works counteract the venom which is poured at school benches and which is still being poured into our souls; they counteract the insanity of valor, the frenzy of false heroism. And in order to destroy this false education and to eradicate the evil of age-old traditions, he has not tried to idealize peace in vulgar, tasteless allegories. He has simply restored, with terrifying accuracy and epic realism, the real image of war: blood, ruins, fire, the naked infamy of slaughter. And for that the remembrance of him will not be effaced from the grateful memory of peoples. Vasily Vereshchagin has served humanity well.[46]

Perhaps the French expected to see Russia's "victory" over Turkey depicted in the Balkan war works, since military pageantry was the staple of battle paintings of pre-bourgeois society (1793); the action in those conventional paintings was confined to heroic feats of a professional, hereditary military caste and to operations proper: the glorification of the skills of military leaders and their victories, broad panoramas of battlefields full of roaring cannons and gunfire, military leaders on rearing white horses, soldiers in action and lying dead, rising gunsmoke, flags, banners, and parades.[47] This form of battle painting served state needs by sanctioning war. What Vereshchagin portrayed in his war paintings was "radically different and in the highest degree contemporary . . . in form and content. No previous period of art would have dared anything similar."[48] As Vereshchagin pointed out to Tretiakov, "between *festive* paintings of war . . . and paintings of war *as such, as it really is*, there is a vast difference."[49] In response to Vereshchagin's exhibition in Vienna in 1881, an Austrian writer explained the critical distinction: "All that battle artists have only seen heretofore is the glory of conquerors and military leaders. Vereshchagin, to the contrary, has observed only people who have become weak through loss of blood and perish, and who pay with their blood and lives for the glory of others. These Russo-Turkish paintings speak, therefore, more than all that has been written in brochures and articles that condemn war and its instigators."[50] In monarchic bourgeois society, however, war involved the large-scale destruction of the common masses for reasons of state, e.g., ideological fanaticism, economic and territorial expansion, and personal aggrandizement. In Vereshchagin's experience, this was the universal meaning of "contemporary" war; its character has not changed but intensified in Draconian forms in the twentieth century. As he remarked, "In war, victory is only ten percent, and ninety percent is horrible mutilations, cold, hunger, cruelty, despair and death in its most staggering manifestations."[51]

In one of his most popular Balkan war paintings, *Shipka-Sheinovo (Skobelev at Shipka)* [1883–88; Pl. 11], Vereshchagin juxtaposes the traditional form of battle painting and the real tragedy of wars whose victims have neither voice nor identity; he vividly shows the tragic human costs of military victory. The action takes place in a snow-covered valley against the background of the Balkan mountains and a partly cloudy sky. The day after his decisive victory at Shipka, Skobelev rides a white horse—followed by Vereshchagin in a white fur coat and by Skobelev's staff saluting the cheering soldiers—between scattered frozen Turkish and Russian corpses in the immediate foreground and a long formation of his troops, many of whom have thrown their caps in the air. He accepts their cheers of victory as he waves his cap and cries out to them, "In the name of our country, in the name of the Sovereign, thank you, comrades." At the extreme left, the raised (probably frozen) arms of a dead Russian soldier in a final, futile appeal or prayer are a grim contrast to the general's victorious salute. This painting also reflects the contradictory roles that Vereshchagin sought to play in his life: on the one hand, his attachment to the military, his love of military action, his passion for objective scientific observation and knowledge of war, and on the other, his condemnation of war and his genuine compassion for the sufferings of the ordinary people. To a certain extent, his life and art closely parallel those of Tolstoy, whose personality was even more divided. Both also condemned war but supported it patriotically when it served noble or just causes. A state perspective on war and on political dissent that has a contemporary resonance is reflected in Grand Prince Alexander's comment upon receiving a copy of the catalogue of Vereshchagin's Paris exhibition: "In reading Vereshchagin's catalogue of paintings, and especially the texts to them, I cannot conceal that it was repugnant for me to read his customary biases that are offensive to our national pride, and one may draw one conclusion from them: either Vereshchagin is a swine or a completely deranged man!"[52]

In March 1880, Vereshchagin, deeply in debt as a result of the costs of arranging his London and Paris shows, had to obtain a loan to hold a forty-day exhibition of his Indian and Balkan war collections in St. Petersburg, where he hoped to sell each collectively. About 200,000 Russians attended the exhibit at a nominal admission fee. In Paris, Grand Prince Alexander had told Vereshchagin that Russians would not understand the war paintings; thus, Vereshchagin added explanatory inscriptions to make them more comprehensible. Grand Prince Vladimir, the head of the Academy of Arts, asked that the inscriptions be removed; Vereshchagin refused and challenged the Grand Prince to order their removal, which he did.[53] Vereshchagin complied, and wrote to the secretary of the academy, who served as the Grand Prince's intermediary: "I am removing the inscriptions, but let his highness the Grand Prince take the blame that people who protest the evils of war be equated with those who are negative to the state."[54]

While the exhibition was in progress, Tsar Alexander II wanted Vereshchagin to bring the entire collection to the Winter Palace for his personal examination. Vereshchagin declined the "honor"; the tsar sent his guards to remove the paintings from the walls and bring them to the palace, thus causing the exhibition to be closed for several days. Vereshchagin did, however, arrange the exhibit for the tsar, but saw no need to tour it with him. He sought to avoid the delicate situation of answering questions from the tsar and his military staff and suggested that his brother Alexander accompany the tsar instead; the tsar agreed.[55] Perhaps the memory of the Turkestan exhibit in 1874, when he destroyed three paintings, played a large role in Vereshchagin's refusal, or the real agenda of the tsar's court in isolating Vereshchagin's works in the Winter Palace may have been to compel him to withdraw objectional paintings from the exhibit. Disillusioned by this experience and on the verge of illness, Vereshchagin noted that if he could escape the poverty of his situation he would abandon St. Petersburg and never exhibit his works there again.[56] The tsar did not offer to purchase the Balkan war series, although the Prussian General Werder Wilhelm, a military attaché in St. Petersburg, advised him to buy the collection and then destroy it.[57] What the Russian Minister of War D. Miliutin wrote in his diary accurately reflects the royal court's reaction to Vereshchagin's Balkan works:

> After my report . . . I dropped into Nikolaevsky Hall of the Winter Palace where Vereshchagin's paintings were on display for the sovereign, paintings which caused such an uproar and aroused bitter arguments between the admirers of his talent, largely by ultra-realists, and the opponents who consider these paintings not a reproduction of the scenes of the former war, but a profanation of war, a malicious caricature of what constitutes the pride and object of worship for national feeling. Indeed, Vereshchagin is unquestionably a talented artist, and has a strange inclination to choose for his paintings the most unattractive subjects: to portray only the unsightly dimension of war and, moreover, to attach to his paintings inscriptions in the form of malicious epigrams with pretensions to being witty. Thus, for example, having depicted in three paintings a sentry covered with snow and freezing to death, he wrote over these paintings 'All Is Quiet at Shipka!' In the painting that depicted the sovereign and his retinue at

> Plevna, in view of the bloodshed, he inscribes 'The Tsar's Name-Day.' This inscription, however, which was flaunted in Paris, disappeared, of course, when it was on display here. Without having had the opportunity to attend the exhibit that has attracted masses of people, I was glad of the convenient occasion personally to confirm the endless talk that I heard of these paintings, and I must admit that having seen the whole series of paintings, I came away distressed. The artist himself was not in the hall. The sovereign, after he wanted to see the paintings, did not want to see the author himself.[58]

A Russian artist close to the royal court recalled a conversation with Grand Prince Alexander after the prince had seen Vereshchagin's paintings:

> Well, let's talk a bit about Vereshchagin and his paintings. My pride as a military man and former witness of the last war did not allow me to acquire paintings of such content, in which I see all bias and falsehood. Let's take the Plevna Highway, scattered with corpses of Turkish soldiers half-covered with snow, over which hovers a flock of ravens. And all this bears the title, 'Our Prisoners.' But weren't our soldiers, horses and military carts lost on the same highway, and all that removed and committed to the earth? I myself witnessed that, and for that reason it is a sickening bias and lie. And the field, where 300 men lie dead, over whom a priest burns incense, behind whom stands a clerk—isn't that blasphemy, when a common soldier was not buried with tens of his fellow soldiers—just where is the truth here? There can be particular instances of confusion, but to generalize them in such a major work is simply dishonest. I won't speak of 'The Tsar's Name-Day,' that malicious irony concerning our defeat [at Plevna]. . . . All this is a product of some malice against our soldiers, a malice that the artist desires to conceal by preaching that he is creating similar paintings to arouse the disgust of people against war. War always was, is, and will be waged for the offended honor of a nation or for something else, and not to heal the wounds of humanity by the vulgar depictions of a profiteer for his fame.[59]

Several days after the tsar examined the paintings, Vereshchagin wrote to a friend in Paris: "The heir and several other highnesses are enraged. The lack of patriotism, almost betrayal—that's what they are accusing me of. But the majority of the public does not share that opinion."[60] Further, a policeman was posted in front of Vereshchagin's residence because Grand Prince Michael, a general and chairman of the State Council, suspected him of being the head of the nihilist movement in Russia. Subsequently, Vereshchagin found it impossible to travel or work in the stifling atmosphere in Russia after the assassination of Tsar Alexander II in 1881.[61]

Vereshchagin was right about the public and press reaction to his exhibit, which, in view of the "enormous sensation" that it created, split the Russian press into two opposing camps. The majority of the newspaper reviews were highly favorable; they saw the Balkan war paintings as highly realistic and faithful representations. In contrast to its reaction to the 1874 exhibit, the autocracy was prepared to launch a sustained assault on Vereshchagin through the reactionary newspaper *New Times,* which served the government's bidding. In a series of articles, the newspaper disparaged Vereshchagin's artistic talent and asserted that the success of his Paris exhibit had been exaggerated, since major newspapers had refused to cover it. It may very well be that the newspaper's objective in vilifying Vereshchagin was to discourage art collectors from purchasing the Balkan war paintings. More importantly, the newspaper excoriated Vereshchagin for his biased and distorted portrayal of the war (the same charge that Grand Prince Alexander leveled at him in Paris), his debasement of the Russian army and his glorification of the Turkish army, and his lack of patriotism. This attack evoked a public response from Vereshchagin:

> I presented the other side of the *Russian* war, and not the *Austrian* or *English* wars, because *I happened to see this war and not those wars.* Without considering a Russian a 'wild beast,' I do not attribute to him any exceptional blood-thirsty instincts peculiar only to him, and assume that it was understood that way, for example, in Paris, where of all the voices of the critics who recognized in my works a perceptible philosophical orientation, not a single critic accused me of bias,

> which it seems is too often hurled here at those who think independently. I can only regret that the abstract-philosophical portrayal of the horrors of war (horrors of which our and other European societies have very confused ideas) could be understood in the narrow sense of a reproach *namely* to a Russian.[62]

However successful his St. Petersburg exhibition, Vereshchagin was unable to sell his Indian and Balkan war paintings collectively. After his shows in Paris, Vienna, and Berlin, he received numerous expressions of interest in as well as private offers to acquire his works. In urgent need of a large sum of money to liquidate his debts and to undertake another journey to India, he decided to auction his Indian collection in St. Petersburg after the close of the exhibit. This precluded the completion of that collection as a "poem." The two-day auction brought 140,000 rubles, which is considerably more than Vereshchagin expected. Tretiakov was the major buyer and paid 75,000 rubles for various pieces. Gratified by the results, Vereshchagin donated 10,000 rubles for the support of art and music schools and for the medical education of women. He later regretted his decision to auction the paintings when he realized that they would have fetched far more in exhibition fees and sales.[63]

After Paris and St. Petersburg, Vereshchagin received numerous invitations to hold exhibits—some seventy five during his life—in other West European locales. In October 1881, his exhibition in Vienna attracted 110,000 viewers (an unprecedented number for that city), received about fifty reviews, and made Vereshchagin the "most popular man," "the hero of the day." Russian church music and folk songs were played during the exhibition. Vereshchagin donated the proceeds from three days of admission fees and the sale of catalogues to the poor of the city, and one day of proceeds to the pension fund of the staff of the Viennese Art Association. Local artists who helped organize the exhibit found it impractical to satisfy Vereshchagin's demand that schoolchildren and soldiers be admitted free.[64]

In view of the stunning success of the first show in Paris, Vereshchagin arranged another there in December 1881. He tried to hold it in a prestigious art club with the help of a committee of French artists, but they hobbled his efforts out of personal rivalry. The exhibition finally opened in the halls of the French newspaper, *Gaulois*, which was owned by a Russian, Ilia Tsion, a former professor. Although it promised to be quite successful, the exhibition had to be canceled because of an altercation between Vereshchagin and Tsion apparently over the rental terms for the hall. During the course of the brief exhibit, Vereshchagin and a friend were speaking with Tsion, who became boorish and arrogant and told Vereshchagin to go to hell. Vereshchagin, standing with hat in his hand, struck Tsion twice in the face with his hat; Tsion bared his revolver, as did Vereshchagin, who pointed his at Tsion's forehead and dared him to shoot. After lowering his revolver, Tsion claimed he had only been joking.[65]

Vereshchagin's February 1882 exhibit in Berlin drew 150,000 viewers and received more than ninety published reviews. A nominal admission fee for the German military attracted many groups of soldiers at the beginning of the exhibit. Like the French, a number of German critics observed similarities between Vereshchagin's art and that of Adolf Menzel (1815–1905), Hans Makart (1840–84), and Eduard Hildenbrandt (1817–68). One critic offered an unusual perspective on the war paintings:

> When one glances at Vereshchagin's striking paintings, it comes involuntarily to mind that here before us are juxtaposed *something higher*, of which human creativity is capable—art, and *something lower*, to which the human spirit is capable of descending—the bloody business of Cain. Murder here is the subject of art, and note, not just common murder, but multiplied, stylized, embellished by ideas and ideals, fringed with shining honors—the murder of whole masses, war. But what acts as the content of Vereshchagin's works is a fiery, angry statement against the mad beast-like nature of war. To be sure, art should not be a school teacher, a preacher; but when it arouses in the viewer such thoughts which carry him far beyond the limits of a painting, when it elevates him, shakes him by means of the tragic element, compels him by paintings about vulgarity and shame to enter into himself—then it achieves only what constitutes its real obligation.[66]

Another critic pointed out the role of music at the exhibit: "Concealed from the spectators is a choir, accompanied by a harmonium, that sings solemn hymns. The artist required this exacting apparatus not for his paintings, the artistic merit of which is beyond question, but because Vereshchagin, by regarding himself to a certain degree an apostle of peace, wants by means of singing, music and art to convince the broad public that war is the most infamous of all."[67]

Vereshchagin accompanied Field Marshal Helmut von Moltke, chief of staff of the Prussian army who believed in the supremacy of military authority in civilian affairs, through the exhibition. When they came to the *Apotheosis of War* (see Pl. 7), Vereshchagin translated and repeated the inscription. Moltke did not react, but shortly thereafter he issued an order forbiding German military personnel and schoolchildren to attend the exhibition en masse.[68] In effect, the order excluded children, but individual German soldiers would quickly examine the works and leave. The exhibition went on to major cities worldwide, including Dresden, Hamburg, Dusseldorf, Bremen, Brussels, Prague, Budapest, Amsterdam, Copenhagen, Stockholm, New York, Chicago, Boston, and Philadelphia.

Chapter Four

NEW DIRECTIONS

The hostile reaction of the Russian royal court to the 1880 exhibit as well as the "white terror," the repressive, reactionary reign that seized Russia after the assassination of Tsar Alexander II in 1881, began to make their full impact on Vereshchagin. From the perspective of the Russian autocracy, his Balkan war paintings were bitter reminders of its failed ambitions of military conquest; its military inferiority, economic backwardness, and diplomatic humiliation; and the onset of a severe domestic crisis. Moreover, his allegedly biased portrayal of the war, the nominal admission fee to his exhibit, and his refusal to accompany the tsar in his review were tantamount to an assault not only against war but against the political order as well. Thus, Vereshchagin's art and behavior were considered revolutionary. The royal court's repeated charge that he was a nihilist distressed him in Paris and almost led to a nervous collapse in 1882. The illness was attended by an attack of malaria that required quinine, morphine, electric shock, and water treatments. A well-known French neuropathologist, Jean Martin Charcot (1825–93), diagnosed exhaustion and strained nerves and advised rest.[1] Vereshchagin believed that he would not survive the crisis and was constantly absorbed by the "thought of approaching death."[2] He became so disillusioned and depressed that he decided to abandon paintings on war: "Not only in Russia, but in both Austria and Germany they recognized the revolutionary orientation of my war paintings. The whole Russian royal court considers me a nihilist. I will find other subjects."[3]

He began to reflect on new subjects in his war against state oppression and state execution of criminals, political dissenters, and revolutionaries.

But he faced a dilemma which he, in a state of pain and despair, tended to exaggerate. Despite his deep love and longing for his native land, he considered the Russian domestic situation stifling and unsuitable for work. He had planned to make studies for the *Trilogy of Executions* in St. Petersburg and to travel to Siberia to create a series on Russian penal servitude and political exiles. These works would be Vereshchagin's way of punishing the punishers.[4] But he was convinced that he could not "breathe freely" in Russia, because he would face constant harassment, interrogation, and bureaucratic red tape wherever he traveled.[5]

During most of 1882, Vereshchagin left the management of his exhibits in Hamburg, Dresden, Dusseldorf, Brussels, and Budapest to his brother Alexander, and he devoted his attention to preparing his articles about the Caucasus, Turkestan, and India for translation into German and French. He also contributed autobiographical data to Stasov, who was writing a study of his life to the year 1882. As his health improved, however, the thought of returning to Russia became irresistible. In September 1882, fearing that he would be accused of sedition, he asked Stasov to obtain from the Ministry of Internal Affairs a special pass that would relieve him of surveillance and interrogation from police and village constables, since it was "unthinkable" for him to travel in Russia without one. He prepared for the trip, but then postponed it after consulting with friends, who advised him to wait for a more favorable political climate in Russia.[6]

In October 1882, he decided instead to travel to India to make sketches and studies of the Himalayas and its peoples in order to supplement his forthcoming exhibits and especially to create one painting about the new target in his war against state violence—capital punishment. He explained his interest in the subject:

> Observing life through all my various travels, I have been particularly struck by the fact that even in our time people kill one another everywhere and under all possible pretexts, and by every possible means. Wholesale murder is still called *war*, while killing individuals is called *execution*. Everywhere the same worship of brute strength, the same inconsistency; on the one hand, men slaying their fellows by the million for an idea often impracticable, are elevated to a high

> pedestal of public admiration; on the other, men who kill individuals for the sake of a crust of bread, are mercilessly and promptly executed—and this even in Christian countries, in the name of Him whose teaching was founded on peace and love. These facts, observed on many occasions, made a strong impression on my mind, and after having carefully thought the matter over, I painted several pictures of wars and executions. These subjects I have treated in a fashion far from sentimental, for having myself killed many a poor fellow-creature in different wars, I have not the right to be sentimental. But the sight of heaps of human beings slaughtered, shot, beheaded, hanged under my eyes in all that region extending from the frontier of China to Bulgaria, has not failed to impress itself vividly on the imaginative side of my work.[7]

The British police in India were hostile to and suspicious of Vereshchagin's art and still considered him an agent of the Russian government; Tsar Alexander III considered him an agent of the Russian revolutionaries and conspirators. Vereshchagin remarked that all that remained was for him to be suspected of being an English agent, despite his nationality.[8] By mid-January 1883, Vereshchagin had lost interest in Indian subjects and had fulfilled his task of making studies for a painting—*English Suppression of an Indian Rebellion* (1884; see Fig. 19)—that was intended to sting the British hide.

During his stay in India, he began to make plans for an exhibit in Moscow, despite a lingering fear of hostilities from the Russian police. Upon arriving in Moscow in March 1883, he arranged an exhibit for April primarily to sell his Balkan war paintings in order to finance a trip to Palestine, where he would create, among other works of the biblical era, another piece in the trilogy, *Roman Execution (Crucifixion)* [see Fig. 18]. The Moscow exhibit was largely satisfactory and received favorable press coverage, but it hardly matched the success of the 1880 show in St. Petersburg. The Russian censor would not allow Vereshchagin to photograph half of his "rebellious" paintings. As in St. Petersburg, he was accused, even more forcefully, of being unpatriotic, a "charlatan, a cosmopolitan, a subversive, a corrupter of the people."[9] Vereshchagin also went to St. Petersburg to make studies for *Execution of Conspirators in*

Russia (see Fig. 20). To be safe, he requested permission from the Academy of Arts to make the studies; the academy, obviously unaware of his real purpose, granted his request. In late March, he offered Tretiakov the entire Balkan war series of twenty-five pieces and about fifty studies for 150,000 rubles. Tretiakov, however, did not like all of the war pieces because they lacked unity and concerned only isolated episodes. Further, he planned to spend no more than 50,000 rubles in acquiring certain works.[10] Unable to sell his paintings collectively, Vereshchagin assigned them to an art broker while the Moscow exhibit was in progress; much to Tretiakov's surprise, the bidding for the paintings was quite competitive, as Vereshchagin had predicted. Tretiakov paid 57,000 rubles for three works: *Alexander II at Plevna on August 30, 1877* (see Fig. 12), *Before the Attack. At Plevna* (see Fig. 14), and *Shipka-Sheinovo (Skobelev at Shipka* (see Pl. 11). Two Kievan industrialists and art collectors, Nikolai and Ivan Tereshchenko (father and son), purchased five pieces and the fifty studies for an undisclosed amount. The proceeds from the sale were apparently ample enough to enable Vereshchagin to donate a large sum to Russian art schools. In 1887, Tretiakov purchased from Vereshchagin *After the Attack. Dressing Station at Plevna* (see Fig. 13) and *The Defeated. Funeral Service* (see Fig. 17) for 12,500 rubles.

The lack of harassment from the Russian government and the desire to sell the remaining Balkan war pieces in Russia prompted Vereshchagin in December 1883 to hold an exhibit in St. Petersburg of his unsold works and his new ones on India. The exhibit created no significant impression, since Russians in St. Petersburg previously had seen many of the paintings. Vereshchagin was unable to sell the remainder of the Balkan pieces, and his Indian works generated no interest. Before the exhibit, he had asked Tretiakov to forward *Before the Attack* without a frame to the exhibit. The latter's refusal evoked a one-line response from Vereshchagin: "You and I are no longer friends." Their friendship, however, was renewed in 1886, and, in a letter to a friend, Vereshchagin admitted that it was stupid and crude to treat Tretiakov as he did.[11] Moreover, Vereshchagin had a personal rift with his long-time friend and supporter, Stasov, who had become "sick and tired" of him. Although this breach terminated their correspondence for nine years, Stasov still wrote favorably of Vereshchagin's art.[12]

In early 1884, Vereshchagin, accompanied by his wife, went to Palestine to make ethnographic sketches and studies and particularly to create *Roman Execution (Crucifixion)* as part of his *Trilogy of Executions.* In Jerusalem, he worked closely with rabbis and Russian monks, including the Russian Orthodox priest Antonin, on archaeological explorations and biblical studies for his paintings. On the basis of his findings, he portrayed the crucifixion close to the walls of Jerusalem; he rendered the draperies of the numerous figures in accordance with historical records and ancient carvings.[13] Upon his return to Paris in late 1884, he began to work on the *Trilogy of Executions* and a series of biblical works in preparation for forthcoming exhibits in Western Europe and America.

The first piece in the trilogy is *Roman Execution (Crucifixion)* [1887; Fig. 18]. Although crucifixion is usually associated with Christ, it was also used by the Romans to execute slaves, foreigners, robbers, and others, for acts of unrest, political subversion, or sedition. The victim was stripped of his clothing, and his hands and feet were nailed to the beams of the cross, which rendered him immobile. His legs were the main support on the crucifix; breaking them or piercing the body with a lance hastened death. Vereshchagin considered crucifixion the cruelest form of capital punishment because it involved slow torture for days and ultimate death by asphyxiation as the body was drained of blood. Figure 18 can easily be taken as the Crucifixion of Christ, since it contains the iconography customarily connected with such paintings. Vereshchagin portrays the more traditional form of the crucifixion, which includes three women, Roman guards, and a large group of diverse figures. His subtle intent, however, was to demonstrate that crucifixion was not unique to Christ; that is was an instrument of Roman political oppression and a not uncommon event.

Vereshchagin depicts the episode on a dark, cloudy day outside the high walls of Jerusalem; on a small slope, figures are being crucified. The extreme lateral view of the crucifixion is quite unusual, if not original, since most Renaissance artists usually fixed it in the immediate foreground. The setting recalls a prison courtyard. The agony in the faces of the three victims is barely visible to the viewer. Vereshchagin informs us that the long-haired figure in the center has "dedicated himself to God"; thus this person was being executed for a religious belief that involved

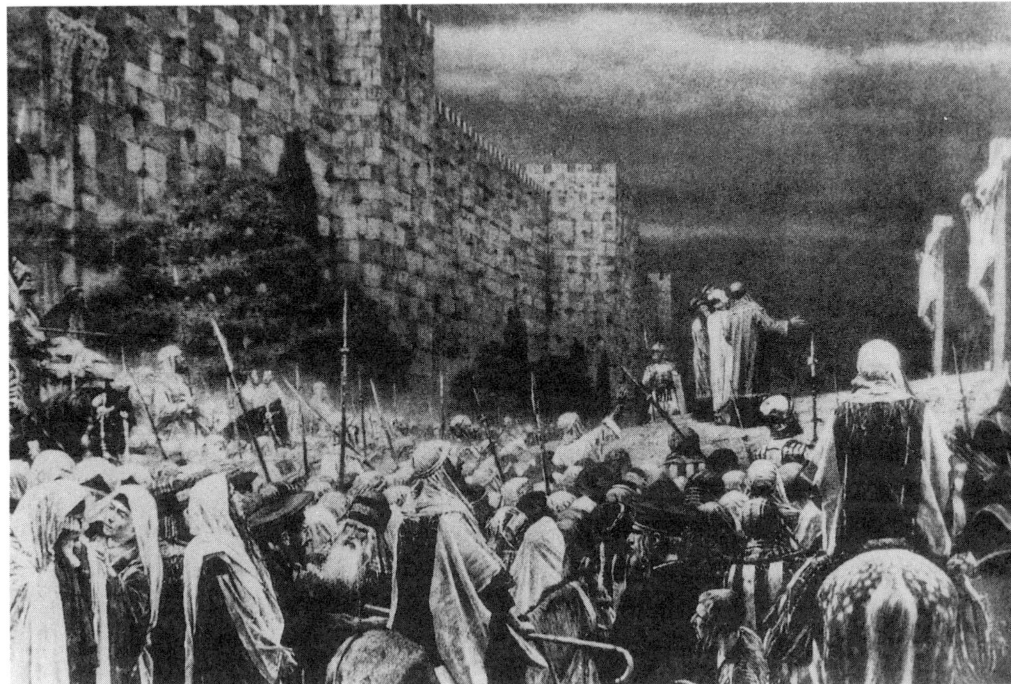

Figure 18. *Roman Execution (Crucifixion)*. 1887. Oil on canvas. 295 × 399 cm. By permission of the Brooklyn Museum, New York.

political dissent and subversion. Two Judaean clergymen are engaged in discussion with a Roman military official who stands between them. They are the key figures in the work. It is difficult to interpret the gesture of the clergyman's hand on the right, although Vereshchagin attempted—quite unsuccessfully—to show that the discussion concerned the guilt of the figure in the center. Perhaps he really meant to signify that the crucifixion was an unavoidable necessity and that the clergy sanctioned the spectacle of agonizing death and were in collusion with the Roman rulers in oppressing their own people. In the foreground, a large group of Roman soldiers have bared their spears and lances, ready to prevent any intervention or disorder. In the immediate foreground, a dense crowd of men and women, representing all social levels, has gathered in grief and curiosity to watch the execution. Vereshchagin has deliberately trapped them between the grim choice of crucifixion for opposition to the political order and acceptance of their confinement in it as symbolized by the high, impenetrable walls to the left. Vereshchagin describes his own work from a historical perspective:

> In the foreground . . . are seen people of every description; some on foot, some on horseback; others mounted on camels or on donkeys. Those are country folk or nomads, who, returning home from market, stopped over on their way for a moment in order to witness the event of the day—the execution of a man, the renown of whose deeds had reached even their huts and tents—a man whose arrest caused almost an insurrection in the city. Among others in the crowd can be noticed a few Hebrew merchants with their characteristic head-gear . . . and Pharisees with the letters of the Law written on the coverings of their heads. One of the Pharisees is discussing something with his neighbor concerning a woman who is seen weeping bitterly, in the corner of the picture, presumably the mother of one of the crucified men. Her face cannot be seen, but her sorrow must be great indeed, and none of the women surrounding her seems likely to be able to console her.[14]

Another woman, probably a relative of one of the victims, watches the crucifixion and weeps. These three women bear the torment of the three victims. The painting conveys the hopelessness, oppression, and suffering that pervaded life under Roman rule.

English Suppression of an Indian Rebellion (1884; Fig. 19) is the second piece in the trilogy. It is based on the 1857 mutiny of the Sepoys—native Indian soldiers who served in the British army—against the westernizing policies that threatened Indian culture during the administration (1848–57) of Governor-General Dalhousie. The mutiny, which was also a function of racial and religious antagonisms, led to an open rebellion against British imperial rule. According to Vereshchagin, "blowing from guns," the form of execution depicted in the work, "was . . . comparatively humane" and "was used by the British authorities in India for many years before and after the Sepoy revolt," despite assertions by the English military that it had been used only "in a few instances."[15] One retired British general proudly confirmed the practice of this form of execu-

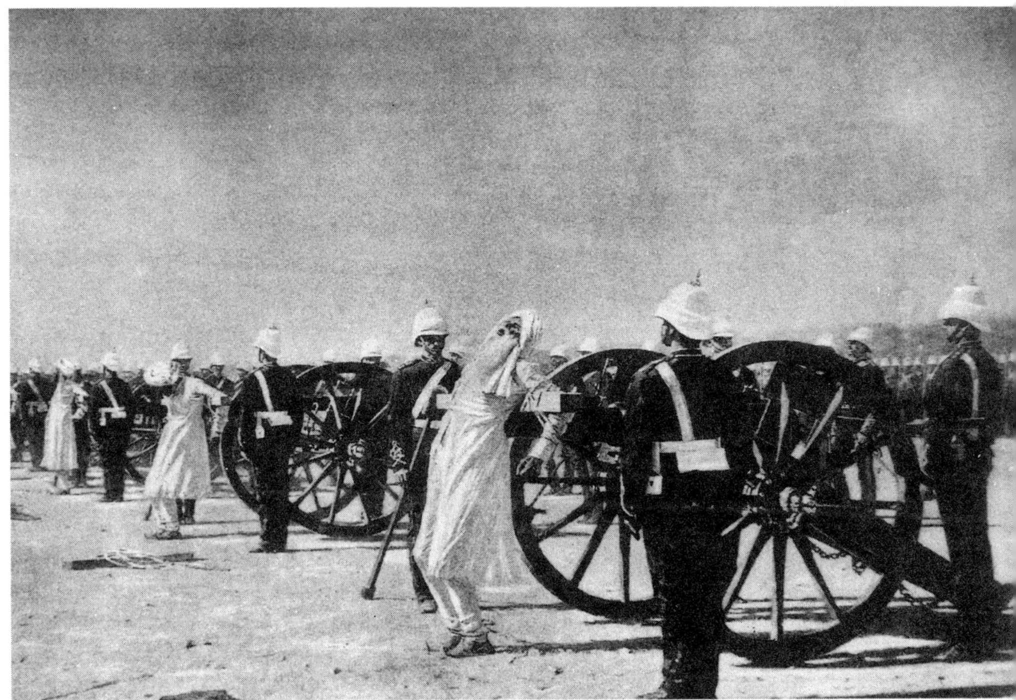

Figure 19. *English Suppression of an Indian Rebellion.* 1884. Oil on canvas. Whereabouts unknown.

tion.[16] Hindus believed that death by bullet or hanging would be regarded in the other world as an expression of martyrdom. Execution by cannon, however, instilled "positive terror into the heart of a native, since such a shot tears the criminal's body in many parts and thus prevents him from presenting himself in decent form in heaven"; therefore, the Hindu did not fear any other form "at the hands of the heathenish, unclean Europeans." In view of this attitude, and, as long as the British sought to impose their economic, cultural, and religious rule on the Indian population, Vereshchagin believed that this method of capital punishment would persist.[17]

The painting does not depict the Sepoys but Sikh peasants who waged a long, bitter struggle against British rule. On a hot, sunny day, four white-robed Sikhs are bound with their backs to the barrels of black cast-iron cannon. It is no accident that the positions of the victims are comparable to those of the three figures in the *Roman Execution (Crucifixion)*: this is another form of crucifixion. On the ground at the left lie the remains of rope and boards that were used to tie them. Awaiting the execution order, the English soldiers stand at puppetlike attention, their rigid positions a contrast to the helpless stances of the victims. The rows of soldiers with their bayonets attached to their rifles in the extreme right background add to the overkill, which is historically accurate in view of the ferocious vengeance the British took on the Indian population for the mutiny. The first Sikh, a tall elderly man is tightly strapped to the gun; he accepts his fate and stoically awaits the imminent explosion. During the executions, many observers were impressed by the "bravery and resignation" of the Indians; as one witness recalled: "Often and often have I seen natives executed, of all ages, of every caste, and every position in society. Yet never have I seen one of them misbehave. They died with a stoicism that in Europe would excite astonishment and admiration."[18] The English soldier who faces the viewer looks at the Sikh with a modicum of pity. The second Sikh is a far more pathetic figure than the first; he can barely stand, and indeed might fall if not for the ropes that bind him to the gun.

The *Execution of Conspirators in Russia* (1884–85; Fig. 20), the last piece in the trilogy, is based on the public hanging of S. Perovskaia, A. Zheliabov, N. Kibalchich, T. Mikhailov, and N. Rysakov, five members of the Russian revolutionary organization, The People's Will, who assassinated Tsar Alexander II on March 1, 1881. During the trial, both the Russian philosopher Vladimir Soloviov and Tolstoy appealed to Tsar Alexander III, as the Christian ruler of a Christian nation, to pardon and exile the revolutionaries.[19] At the trial, Zheliabov described the objectives of the organization and the transformation of the movement from peaceful to revolutionary aims to topple the political order:

> We have tried in several different ways to act on behalf of the people. At the beginning of the seventies we chose to live like workers and peacefully propagate our Socialist ideas. The movement was absolutely harmless. But how did it end? It was broken only because of the immense obstacles in the form of prison and banishment with

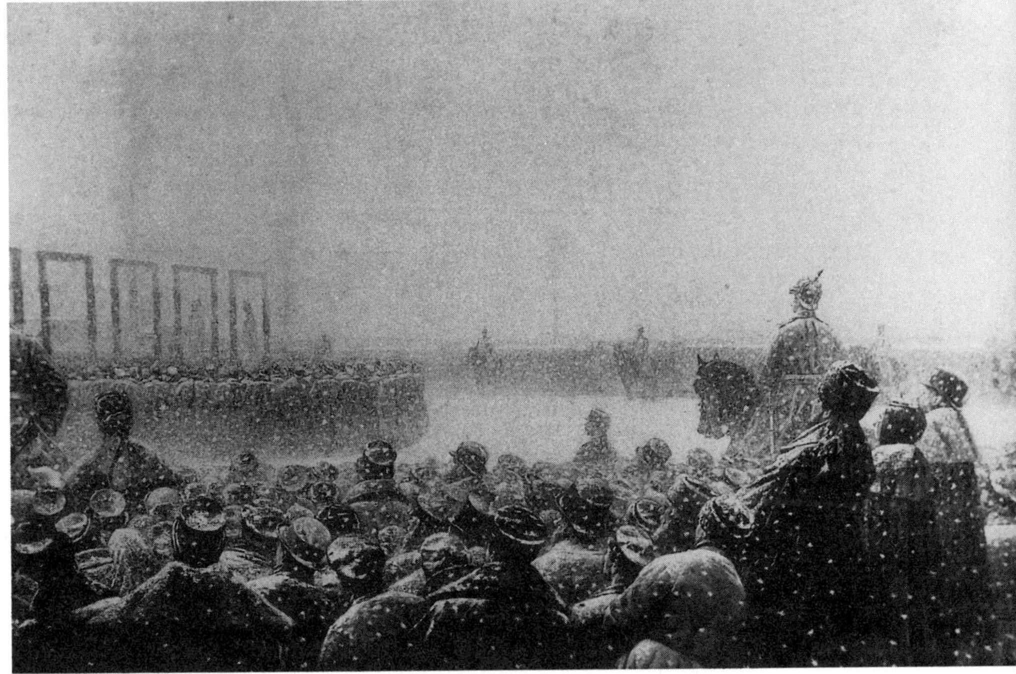

Figure 20. *Execution of Conspirators in Russia.* 1884–85. Oil on canvas. 285 × 400 cm. Museum of the Great October Revolution, St. Petersburg.

which it had to contend. A movement, which was unstained by blood and which repudiated violence, was crushed. . . . The short time that we lived among the people showed us how bookish and doctrinaire were our ideas. We then decided to act on behalf of the interests created by the people, interests which were inherent in its life and which it recognized. Such was the distinctive character of Populism. From metaphysics and dreams we moved to positivism, and kept close to the soil. . . . Instead of spreading Socialist ideas, we gave first place to our determination to reawaken the people by agitation in the name of the interest that it felt; instead of a peaceful fight we applied ourselves to a fight with deeds. We began with small deeds. . . . It was in 1878 that the idea of a more radical fight first made its appearance—the idea of cutting the Gordian knot. The party had not yet seen clearly enough the significance of our political structure for the destiny of the Russian people, though now all its forces drove it to battle against the political system.[20]

Before the execution, Rysakov attempted to save his life by offering to work for the Russian police; his proposal was rejected. Perovskaia wrote to her mother that she had lived according to her convictions and awaited her fate "with a clear conscience." She and Zheliabov refused to see a priest; Mikhailov made his confession, as did Rysakov, who received the Eucharist. On the bright morning of April 3, 1881, the five prisoners were brought to Semionovsky Square in St. Petersburg, where 100,000 people had gathered to watch the hanging. One witness remarked that the prisoners looked like victors riding in triumph. Five priests in separate carriages followed the procession. The police restrained the angry crowd from attacking two women who waved handkerchiefs at the condemned prisoners. As the revolutionaries came up to the gallows, the verdict was read, and the five priests approached them to kiss the crucifix, after which they all kissed each other farewell. Their heads and faces were then covered with white shrouds. The beat of drums added drama to the state spectacle of death. The hangman removed his coat to prepare the noose for the first hanging. For the second, the rope snapped twice under the heavy weight of Mikhailov's body. The crowd, initially hostile to the prisoners, became angry; it now saw the twice-broken rope as a sign of divine intervention for pardon. When the rope appeared to break again, the hangman added another noose which held. The other executions were completed without interruption. The proceedings lasted about forty-five minutes, after which the condemned were removed from the gallows, placed in black coffins and carted away for burial in an unmarked grave.[21]

Vereshchagin's rendition of the slow, cruel death by hanging, which marked a moderate advance in reducing the victims' suffering, occurs on a cold, snowy morning, symbolic of the "white terror" that had gripped the country after the assassination of Alexander II. Like the crosses in *Roman Execution (Crucifixion)* [see Fig. 18] the gallows are relegated to the background, but their position is reversed to the left. Two figures already hang from the gallows. Beyond them in the background, smokestacks suggest that execution is a normal feature of daily production. Before the gallows is a small group of government officials and military figures who hope to obtain a piece of the hangman's cord which they believe will bring luck at cards.[22] Policemen on horseback maintain order and keep the crowd at a distance. Like the clergy in *Roman Execution (Crucifixion)*, the priest in the extreme right foreground is a focal figure. Although he looks passively on from a distance, he is linked to the policeman on horseback to his immediate right, who symbolizes the state.

Vereshchagin also painted a series of works on various episodes in the life of Jesus. Two of these invite attention in view of the controversy and sensation they created when they were exhibited in Vienna in 1885. The first, *The Holy Family* (1884–85; Fig. 21), is Vereshchagin's interpretation of the family of Jesus. Renaissance artists almost always represented the child or infant Jesus and his mother Mary; Joseph was portrayed as a marginal figure, often an observer, smiling or adoring the scene against the background of a beautiful landscape and horizon. Some versions depict Joseph holding Jesus, who extends his arms to Mary. St. John, Elizabeth and Zachariah, angels, doves, cherubs, crowns of flowers, various animals—oxen, dogs, sheep, cats (Rembrandt)—often attend the scene in a variety of interactions. The Spanish artist Bartolomé Murillo (1617–82) portrayed many versions of the Holy Family in which he included a basket containing Joseph's tools. Often mother and child were the only figures in a garden or a meadow as Mary held, embraced, admired, or nursed the infant Jesus or as he sat or stood on her lap or at her knees.[23] In Roman Catholic dogma, the Holy Family consisted only of the Virgin Mary, Jesus, and Joseph; the brothers and sisters of the family were rarely, if ever, included in the iconography.

Vereshchagin's *The Holy Family* is perhaps the first work that treats, from a rationalist or positivist stance, the humble origins and the daily life of Jesus' family. The scene is a small shady courtyard littered with pieces of wood, chicken feathers, and other debris. Jesus' four brothers and two sisters are in the work. Two brothers sit face to face playing, while six chickens roam the yard in search of food. One brother helps his father, Joseph—with back to viewer—at carpentry. Mary sits in the background nursing an infant as one of her daughters looks on. The children's laundry had been hung out to dry as the sun begins to penetrate the

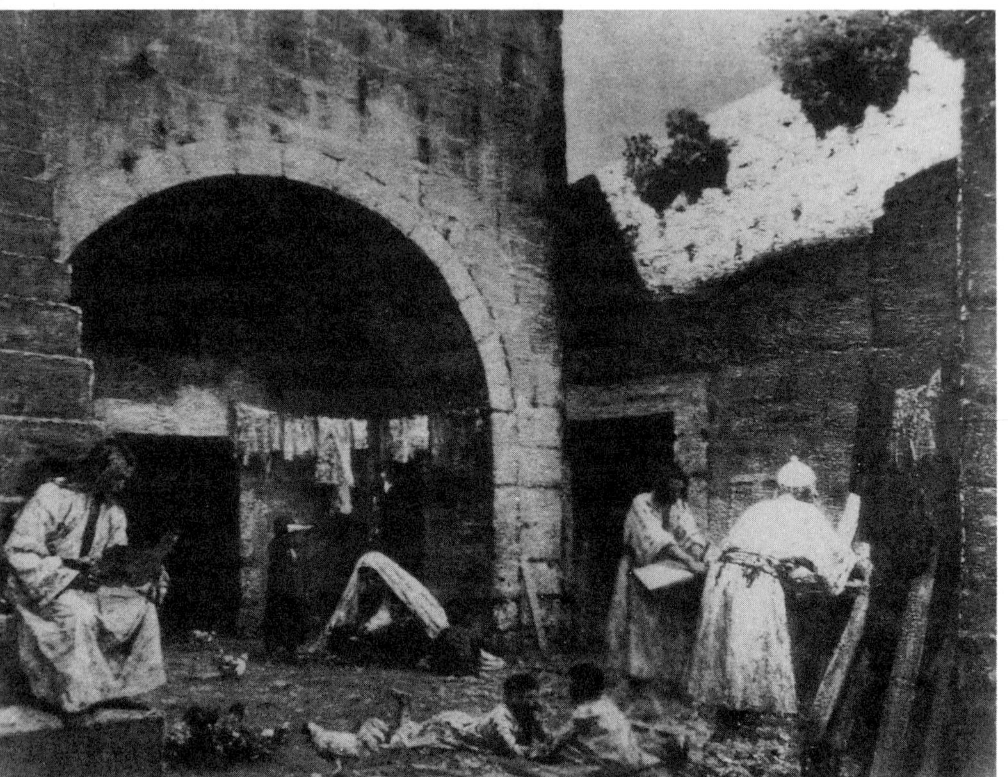

Figure 21. *The Holy Family.* 1884–85. Oil on canvas. Whereabouts unknown.

courtyard. Jesus sits in the left foreground, absorbed in reading the holy scrolls and thus concerned with his religious mission and his basic prophecy that the Kingdom of God was at hand.

Vereshchagin found scriptural support for his portrayal of the Holy Family especially in Matthew 13:55–56, Mark 6:3, and John 7:3.[24] That the depiction has foundation in historical fact is at least possible, as one critic pointed out: The "picture comes nearer to being a representation of facts than do those of the same subject by Raphael and other masters of the Renaissance, who merely painted comely Italian women in conventional robes of blue and red, and beautiful children; or than those by Rembrandt do, who painted the common people of his native town in their everyday costume as the companions of Christ."[25] In representing a daily scene in their prosaic life, Vereshchagin was explicitly challenging the concept of the Holy Family, although he had great respect for the idea of Christianity and its founder.[26]

The second piece is *The Resurrection of Christ* (1884–85; destroyed). Historically, Renaissance and other artists treated the Resurrection in various ways; for example, usually two to six Roman soldiers sleep, watch, or flee while Christ, accompanied, surrounded, or supported by angels, arises in a radiant light from the tomb, carries a cross staff or banner cross in his left hand, points upward with his right hand, and appears to Mary or Mary Magdalene. Other versions depict angels removing the stone from the entrance to his tomb and Christ—having risen—floating on a cloud, blessing the world.[27] In Vereshchagin's painting, Christ's tomb is embedded in a small hill against the background of the walls of Jerusalem. Jesus, wearing a long wing-shaped head-piece, peers out of the entrance to the tomb as if he had just awakened from sleep and attempts to recover his bearings. Two Roman guards, alarmed by Christ's appearance, flee the scene. This treatment was, to be sure, a radical departure from the traditional iconography of the Resurrection and was certain to arouse controversy and protest.

Because of the censor's ban, Vereshchagin never exhibited the *Trilogy of Executions, The Holy Family,* and *The Resurrection of Christ* in Russia, and reproduction of them was forbidden. One religious journal called Vereshchagin's explanatory remarks about *The Holy Family* "deranged." Another newspaper questioned Jesus' reading of holy scrolls at age twelve on the grounds that he was more intelligent than all his contemporaries and would already have been preaching at that age.[28]

In October 1885, in a joint exhibition with Viennese artists, Vereshchagin displayed his biblical, Indian, and other works in Vienna. Even before the exhibit opened, artists questioned the biblical interpretations of the paintings in the descriptions Vereshchagin wrote for the catalogue. The exhibit initially attracted relatively few spectators, but it was well received; Vereshchagin hopefully remarked to his wife that it would attract greater crowds and attention as it progressed.[29] Two works from the *Trilogy of Executions—Roman Execution (Crucifixion)* [see Fig. 18] and *Execution of Conspirators in Russia* (see Fig. 20)—made a considerable impression on the public.

Shortly after the exhibit opened, an official of Vienna's Catholic Diocese brought the catalogue to the attention of Cardinal Ganglbauer, especially in relation to *The Holy Family* and *The Resurrection of Christ*, which he found objectionable. He demanded that they either be removed from display or the exhibit be closed. In a letter to the local press, the cardinal reiterated the fundamentals of Catholic dogma, stated that Vereshchagin's interpretation of the Scriptures was tendentious and false and that his works undermined "the belief in the redemption of humanity by the Embodiment of the Son of God," and appealed to Catholics to boycott the exhibit. He also suggested that the paintings were counter to Raphael's inspired and "immortal artistic creations" of the Holy Family. Hence, Vereshchagin's work on that subject was "sacrilegious" and his *The Resurrection of Christ* a profound insult to the Catholic Faith, a "profanation of the loftiest ideal in Christian art." For that reason, the cardinal continued, it was his

> obligation to take the trouble of having these paintings . . . removed from the view of the visitors of the exhibit and, moreover, as far as possible, quietly and noiselessly. But my efforts were unsuccessful and even, to my extreme regret, were exploited daily in various newspapers as an advertisement for these sacrilegious works. I have no choice, as a Bishop who is obliged by virtue of his vows, not only to preach our holy Catholic doctrine, but also to defend it against all encroachments . . . I appeal to all faithful Catholics with the exhortation that they not participate in this blasphemy by their presence at the exhibit, and on behalf of all who are faithful to my Diocese, I pray to God Incarnate, our Savior, not to be angry at the humiliation to which He has been subjected by the exhibit of these paintings in the Catholic city of Vienna.[30]

The letter evoked a public response from Vereshchagin, who wrote that the cardinal's criticism of the paintings honored them. Vereshchagin remarked that he would eschew strident expressions that would violate the Christian spirit. He understood the cardinal's pique concerning the conflict between his own biblical interpretation in the pieces and official Catholic doctrine. Vereshchagin was somewhat disappointed that the cardinal did not cite support for his views in the scriptures, which embodied the spirit of Christianity in all its simplicity and grandeur, whereas legends multiplied and became deeply ingrained in the realm of imagination. As for *The Resurrection of Christ*, which the cardinal believed contradicted Catholic doctrine, Vereshchagin asserted that the Resurrection of the Savior occurred in the opening through which his body was placed in the tomb, and he asked the cardinal: "Doesn't the New Testament speak of an angel who removed the stone from that very opening?" For Vereshchagin, the conflict between Catholic doctrine and the New Testament was even greater since the latter holds that the Holy Family consisted of many members; he cited various passages from the New Testament to support his contention that in addition to Jesus, the first child, the Holy Virgin had seven or eight children. To resolve the doubts and perplexities that spawned the conflict, Vereshchagin suggested that a Universal Assembly be called immediately to settle the controversy, and he pleaded for religious tolerance pending the convening of the assembly.[31]

In another letter to Cardinal Ganglbauer in response to Jesuit attacks on his paintings, Vereshchagin pointed out that the concept of Mary's virginity, which Jesus, the apostles Peter and Paul, and the New Testament did not mention "during her whole life," took shape substantially later and could be "viewed as an attractive and poetic heresy." That Matthew 1:25 stated that "*before the birth of Jesus Mary did not know Joseph*" did not preclude Mary giving subsequent birth to children by Joseph; and since Christ, the apostles, and the New Testament affirmed the existence of the children who were born later, Vereshchagin considered the issue of Jesus' brothers and sisters resolved.[32]

Vereshchagin's response hardly ended the dispute, and his conflict with the Catholic Church took an ominous and violent turn. As the cardinal noted, his own exhortation excited the curiosity of Catholics and others about Vereshchagin's exhibit in a way that no publicity could have achieved. One newspaper reported that the exhibit became the focal point for the whole of Vienna; huge crowds flocked to see it and gathered around the two paintings. Another newspaper observed that if Vereshchagin had called the painting *The Interior of a Home in Nazareth*, no one would have taken it for a representation of the Holy Family. The

Viennese press defended Vereshchagin's right to express his interpretation of the scriptures in his art. When asked if he would remove his paintings, Vereshchagin replied that he had devoted a great deal of time to them, and would do so only if compelled to by the Austrian police. When Vereshchagin cited the Scriptures in creating his works, Catholic priests replied, "We don't want to know what's in the New Testament, we know the tradition of our Church and nothing else."[33]

When his appeal for a boycott of the exhibition failed, Cardinal Ganglbauer met with Archduke Karl, the head of the Society of Artists, to urge him to remove Vereshchagin's works. The archduke examined them and promised, as rumor had it, to remove them but never took any decisive action. The exhibit also became an issue in the Austrian Parliament, when one of its members asked why the police had not removed the paintings and brought Vereshchagin to trial. In fact, Vereshchagin was fined by an Austrian court for unauthorized sale of photographs of his two biblical pieces. The exhibition continued to draw large crowds; the Catholic Church held a three-day mass of repentance and a religious procession to atone for the "sin" of Vereshchagin's works. Catholics were exhorted to pray, as the cardinal had suggested in his letter, to mollify God's justice and to avert His anger against the paintings. One Catholic monk wildly hurled a bottle of vitriol at six paintings, whose frames and burnt canvases required repair. The damage was not serious, although the "whole right half" of *The Resurrection of Christ* needed reworking. Vereshchagin remarked to his wife that the monk did not damage the paintings as much as he wanted to. *Figaro*, a French newspaper, published a cartoon of Vereshchagin burning atop a pile of his paintings (Fig. 22); the caption claimed that he was fortunate to be living in those times, for in another era his clash with the Church Fathers would have ended differently (i.e., he would have been burned as a heretic).[34]

Frightened by these events, Vereshchagin moved his revolver from his rear to his side pocket.[35] He realized that he could not exhibit his biblical works in other Catholic countries. He later remarked to a German newspaper correspondent:

> One man is unable to wage a struggle against the [Catholic] Fathers. I am tired and do not intend to do so any longer . . . The Fathers

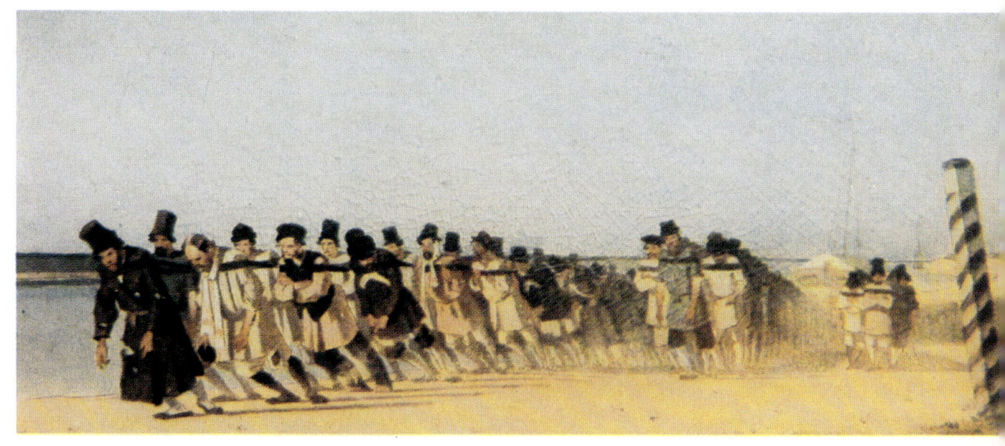

Plate 1. *Boathaulers.* Sketch of unrealized painting. 1866.
Oil on cardboard. 17.5 × 33 cm. Museum of Russian Art, Kiev.

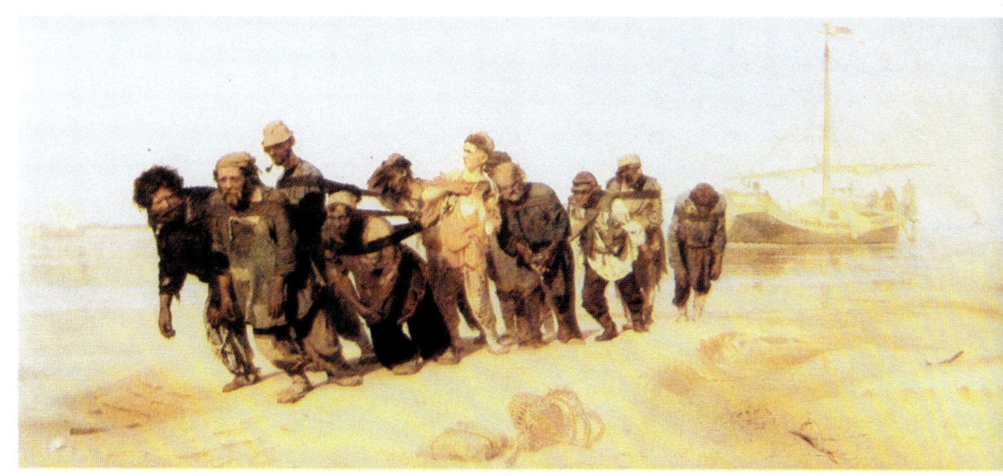

Plate 2. Ilia Repin, *Boathaulers on the Volga.* 1870–73.
131 × 281 cm. By permission of the Russian Museum, St. Petersburg.

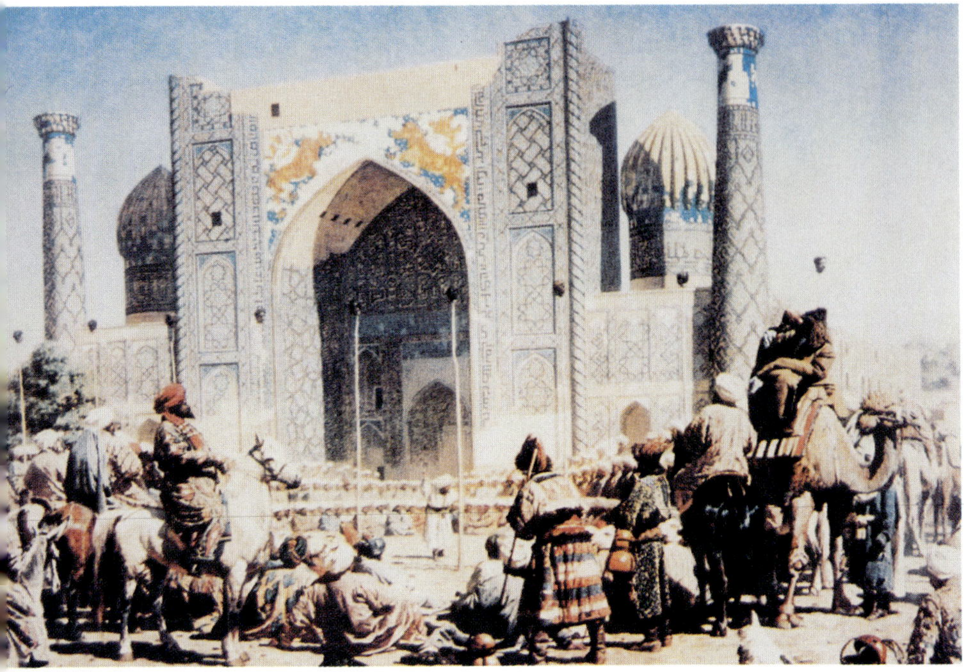

Plate 3. *Rejoicing*. 1872. Oil on canvas. 195 × 257 cm. Tretiakov Gallery, Moscow.

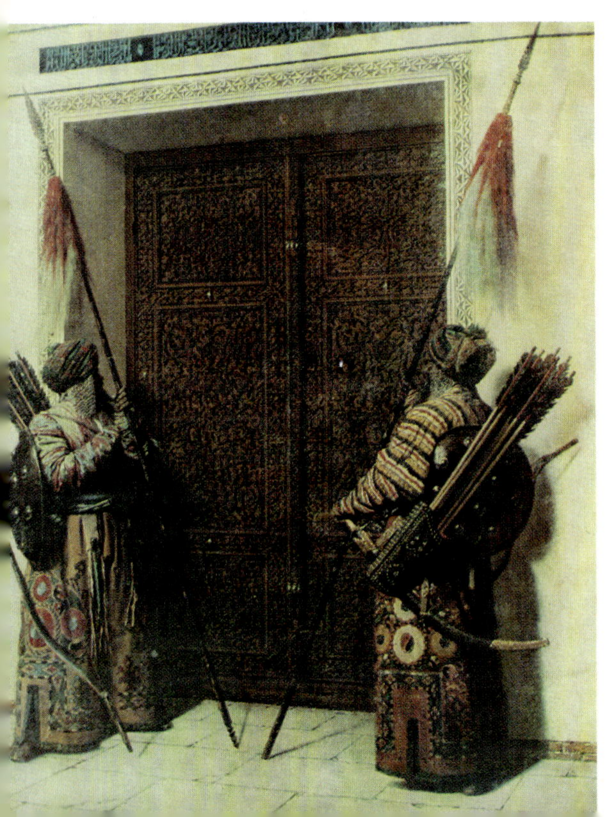

Plate 4. *Doors of Tamerlane*. 1872–73. Oil on Canvas. 213 × 168 cm. Tretiakov Gallery, Moscow.

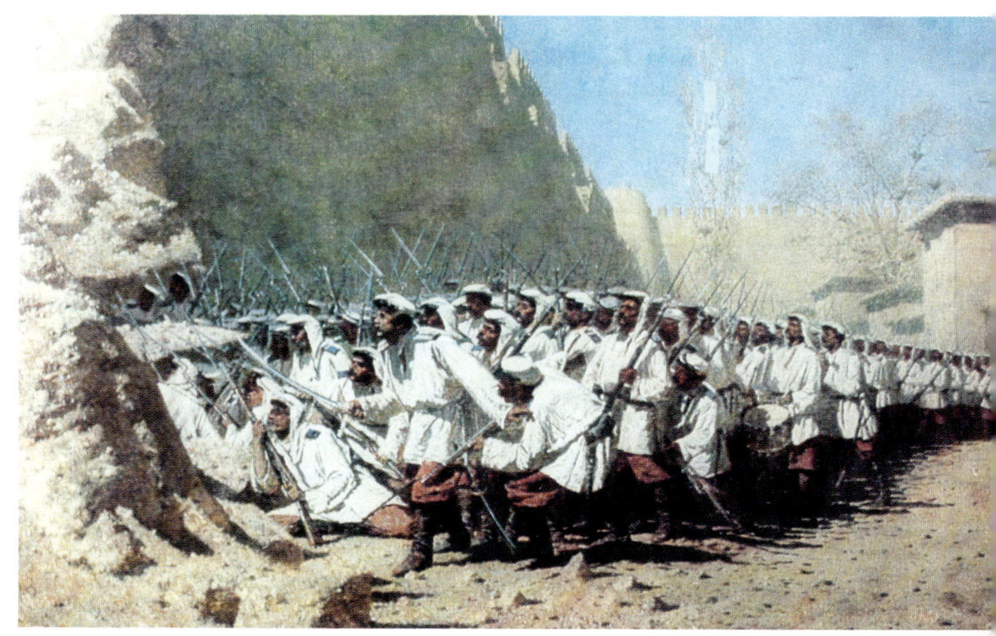

Plate 5. *By the Fortress Wall. Let Them Enter.* 1871. Oil on canvas. Lost.

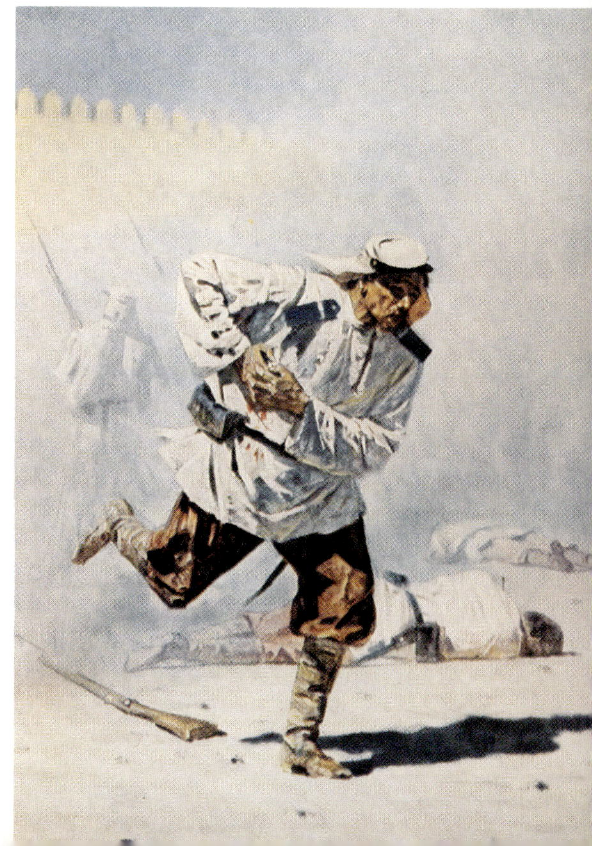

Plate 6. *The Fatally Wounded Soldier.* 1873. Oil on canvas. 73 × 56.6 cm. Tretiakov Gallery, Moscow.

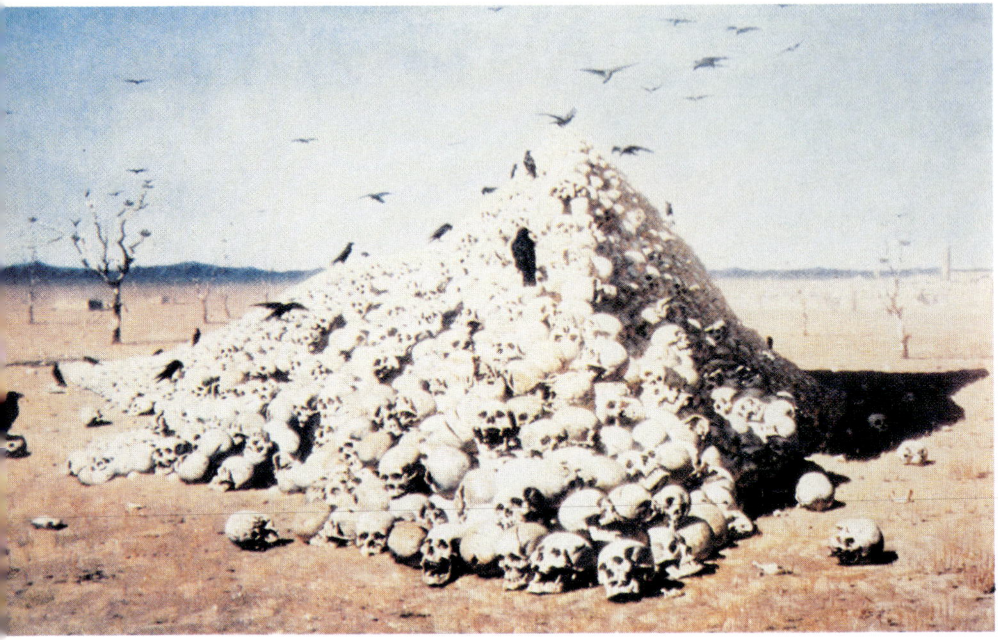

Plate 7. *Apotheosis of War*. 1871. Oil on canvas. 127 × 197 cm. Tretiakov Gallery, Moscow.

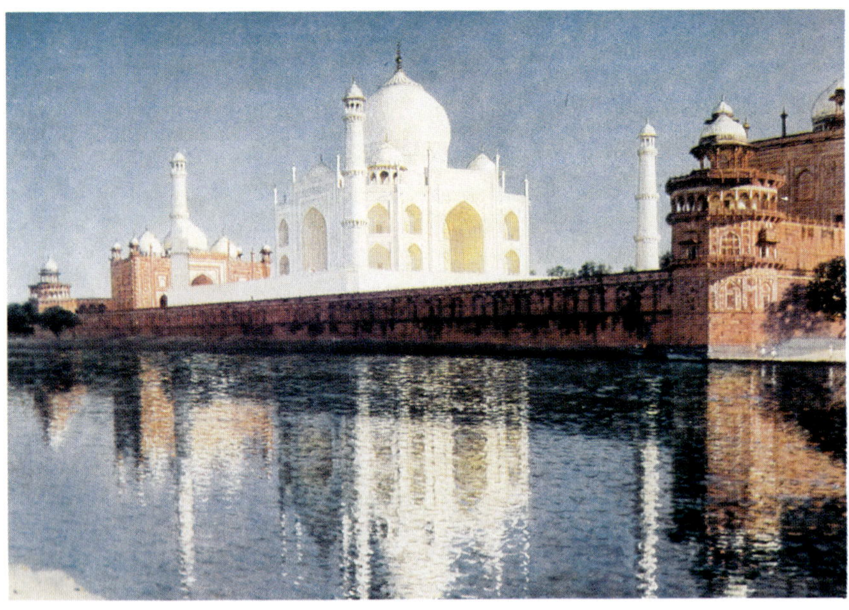

Plate 8. *Taj Mahal Mausoleum in Agra*. 1874–76. 40.5 × 55 cm. Tretiakov Gallery, Moscow.

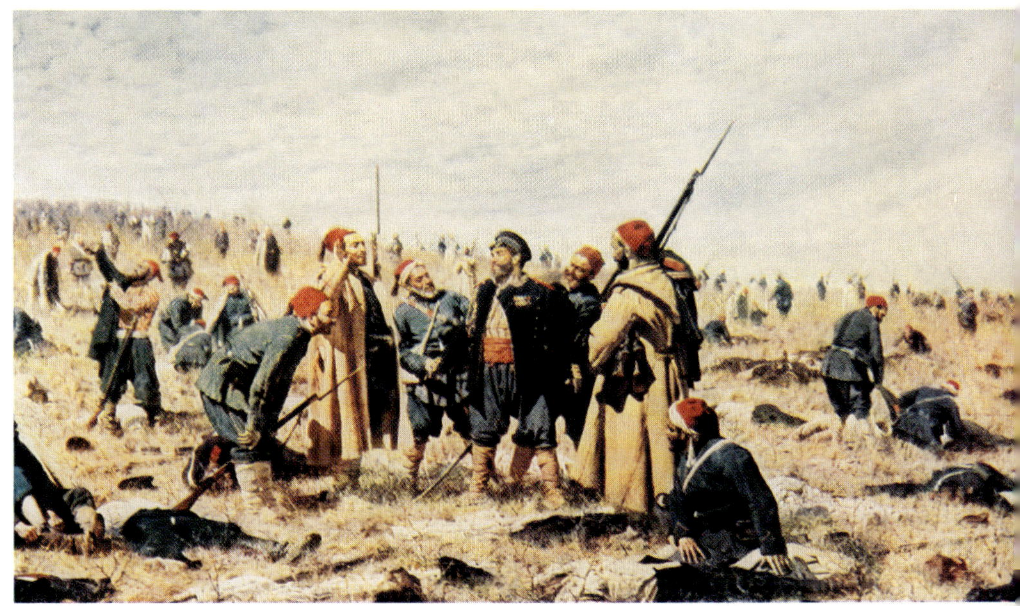

Plate 9. *The Conquerors.* 1878–79. 180 × 301 cm. Museum of Russian Art, Kiev.

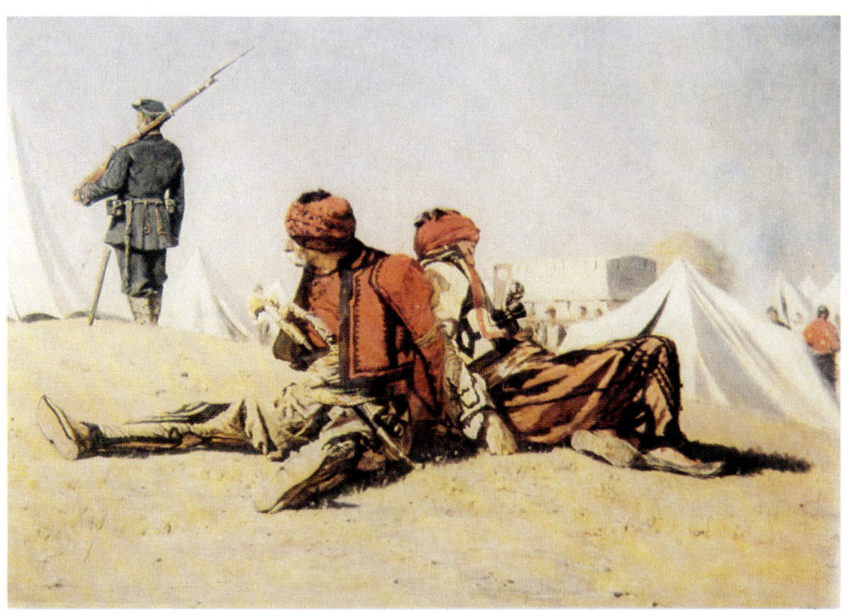

Plate 10. *Two Hawks (Bashi-Bazouks).* 1878–79. 78.5 × 110 cm. Oil on canvas. Museum of Russian Art, Kiev.

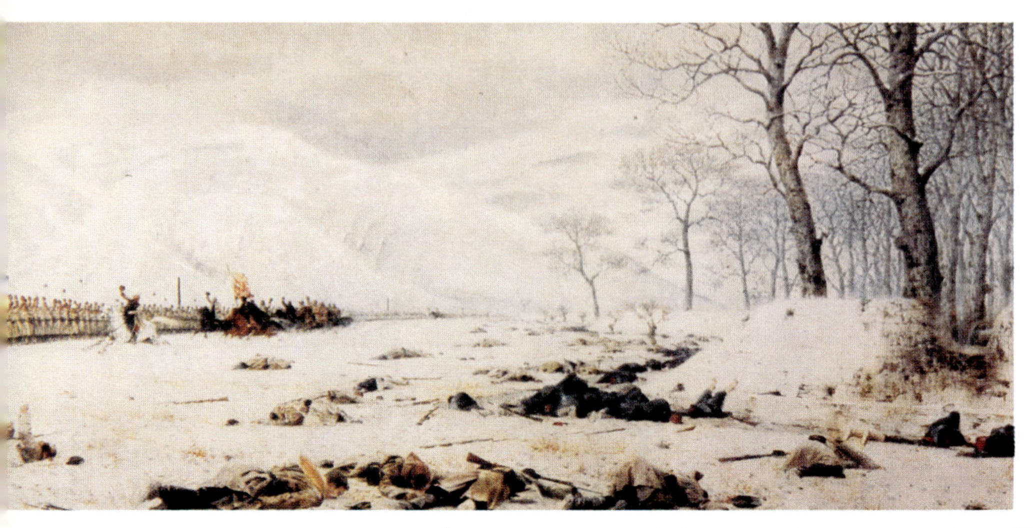

Plate 11. *Shipka-Sheinovo (Skobelev at Shipka)*. 1883–88. 188 × 405 cm. Russian Museum, St. Petersburg.

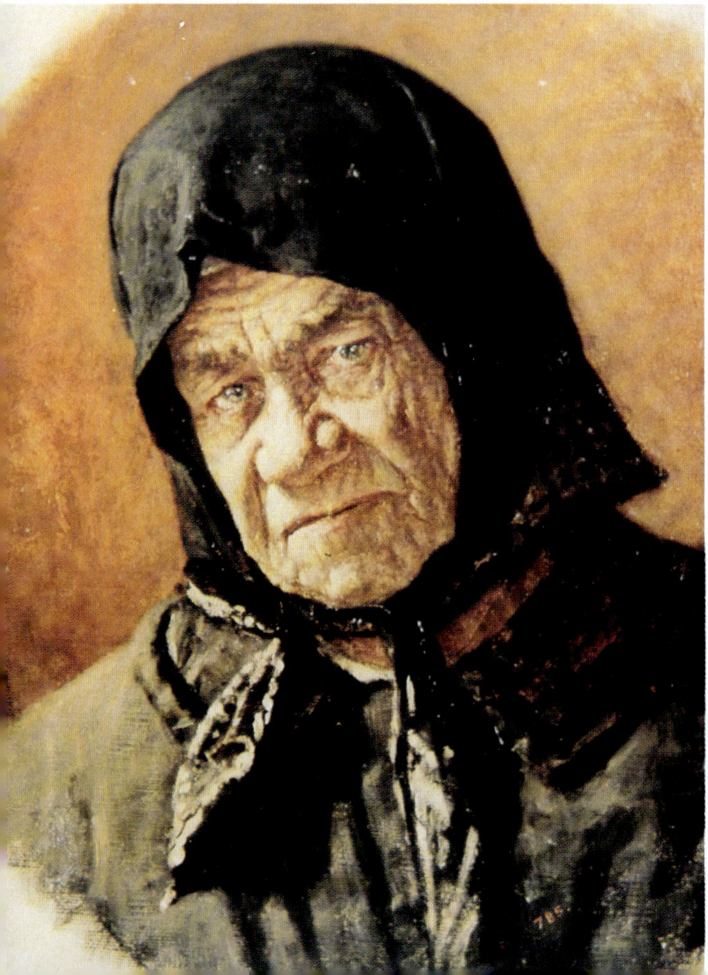

Plate 12. *The Old-Woman Beggar. Ninety-Six Years Old*. Circa 1891. Oil on canvas. 29.5 × 23 cm. By permission of the Russian Museum, St. Petersburg.

Plate 13. *Near Moscow Waiting for a Boyar Delegation.* 1891–92. Oil on canvas. 135 × 109 cm. Historical Museum, Moscow.

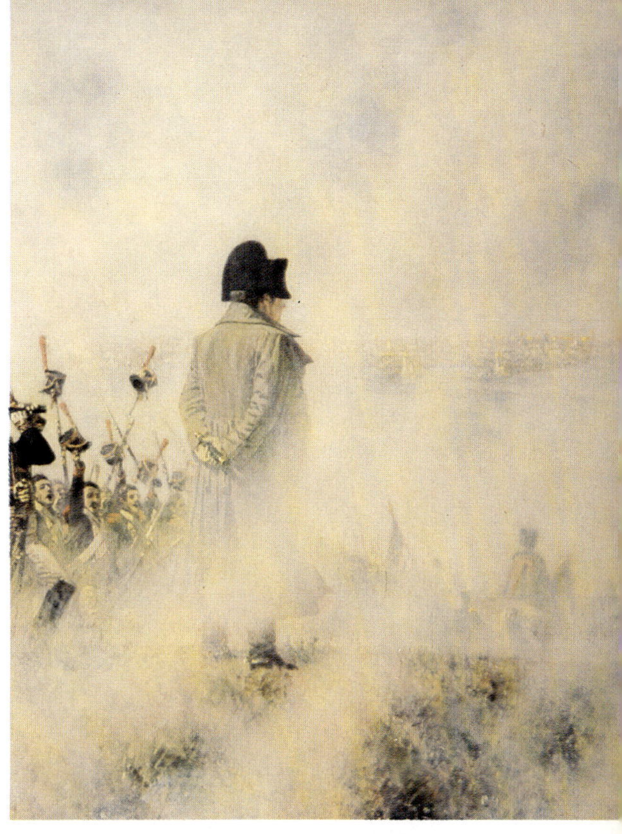

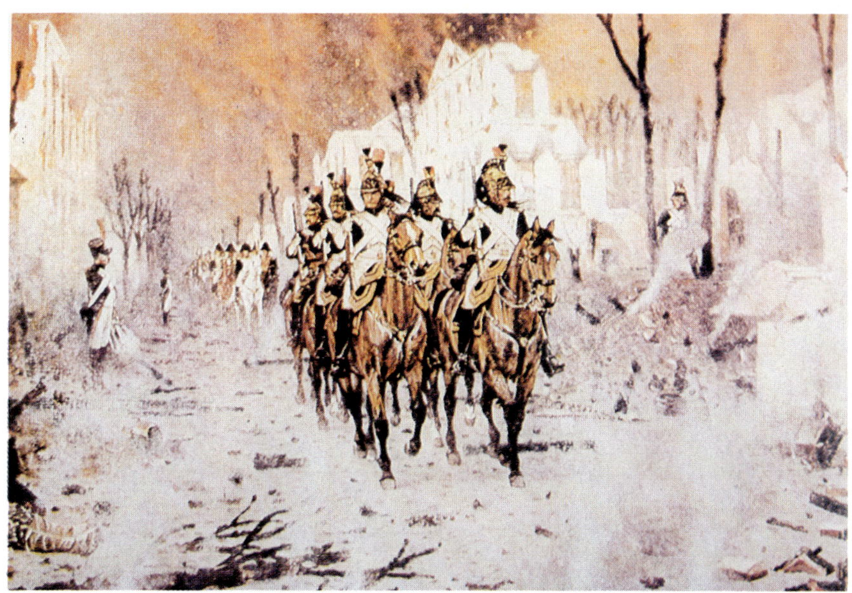

Plate 14. *Return from the Petrovsky Palace.* 1895. Oil on canvas. 87 × 135 cm. Picture Gallery of Armenia, Erevan.

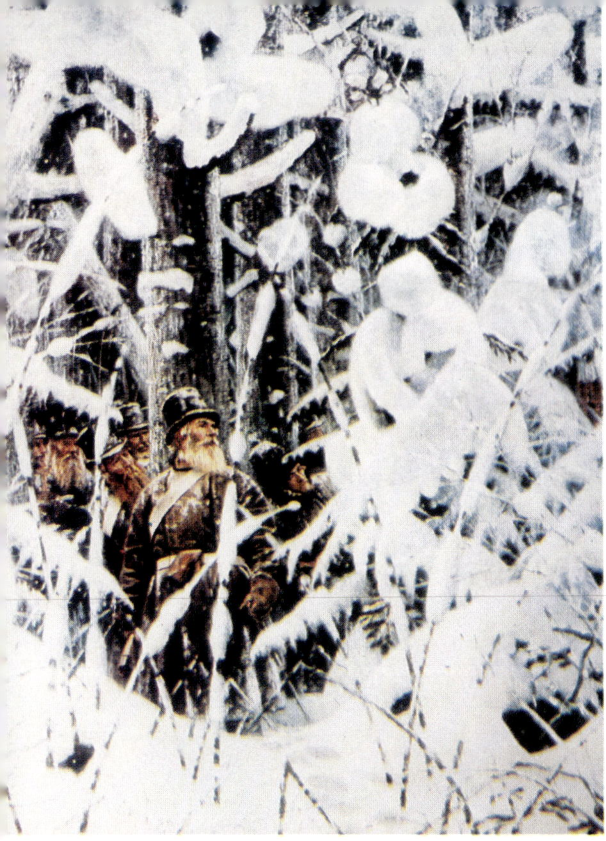

Plate 15. *Wait! Let'em Come Nearer!* 1887–95.
Oil on canvas. 198 × 149 cm.
Historical Museum, Moscow.

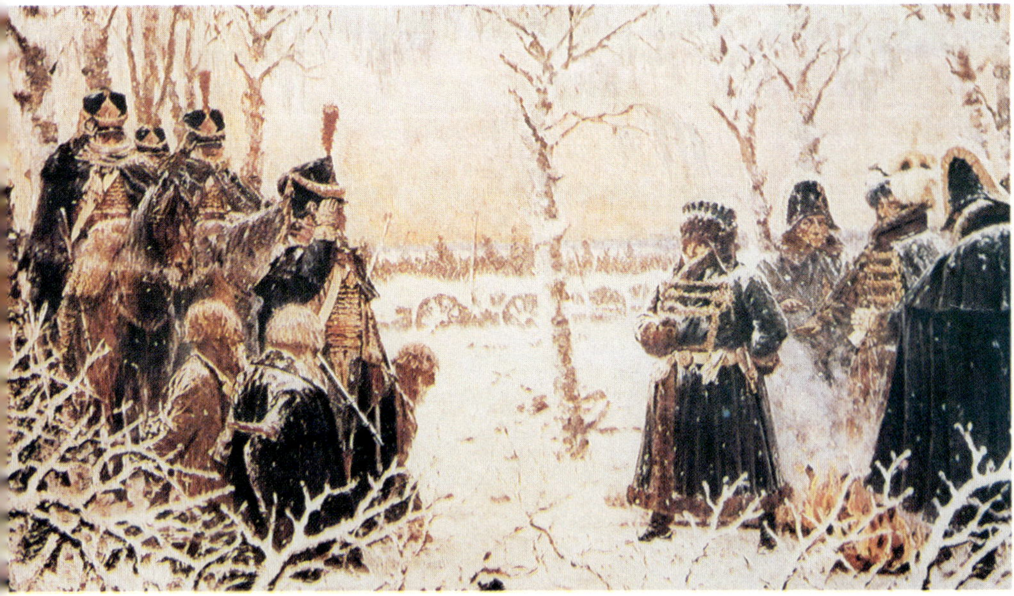

Plate 16. *Captured with Arms? Shoot Them.* 1887–95. Oil on canvas. 142 × 185 cm. Historical Museum, Moscow.

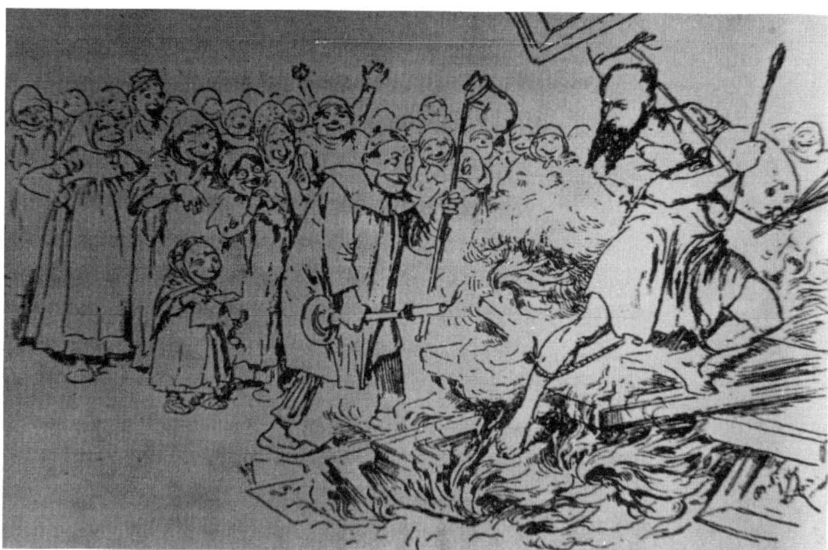

Figure 22. Caricature of V. V. Vereshchagin in *Figaro*, 1885. From A. Lebedev and A. Solodovnikov, *V. V. Vereshchagin* (Moscow: Iskusstvo, 1988).

> are clever . . . they know how to present a matter in a way that has now deprived me of artistic fame. Some think that I am a hero of publicity, others claim that I am a swindler, and there will be even others who are ready to state under oath that I have gone mad. I will no longer exhibit my works of a religious nature in Catholic countries. What I had to experience in Vienna was quite enough. That is why I did not exhibit those paintings in Budapest.[36]

Concerned about recovering his costs in arranging the Vienna exhibit, Vereshchagin wrote to his wife: "Don't forget, we are poor if the exhibit does not produce money and if they don't sell my paintings."[37] There is no evidence any of his paintings were sold there. Even after the exhibit ended in November, the controversy continued. One critic considered Vereshchagin an agent of the Russian autocracy in fomenting discord and his exhibit a kind of Trojan Horse for the sinister political aims of the Russian state in conquering the world. Another made a preposterous but telling observation about the threat that Vereshchagin's art, in service of the Russian government, posed to the world:

> His art goes to India ahead of Russian bayonets and makes, if only on canvas, the enchanting palaces of Delhi, Agra, and others Russian property. The Russian hospital in Jerusalem has for a long time served as evidence that even Palestine has been included in future Russian plans. Situated in a strategically important region, this building has with complete suddenness been crystallized into a powerful citadel. Having visited the Holy ground of Palestine, the artist has placed this land and its people under the command of his art.[38]

In 1886, Vereshchagin went to Budapest to hold another exhibit, but he deliberately excluded his controversial biblical pieces. The Catholic cardinal there, apprised of the events in Vienna, announced he would oppose it if it contained the biblical paintings. Nevertheless, the exhibit proceeded well. Before it opened, Vereshchagin, in an attempt to make his works more acceptable to the Hungarian public, delivered his first public talk on the role of art in society. His views were the basis of two pieces which he later published as *Realism* and *On Progress in Art.*

Vereshchagin's unusually prescient talk was typically Russian in yoking art and "civic responsibility," but it still reflected in attenuated form the nineteenth-century belief in Progress through education, reason, persuasion, and commitment. He pointed out that artists were not as a whole very well educated because they commonly believed that a basic education was unrelated to their artistic talents; and it was for this reason that art, which during the preceding centuries had been a potent social influence, had been unable in modern times to abandon its role as a humble and pleasing servant of society and to fulfill its primary task not only in the aesthetic but in the more important psychological development of society. That artists were largely enthralled by and slavishly imitated the great masters of the past served to limit the creative parameters and social role of art. Vereshchagin did not mention the specific aim of art's psychological role, but that became clear as he proceeded to draw the relationship between art and the political currents of the time.[39] He asserted that art could no longer be a piece of furniture, an idle amusement, or a relief from the restraints or limitations of time and place; art had to reflect progressive tendencies in view of the serious threat that socialism and anarchism posed to the social fabric. He elaborated:

> The masses that have been for centuries leading a life of expectancy while hanging on the very borders of starvation, are willing to wait no more. Their former hopes in the future are discarded; their appetites are whetted and they are clamoring for arrears, which means now the division of all riches, and so as to make the division more lasting, they are claiming that talents and capacities should be leveled down to one standard, all workers of progress and comfort alike drawing the same pay. They are striving to reconstruct society on new foundations, and in case of opposition to their aims, they threaten to apply the torch to all monuments pertaining to an order that, according to them, has already outlived its usefulness; they threaten to blow up public buildings, the churches, the art galleries, libraries and museums—a downright religion of despair.[40]

According to Vereshchagin, although society "at large" was responsible for the conditions of the masses, it could not, in the long run, depend on military strength and the church to defend it against the onslaught of socialism and anarchism. One day the army would refuse to shoot its own people; the church—blinded by mutual hatred and torn by doctrinal conflict and petty controversy—had neglected its lofty mission on earth and would eventually lose its hold on society. The defense of an open, rational, and humane society now depended on talented scientists, writers, and artists who would "defend and advocate the improvement of existing things by peaceful and gradual means." In alluding to his own struggle, Vereshchagin remarked that society was invariably hostile to the mission of men of talent, and he pleaded for tolerance of artistic and scientific innovation and discovery, including his own art as a defense of, and not a threat to, the existing order:

> In this society of ours anything that is common and conventional is shielded by all kinds of rights and privileges, while anything that is new and original is bound to awaken animosity and censure, has to

go through a severe struggle under the pressure of wide-spread cant and hypocrisy.

Try to create anything ingenious in any of the regions of science and literature, try to present in graphic or plastic form the most original, striking conception, but only forget or refuse to surround it with the conventional layer of triviality and vulgarity so dear to the heart of society, you will be done for, you will not even obtain a hearing, you will be called a charlatan, if nothing worse than that.

Why is that so? Was it society that has shown the way to all great discoveries? No, it has always detained them, has always put brakes on them.

Has society, in its collective form, ever evoked any of the great manifestations of art or literature? No; society was always eager to worry, to persecute men of talent, though it was erecting monuments after their death . . . It is high time, it seems to me, to understand the necessity of treating art with tolerance and confidence, if we want it to fraternize with society, to become as one with it, to serve it faithfully and well in the present troubled times when the poet and artist are soldiers on their posts.[41]

During the mid-1880s, Vereshchagin's fame and reputation grew to the extent that he had to decline invitations to display his works in various European cities.[42] From 1886 to 1888, he held exhibitions in Berlin, Frankfurt-On-The-Main, Prague, Breslau, Leipzig, Koenigsburg, Amsterdam, Stockholm, Copenhagen, London, Liverpool, and Paris. At some of these exhibits, Vereshchagin would join the spectators in the evenings to answer their questions about his life and art and to address the major social and political issues of the day. His London exhibit of 1888 was well received despite objections to his offensive painting, *English Suppression of an Indian Rebellion* (see Fig. 19). One critic offered a perceptive, incisive assessment of Vereshchagin as an artist, placing his status among other artists in historical perspective:

M. Verestchagin is a prince among illustrators. Let him go into ever so strange and remote country, amidst ever so bewildering a turmoil of incident; add even the dangers and confusion of battle; he will pounce like a hawk upon his impression and bring it out reeking with human interest and emotion. The exhibition of his works at the Grosvenor is full of instances of his intuitive power of perceiving what is striking and suggestive in a scene. Yet his work is more than an enlarged graphic illustration, for he has successfully resolved the problems of bold handling and broadly atmospheric color. His solid French training . . . enables him to treat his idea with all the resources of modern realism and to invest it with all the thrill of actuality. He draws admirably with the brush, and has a keen eye for facial type and expression. Still it cannot be said that his art is of the highest order; it may be among the best of its kind, but that kind is not of the royal type. It might be unnecessary, perhaps, to say this, but that so many people in England are apt to judge of the rank of a painter solely by the interest of the momentary novelty of his subjects. It should be remembered that when these become stale, or go out of fashion, a picture has nothing to depend on but the imposing grandeur of its style and plastic ideal. Now, in his treatment of kindred subjects, M. Verestchagin shows but little of the pictorial magnificence of Velásquez [1599–1660] in the *Surrender of Breda* [1634–35], Delacroix [1798–1863] in the *Crusaders at Constantinople* [1840], or Regnault [1843–71] in *Marshal Prim* [1869]. He aims differently from these men, and his work does not even belong to the same category. M. Verestchagin can realise vividly what he has seen with poignant, but not with a grand or triumphant imagination. He feels more deeply what is humanly interesting and touching in actual scenes than what is ideally noble on canvas. His technique is of that broad, efficient sort which has become perfected and placed at the service of modern painters by the great French revival of this century. The chief men of that movement had not M. Verestchagin's experience, or perhaps his peculiar character and widely developed sensitiveness to human affairs; but they made his ideal of art for him, and their use of it far surpassed his in nobility and delicacy. They taught him, in fact, that it was possible to apply decorative breadth and pictorial grandeur of the ancients to the treatment of modern subjects.

> In his methods of putting this lesson into practice M. Verestchagin displays originality both of vision and treatment. The composition and choice of *motif* displayed in his big battle pieces of the Russo-Turkish war are bold innovations upon the ordinary practice of battle painters. If the germs of his pictorial development are to be found in the work of the excellent school of modern illustration of the last twenty years, it would be unjust to deny that he has shown real genius in making use of so slight an indication to found a system of large figure painting.[43]

In 1887–88, Vereshchagin traveled to the central Russian cities of Yaroslavl, Rostov, Kostroma, and Makarev to make studies of the region's cultural and religious monuments and ethnographic types. His return to Russia perhaps reflected a longing to reunite with his motherland and its culture and to recover the placid, happy years of his childhood among ordinary Russians. In *Illustrated Autobiographies of Several Unremarkable Russian People* (1895), he wrote of his encounters with them and sought to embody pictorially the character and fate of particular Russians. These studies were a reaffirmation of his abiding commitment and devotion to the ordinary people; the book contains no portraits of any members of his class. The works take on added significance in view of Vereshchagin's distaste for portrait painting.

Two portraits of unremarkable Russians invite discussion, for they evince a formidable dimension of Vereshchagin's artistry. He invests these personalities with psychological depth, sympathy, warmth, and understanding. The first is *The Retired Butler* (1888; Fig. 23), a man who, through cunning and tenacity, was able to escape the ranks of serfdom. The bearded, toothless butler is portrayed against a gray-brown background, his face and head delineated by oblique shafts of light and shade. His rather complacent smile and his intelligent, playful, proud dark-brown eyes express a confident sense of accomplishment in, and triumph over, his lot in life. The wrinkles on his face, on his prominent forehead, and around his eyes speak of his persistence and shrewdness in overcoming life's ordeals.

If the butler expresses triumph over adversity, *The Old-Woman Beggar. Ninety-Six Years Old* (1891; Pl. 12), is a more engaging study. The old

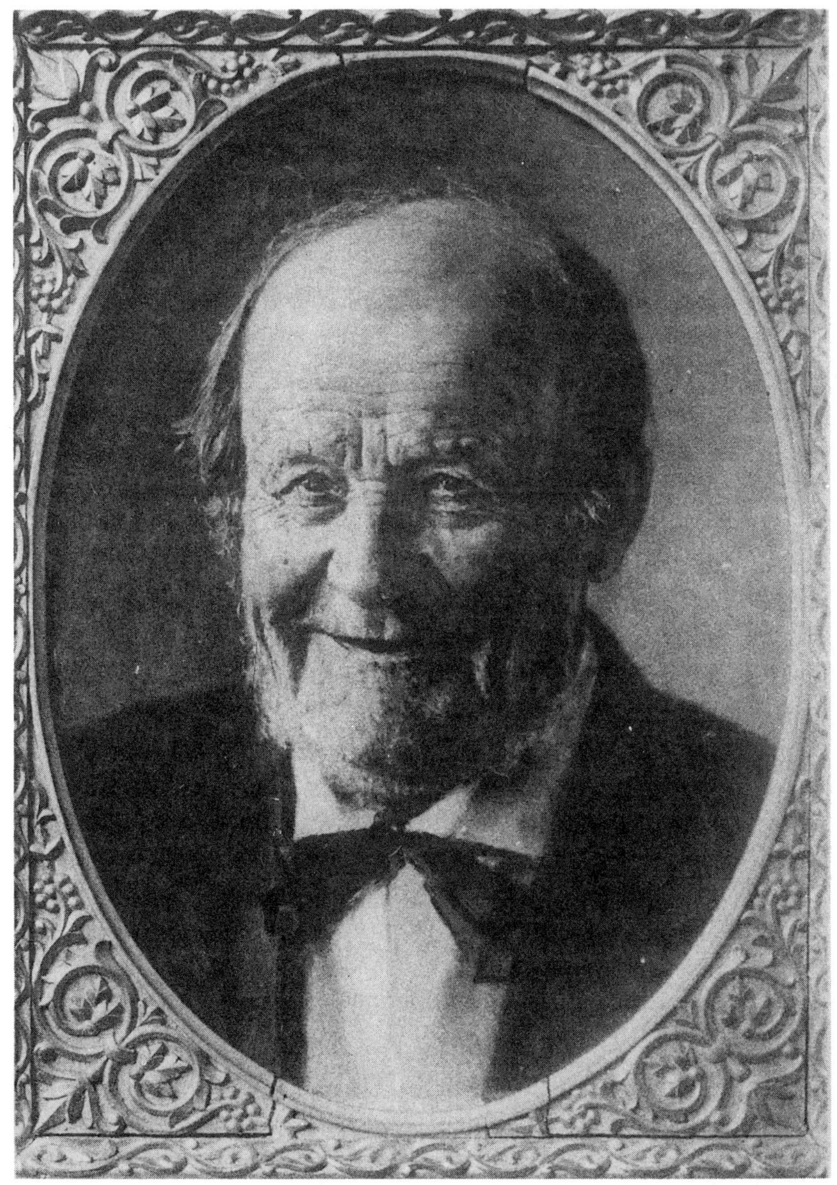

Figure 23. *The Retired Butler*. 1888. Oil on canvas. 47 × 32 cm. Russian Museum, St. Petersburg.

woman, perhaps symbolic of Mother Russia, expresses a completely different character. Vereshchagin called her the "personification of eighty-five years of uninterrupted suffering."[44] The embroidered black shawl gives focus to her illuminated face, large nose, and slightly distorted mouth. Through large red-rimmed, bright blue-green eyes she looks somewhat inquisitively at the viewer with a deep sense of grief, suffering, and poverty, as if she had just related the struggles of her painful life. Her wrinkled skin hangs as if it contained all her past burdens. She wishes that her life had been gentler and far less burdensome, although her expectations were minimal. Yet there is also a sense of her understanding of and sympathy for others, as well as fortitude and courage to overcome her past. She seeks no pity, but rather expects to be understood and accepted on her own terms. She has borne so much that she will surmount anything in the few years left in her life, for nothing can deter her will to survive. Endurance is the one quality that she shares with the butler, as well as with the Russian people in general and with Russian women in particular.

In September 1888, Vereshchagin arrived in New York City to hold an exhibit, to publicize his art, and, primarily, to sell the paintings he was unable to sell to Tretiakov and Tereschenko, two of the more prominent art patrons in Russia who could afford to purchase his works en masse. Above all, he wanted as many of his works as possible to remain in Russia, although he probably could have sold them individually during his exhibits in Western Europe. That several of his biblical history pieces and the *Trilogy of Executions* could not be shown in Russia precluded their sale there. On many occasions, he offered to sell Tretiakov his works much more cheaply than earlier and more cheaply still if they could be lent for his exhibits, but Tretiakov refused further acquisitions. In a letter to him in February 1887, Vereshchagin still expressed some hope that Tretiakov would acquire the works before his trip to New York: "They are suggesting that I exhibit and sell my works abroad; it is horrible to think that somewhere in America and not in Russia my best works will come to find their place and buyer."[45] A major reason for the American exhibit, however, was to acquire enough money to enable Vereshchagin to devote a long period to creating a new series of paintings.[46]

Vereshchagin roamed New York and became familiar with its landmarks and their architectural details. During the course of his exhibit, he became so popular that he was recognized on the streets.[47] New Yorkers were impressed with his childlike charm, congenial personality, and fluent English. One critic, with whom he developed a friendship, observed that Vereshchagin was "a man as strange and as interesting as his works, and far more many-sided; in many respects a king among men, yet possessing traits characteristic of the most common-place. Certainly such a character is worthy of study."[48]

In the early 1880s, America had experienced a cultural revival. The demand for, and the rapid acquisition of, art reached epidemic proportions. As in Western Europe, art in America became the ultimate symbol of affluence and cultural attainment; a market swiftly developed and auction galleries were established.[49] Americans considered European art superior to their own, and the affluent bought works by Gérôme, Meissonier, and the French Impressionists, among others; such works were purchased or imported for auction in New York City. The cost of art in America increased in proportion to rising incomes and affluence until World War I, despite the import duties that the U.S. government imposed on foreign works.[50]

In November 1888, Vereshchagin's exhibition opened in the luxurious American Art Galleries on the south side of Madison Square, which was, "more than any other spot in the United States, the focal point of cosmopolitan society."[51] It was arranged and vigorously promoted by James F. Sutton, a zealous art patron and dealer who was determined to make a fortune in art as well as on Vereshchagin's exhibit. Sutton had recently formed a partnership with Thomas E. Kirby—the leading art auctioneer of his time—to head the American Art Association, which operated and held auctions at the American Art Galleries. Apparently, Sutton, who frequently traveled to Paris to purchase art, had met Vereshchagin or his agent there in the mid-1880s and suggested a New York City exhibit.

Vereshchagin's two-month show marked the first major display of Russian art in America. Highly successful, it drew thousands of curious viewers; no other foreign artist had ever received as much attention and praise in America.[52] What probably appealed to Americans was the strong antiwar orientation of the paintings; the works graphically echoed the tragedies and suffering of the American Civil War which had ended twenty-four years earlier. In addition, customs and costumes of India and Central Asia were a considerable source of novelty and curiosity for some, perhaps appealing to a developing spirit of imperialism; others could readily relate to the exotica, which was well-illustrated in American literature, particularly Bibles.

As in his previous exhibits, many Oriental rugs, tiles, pottery, draperies, and other artifacts were used to decorate the galleries. Vereshchagin brought with him a small group of Russians who, during the exhibit, wore black and red costumes and sang Russian songs. Russian classical and folk music was played by Lidiia V. Andreevskaia (1865–1919), a young Russian pianist and organist; a recent graduate of the Moscow Philharmonic Musical-Dramatic School, she had been invited to New York by the American Art Galleries. In 1891, she and Vereshchagin were married. His previous marriage had been faltering well before he met Lidiia, and in 1890 he obtained a divorce from his first wife; she was given one-thousand rubles annually during Vereshchagin's life, and payment continued for some time after his death.[53]

During his exhibit, Vereshchagin often held talks with spectators on a wide range of issues. In one discussion, he suggested that monies designated for war be used instead to eliminate poverty. He came to focus increasingly on women and their "significance and future in the current epoch and in coming historical periods." Historical progress for Vereshchagin now seemed to lie in the active involvement of women in political affairs and in the work force. A woman could become queen or empress, he pointed out, but could not be a high government official. He believed that greater participation of women in political life would eliminate poverty and particularly war, because women would refuse to assign funds for it.[54] In another discussion, he looked forward to the day "when a new life-giving idea takes root in the civilized world, appealing to the minds of men. From where is this appeal to come? Are we to look for a new revelation, or will the practical experience of life work out a higher code of social and moral principles, applicable to all?" Once again, he appealed for ideological and religious tolerance and diversity. He also observed "one silly fact" during times of war: "the more society sympathizes with the wounded, the less interest does it take in the sick. All the enthusiasm is for the former, and but little care or nursing is voluntarily bestowed on the latter. How such and many other things can be made to agree with the spirit of Christianity is inconceivable."[55]

The exhibit reviews were overwhelmingly positive; a few were negative perhaps because Vereshchagin had offended American artists by criticizing the state of American art.[56] Clarence Cook (1828–1900), a leading American art critic, called the show "an intellectual feast, such as none other presented to the public for the past twenty-five years."[57] General William T. Sherman, the American commander of the Union troops during the Civil War, stated that Vereshchagin was "the greatest painter of the horrors of war that ever lived."[58] Another critic pointed out relative to the war pieces that, "However frightening these paintings are with their realistic portrayal of death in its most startling manifestations, nevertheless when seeing them one feels that the artist created them not out of love for the horrible, but with a heart full of compassion and genuine indignation."[59] Vereshchagin was considered "the first artist of peace," and his works were of "incalculable importance for the development of an American school of art." According to this critic, some American patriots expressed a desire not only to retain Vereshchagin's paintings in America, but to persuade him to stay "so as to lay the foundations of a national-American art."[60]

Perhaps the most balanced review of the exhibit was written by an anonymous critic who took Vereshchagin to task for failing to practice what he preached to other artists: the need to render outdoor events *en plein air*, not in studios. *Roman Execution (Crucifixion)* [see Fig. 18] did not meet Vereshchagin's own criterion: "Does this picture look like a scene out of doors? Is there any air in this pasty gray and black sky?" Perhaps that was precisely the point of the painting—the gloomy, stifling, and oppressive ambience of life under Roman rule. He wrote of Vereshchagin's marked tendency "to force a scene from life with its irregular grouping into arbitrary lines" in the *Trilogy of Executions*, although he believed the artist successfully represented "difficult effects on a large scale." The reviewer found the Balkan war pieces mediocre and commonplace, the character studies adept, and the pencil and oil drawings "excellent, and some even admirable. They are among the most interesting things in the exhibit." In the biblical works, particularly *The Holy Family* (see Fig. 21), the reviewer saw "not so much ground for impugning the artist's motives as the sensational incident which occurred when they were exhibited in Vienna might have led us to expect." Despite the fine technical command and "atmosphere" of the piece, it was "not otherwise remarkable."[61]

The exhibit impressed a major American writer, Theodore Dreiser (1871–1945), who noted its impact on, and inspiration for, the central character of his autobiographical novel, *The 'Genius'* (1915):

> Once there was an exhibition of some of the war pictures of Verestchagin, a great Russian painter who had come West for some purpose[!]. Eugene saw them one Sunday afternoon, and was enthralled by the magnificence of their grasp of the elements of battle; the wonder of color; the truth of character; the dramatic quality; the sense of force and danger and horror and suffering which was somehow around and in through everything that was shown. This man had virility and insight; stupendous imagination and temperament. Eugene stood and stared, wondering how such things could be done. Even afterward the name of Verestchagin was like a great call to imagination; that was the kind of artist to be if you were going to be one.[62]

From New York, the exhibit went to Chicago, St. Louis, Philadelphia, Baltimore, and Boston. Vereshchagin, however, remained in America only until the close of the New York show, after which he returned to Paris to undertake a new project. When the tour ended in 1891, the works returned to New York City, where the entire collection of 110 pieces from the Indian and Balkan war series and the *Trilogy of Executions* was auctioned for $84,300.[63] In terms of rubles, this represented double the dollar amount, which is what Vereshchagin probably would have accepted from Tretiakov. When Vereshchagin returned to New York in 1891 specifically for the auction, he was ignorant of the operations of the art market there and refused, on ethical grounds to deal with "profiteers" (Sutton and Kirby), who suggested that the prices of his works be inflated, presumably in order to obtain higher commissions. One historian who briefly wrote of the exhibit notes cryptically that "Vereshchagin *might have made a lot of money for the AAA* [American Art Association], but he was very temperamental."[64] Kirby said of Vereshchagin that, "Like all geniuses, he was very erratic, a queer type of man," but, despite his "terrific handicaps to popularity, his exhibitions were a great success."[65]

In 1891, Vereshchagin returned to Paris and shortly after settled permanently with his wife and their first child in a newly built home in a village near Moscow. A year later he sold his Paris studio to Konstantin Makovsky (1839–1915), a founding member of the Itinerants. Vereshchagin devoted the remainder of his life largely to the historical study and creation of a major series of paintings on Napoleon's invasion of Russia in 1812.

Chapter Five

VERESHCHAGIN AND NAPOLEON IN RUSSIA, 1812

Vereshchagin had two principal objectives in creating a series of twenty paintings of major episodes from the War of 1812, in which Russia defeated Napoleon and his Grand Army: to portray the extraordinary spirit of heroism and sacrifice of the Russian people in the struggle against the French and to shatter Napoleon's image as a liberator and a military genius.[1] Although Vereshchagin pointed out that Napoleon's debunking was of minor relevance, the emperor is depicted in the overwhelming majority of the paintings: he appears as a troubled, tormented, indecisive man and emerges as the dominant figure of the series. Only three paintings are devoted to the Russian people. The first, *In Defeated Moscow* (*Arsonists or Shooting in the Kremlin*) [1897–98; see Fig. 29], portrays a group of Russians being executed by the French for burning Moscow. In *Wait! Let'em Come Nearer!* (1887–95; see Pl. 15), perhaps the best work in the series, a small group of sturdy, determined Russians stand in a snow-covered forest waiting to ambush the enemy. The third painting is the sequel to the second; in *Captured with Arms? Shoot Them* (1887–95; see Pl. 16), three captured Russians heroically kneel before Napoleon and await execution. One minor painting is devoted to the Russian army, *Bayonet Charge. Hurrah! Hurrah!* (1887–95). Curiously, General Mikhail Kutuzov and Tsar Alexander I are completely absent from the paintings, although Vereshchagin planned to include them in another series—one that never materialized—on the War of 1812. On balance, it appears that Vereshchagin, in creating a major series that would embody his views as a whole, was far more interested in depicting Napoleon's defeat and psychological torment in Russia precisely because he symbolized the organized violence and barbarism of the state against the common masses. Vereshchagin's animus against the Russian autocracy and the military probably explains the exclusion of the tsar, Kutuzov, and the Russian army from the paintings. To this extent, Vereshchagin and Tolstoy's *War and Peace* are in philosophical accord: great historical figures suffer from the illusion of shaping the destinies of nations, but the common masses are the true engines of history.

Vereshchagin was aware of the power of Russian nature (the snow and cold which led to lack of discipline, low morale, desertion, sickness, and starvation), and he understood that it was not solely the Russian people, or the tsar, or the Russian army, or the Cossack horsemen, or the peasant guerrillas which ultimately vanquished Napoleon and expelled him from Russia. To attempt to portray all of these factors would have been extremely difficult and would have surely detracted from the principal role of the Russian people. In his valuable book on the war, however, Vereshchagin clearly deals with the multiple factors responsible for Napoleon's defeat and indicates he knew of the antagonism between Tsar Alexander and Kutuzov before and during the war.[2] What he was able easily to include and explain in a book he simply could not do in his paintings, despite their narrative form. Vereshchagin, therefore, perhaps shrewdly, perhaps unconsciously, circumvented a highly delicate situation by excluding Tsar Alexander and Kutuzov and his army from the paintings. Critics, however, could not determine from the ten works—eight of which included Napoleon—that were exhibited in Moscow in 1895 and in St. Petersburg in 1896, why or how Napoleon was conquered in Russia, or the precise substance of the glorious Russian victory. One critic remarked that Vereshchagin portrayed the conquered (Napoleon) but not the victors.[3] Thus, instead of arousing pride and patriotism, the works evoked dismay, disappointment, and anger; critics claimed that the paintings lacked a tangible hero, had no effect on Russians, and contained little or nothing of historical significance for the Russian people.[4] Possibly, Vereshchagin's primary aim was to counter the legend of Napoleon, in whom there was renewed interest during the 1880s in Western Europe.[5] Napoleon begins and ends the series; his initial poses and expressions indicate dissatisfaction and culminate in raging, mad fury and ultimate humiliation, as he leaves Russia, a crippled man with a devastated army. Thus, the series, which seems to have taken a direction contrary to Vereshchagin's initial intention to focus on the Russian people, may very well be called "The Disintegration and Defeat of Napoleon in Russia."

For that reason, Vereshchagin was unable to sell (indivisibly) the series in Russia, let alone in France during the exhibit there in 1896–97, although a relative of Napoleon expressed some interest in purchasing *Near Moscow Waiting for a Boyar Delegation* (1891–92; see Pl. 13). Vereshchagin hoped that Tretiakov would eventually buy the entire series, but the negative critical reaction to the first ten works probably left the latter indifferent or skeptical; when Tretiakov died in 1898, before the series had been completed, Vereshchagin lost a key potential buyer. In 1901, however, Vereshchagin received a second attractive offer to exhibit his works in America, and returned there to recover his large investment in them, liquidate his debts, and begin the second series of some eighteen paintings, among other projects. The Russian autocracy, when Vereshchagin's agent informed it by telegraph of the exhibit and forthcoming auction in America, agreed to purchase the works for 100,000 rubles ($50,000) primarily in view of the approaching centennial (in 1912) of Napoleon's defeat. As for the second series on the War of 1812, of which he had no clear conception, Vereshchagin faced a dilemma: on the one hand, he wanted to demonstrate the role of Kutuzov and the Russian army; on the other, he feared that the paintings would suffer the same fate as the first series. Further, to emphasize the role of Kutuzov or Tsar Alexander would, conceivably, have negated or contradicted the first series and perhaps would have created even greater confusion concerning the real hero of the war. Vereshchagin also realized that the Russian autocracy, which was not favorably inclined toward his work, would be the most likely buyer of the series if he wanted his paintings to remain in Russia. He thus proposed that the autocracy purchase his paintings on specific subjects as they were completed. But the Russian court, represented by Vladimir Frederiks, naturally wanted the paintings to emphasize the role of Tsar Alexander in Napoleon's defeat, and that emphasis would be contrary to Vereshchagin's view of the national, public character of the victory. Moreover, the Russian court was suspicious of the alleged bias in his paintings, although Vereshchagin was by far the most knowledgeable artist on the war. The court thus stipulated two conditions of purchase: that he work under the court's supervision and that sketches of his paintings be presented for its approval before completion. Both were totally unacceptable to Vereshchagin, who never worked in that mode. Nevertheless, he countered with his own proposal of four paintings, which would include two on Kutuzov but none on Tsar Alexander. He perhaps unwittingly taunted the Russian court by suggesting a painting of General Kutuzov at Fili, a village near Moscow, where the general held a staff conference on September 13, 1812, to decide whether to defend Moscow or abandon it to Napoleon. The court rejected the proposal, obviously because it excluded Tsar Alexander from a major military decision; it informed Vereshchagin that he was free to submit his work on the War of 1812 for its consideration, but there would be no guarantee of purchase.[6]

Vereshchagin's work on the War of 1812, both graphic and written, is of enormous scope and effort that entailed almost twenty years of labor. The paintings required the diverse skills of a painter of portraits and of genre, landscape, and battle scenes; they involved extensive research in French and Russian libraries and archives, prolonged tours of battlefields, and the study of artifacts collected from the war. Almost all the paintings have explanatory texts that document their historical accuracy.[7] Thus, Vereshchagin's portrayal is probably the most accurate and potent rendition of the War of 1812. In addition, he was guided in the presentation of certain episodes by his own experiences in the Russo-Turkish War of 1877–78. For example, two paintings, *Napoleon I at the Borodino Heights* (1897; see Fig. 24) and *Night Bivouac of the Grand Army* (1896–97; see Fig. 30), are similar to *Alexander II at Plevna on August 30, 1877* (see Fig. 12) and *Halt of the Prisoners of War* (1878–79), respectively. Despite their historical accuracy, some of the paintings are dry and rather unimaginative (e.g., *At Gorodnia. Breakthrough or Withdrawal* [1887–95], *Marshal Davout in the Chudovo Monastery* [1900], *On the Way. Bad News from France* [1887–95]), although three episodes, described below, are recreated with artistic authority.

On the evening of June 23, 1812, Napoleon Bonaparte amassed his glorious and invincible Grand Army—the dread of the European continent—on the Russian-Polish border to invade Russia without any declaration of war; the Russians, however, had prepared for the invasion. Napoleon expected to settle a personal score with Tsar Alexander I, who failed to adhere to Napoleon's Continental System (an economic blockade of Britain) and who opposed Napoleon's marriage to his sister.[8] The Grand Army consisted of some 500,000 diverse troops of various nationalities, 6 companies of engineers, 1,372 cannon guns, thousands of artillery and hospital wagons, countless wagons of provisions, and some 100,000 horses for the cavalry, cannons, carts, wagons, and artillery. But the Grand Army, however formidable, was not without its problems in the Russian campaign:

> The Grande Armée of 1812 was the most carefully and completely organized force Napoleon had ever commanded, with the most thoroughly prepared supply system. Its supply train troops were militarized, as was part of its medical service. Most of the troops were well trained, though a good many were not sufficiently hardened for such a demanding campaign, and the Administration included too many cowards and incompetents. In summation, however, *this* Grande Armée was too big . . . at least for the corps commanders that Napoleon had.[9]

A Russian patrol guard approached to ask the advancing soldiers who they were and why they were there. "To make war on you! To take Vilna and set Poland free."[10] This reply marked the spirit of enthusiasm and courage of the French forces as they prepared to cross the Niemen River into Russian territory. "Every subaltern regarded a campaign in Russia as a pleasant six months' outing. The whole army, fully assured of speedy success, looked forward to the war as a means of rapid promotion."[11] The Grand Army was so enormous that it took more than two days to ford the Niemen into Russia.[12] Shortly after it crossed the border into the vast, dense, unfamiliar land of soggy, poor roads, the weather took an ominous turn; intolerable heat became a treacherous stormy, and windy, freezing downpour. "Ten thousand horses perished along the way or later in the forced bivouacs. Great quantities of provisions were abandoned on the sand, and many men died from exposure to the elements."[13] Thus began what would become one of the greatest, most dramatic, heroic, and savage confrontations in military history, one of staggering human and physical losses that ended in disastrous defeat for Napoleon and the almost total destruction of his Grand Army.

The deeper Napoleon penetrated into Russia, the more the illusion of victory propelled him further into the Russian heartland. There, he would eventually discover that, in pursuit of the Russian army, he had entered a land that had been abandoned and razed and that he would wage a war not only against the army of Tsar Alexander I, but against the Russian people and a hostile nature more exacting than mere battle.

Clearly, the Russian military, aware of its weakness and inferior in strength by some 300,000 soldiers, did not seek to engage the Grand Army as it entered Russia, for that would have meant almost certain defeat. Napoleon did not expect this initial lack of opposition. Scorning national sentiment and cultural traditions, he made no appeal to the Estonian, Latvian, and Finnish peoples to revolt against Russian rule. He refused, despite frequent requests at Russian villages, to declare the liberation of the peasant classes in order to enlist their support against the Russian feudal order.[14] Napoleon's military objective was not so much to liberate Russians and others from autocratic rule but to conquer and subjugate them. As one Russian officer put it:

> There is no denying the fact that there was discontent among the people, and the further the enemy advanced, the more the discontent spread. The attitude of the people was extremely doubtful, but it was Napoleon himself, or rather his troops, who contributed most to destroy the confidence of the peasantry in the sincerity of his promises. Rumours soon began to spread that the enemy was plundering all along the line of march; that they were turning the churches into stables, trampling the holy images under-foot or chopping them up for firewood; that they were ill-treating the inhabitants, women, girls, and even young children, suffering at their hands. Small wonder that the peasants betook themselves to the woods, taking with them everything that they could carry, and burning whatever they were unable to move.[15]

The Russian defensive strategy, as determined by General Michel Barclay de Tolly, who was also the Russian Minister of War, was "to outwit and outmanoeuvre the enemy rather than destroy him by a decisive stroke, most of all to be able to take up winter quarters in his territory and lay it under contribution, depleting his resources while economizing one's own," or, to achieve one's objective by "sagacious and sure manoeuvres, without incurring risk."[16] Therefore, Barclay's aim was to avoid a major confrontation with Napoleon's forces, to retreat with his own troops, and to raze and burn villages and towns in order to leave nothing for the French army; by these means he would draw the enemy into the Russian interior, away from its supply center, to isolate, weaken and exhaust it and ultimately drive it out of Russian territory. Napoleon based his military strategy on a "single overwhelming blow."[17] He thus pursued an ever-elusive enemy until the battle at Smolensk on August 15, which marked the first clash between the French and Russian forces. The Russian army resisted Napoleon's onslaught but retreated farther east. In effect, the Russians had established the terms of the war against Napoleon even if his steady advance could not be checked, and even if this entailed the destruction of Russian towns and villages and their inhabitants. Yet there seemed to be a point at which Barclay was compelled to take a stand against Napoleon. Barclay's strategy, which had already eroded one-third of Napoleon's army after five weeks, eventually met with "universal disfavor" among the Russian military, especially after Napoleon defeated him at the Battle of Smolensk on August 17–18, after which Barclay surrendered his command to General Mikhail Kutuzov, who would engage French forces in a major battle at Borodino, some seventy miles west of Moscow.[18]

On September 6, Kutuzov, with an army of 120,000 men, surrounded himself with majestically robed Russian priests bearing religious symbols, including "the beloved icon from Smolensk, which they claimed had been miraculously saved from the profanation of the sacrilegious French." The clergymen conducted a religious ceremony, the purpose of which was to "reinforce military discipline." After noting how the ritual had profoundly touched his men, Kutuzov delivered a passionate appeal to their patriotism to defend their homeland, their tsar, their wives and families, and the Orthodox faith against Napoleon's tyranny and enslavement.[19] The Russian people were defending God's last outpost of freedom in the universe, and it was a battle they could not and would not lose. The battle of Borodino on September 7, which proved to be the bloodiest, fiercest, and most heroic of its time, was largely inconclusive despite Kutuzov's retreat to Moscow in order to preserve his army for a counteroffensive against much weaker French forces; but it proved to be a turning point in the war as it marked the beginning of the end of Napoleon's Grand Army.

In Vereshchagin's *Napoleon I at the Borodino Heights* (1897; Fig. 24), a frustrated Napoleon sits on a hillside, his left foot resting on a drum. The military genius is restless and impatient because his Grand Army has encountered stiff resistance from the Russian forces, and the outcome of the battle is in doubt. His bent head, his hands folded across his chest, and his facial expression—all reflect his discontent with the course of the battle. Clouds of gunsmoke conceal the action from him and the

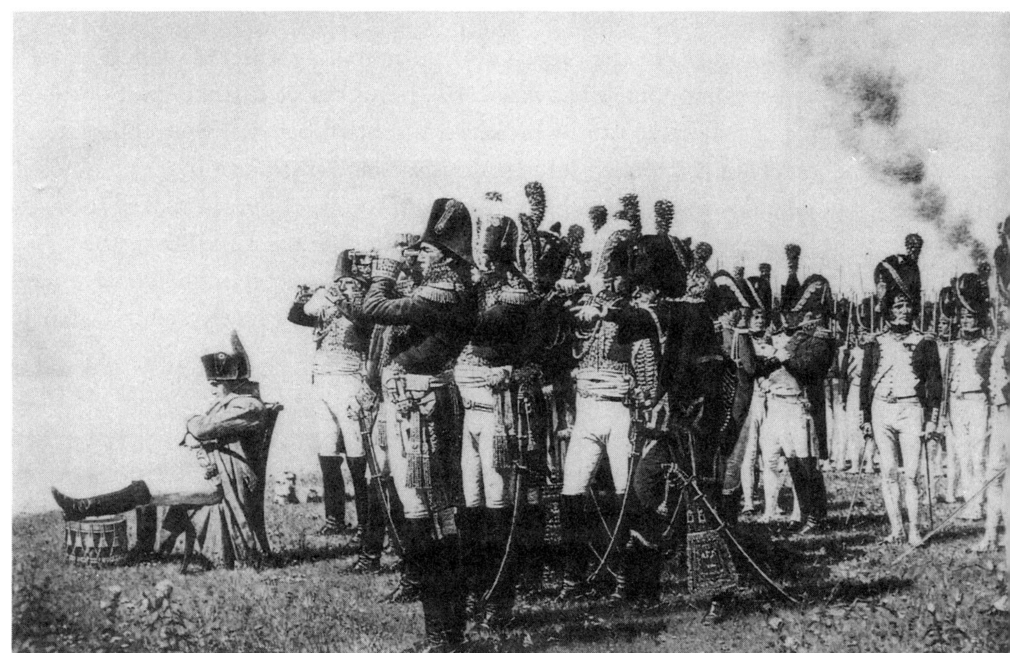

Figure 24. *Napoleon I at the Borodino Heights.* 1897. Oil on canvas. 107 × 157 cm. Historical Museum, Moscow.

pompously dressed generals behind him who are probably officers of the elite Imperial Guard, which Napoleon failed to deploy against the Russian army. In contrast to Napoleon, they seem to pretend to be watching seriously the course of the battle that is quite beyond the ken of the military genius. Some discuss the battle, and others vainly attempt to observe its momentous course with their telescopes, while Napoleon finds no need for one.

In *The End of the Borodino Battle* (1899–1900; Fig. 25), Vereshchagin depicts a major Russian stronghold—barely visible at the extreme right center—which the French finally captured after suffering heavy casualties. Russian and French troops and their horses lie dead and wounded in the ravine and beyond. A number of French soldiers triumphantly salute Napoleon with their helmets, swords, and rifles as he tours the battlefield in the left center. But the heaps of dead surrounding the jubilant officers suggest that the French victory is largely hollow. One French colonel pointed out the cost of the victory:

> Not only had the French army never before suffered such losses as at Borodino, but, what was worse, never before had the spirit of the soldiery been so utterly broken as after that battle. The irrepressible gaiety of the French soldiers vanished, and instead of the songs and jokes in which it had been their wont to forget the fatigues of their long marches, a death-like silence reigned in the camp. Even the officers, it appears, utterly lost heart. Such depression is intelligible when it follows defeat, but it was certainly not to be expected after a victory which had thrown open the gates of Moscow.[20]

Both the French and Russians claimed victory. Tsar Alexander, who, Vereshchagin points out, reluctantly chose Kutuzov as commander of the Russian army, later asserted that when the French momentarily ceased fire during the battle, "Kutuzov lacked the daring to attack the enemy in turn. This unforgivable mistake involved the loss of Moscow."[21] The Russians lost forty thousand men, and the French fifty thousand.[22]

As Kutuzov retreated to Moscow to revitalize his army, Napoleon, "intoxicated with the enthusiasm of glory," advanced his troops to Moscow, the beautiful symbol of the whole Russian empire. If he had

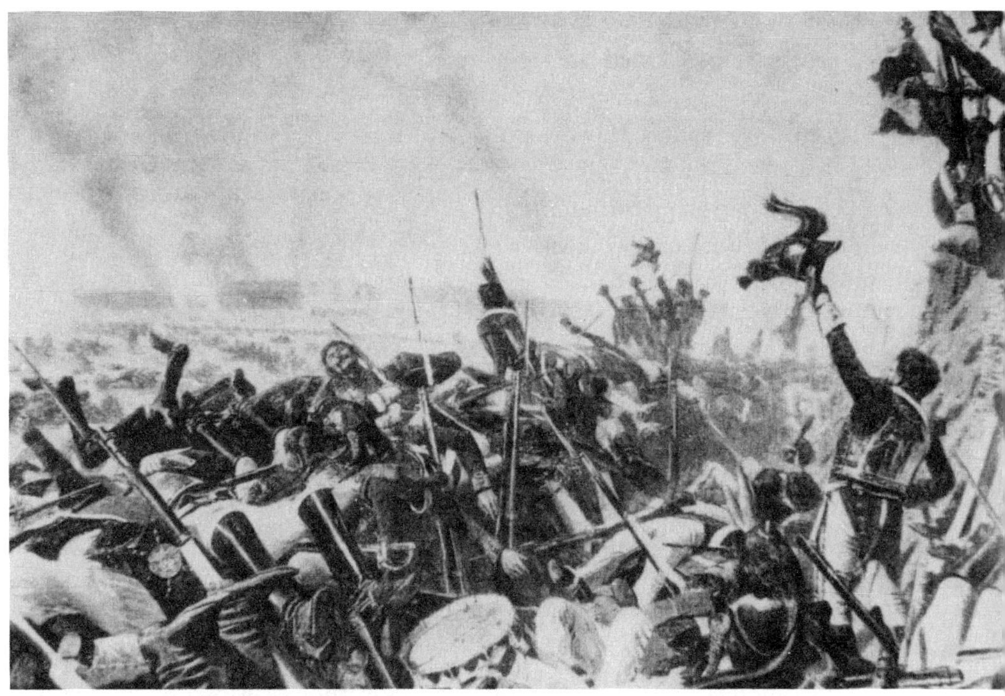

Figure 25. *The End of the Borodino Battle.* 1899–1900. Oil on canvas. 165 × 229 cm. Historical Museum, Moscow.

captured it, Napoleon would have achieved what no one had done before.[23] The Russians, however, had made extensive plans to deprive Napoleon of his prize, plans that utterly puzzled him as he stood at the threshold of his final, most glorious conquest. In *Near Moscow Waiting for a Boyar Delegation* (1891–92; Pl. 13), Vereshchagin portrays Napoleon looking at Moscow from Poklonny Hill; his hands are folded to his back while he vainly waits for Boyars (noblemen who were part of the tsar's administration) to present him with the keys to the splendid city, which lies in the background. The emperor no longer needs his telescope to ascertain the arrival of the Boyars, for he is reconciled to the fact that they will never appear. The rising dust from the French cavalry's descent into Moscow creates another illusory triumph for Napoleon. The Grand Army, still confident of Napoleon's genius, hails the emperor, but he remains unmoved. When a deputation did arrive, however, it consisted of a few "poor aliens, headed by a French compositor." A Russian prisoner who witnessed the scene describes Napoleon's reaction:

> He was thoroughly overcome and completely lost his self-control. His calm and regular step was changed into a quick, uneven tread. He kept looking around him, fidgeted, stood still, trembled all over, looked fierce, tweaked his own nose, pulled a glove off and put it on again, tore another glove out of his pocket, rolled it into a ball, and, as if in deep thought, put it into his other pocket, again took it out, and again put it back, pulled the other glove from his hand, and then quickly drew it on again, and kept repeating the process. This went on for an hour, during which the generals standing behind him remained like statues, not even daring to move.[24]

Two weeks before Napoleon invaded Russia, valuable possessions and financial and commercial records and documents had been removed from Moscow to other areas of the country. Almost the entire population of the city, some 300,000 inhabitants, had prepared to abandon it with their belongings upon the invasion. The Governor of Moscow, Fiodor Rostopchin, had secretly recruited a crew of patriots to mine and set fire to the city's palaces, churches, shops, and dwellings to deny Napoleon shelter and supplies. Tsar Alexander had ordered the construction of a huge fishlike balloon outside of Moscow; it was to fly over the French army, crushing it with steel and fire, but the balloon, which took five days to inflate, could not be launched because of technical difficulties.[25]

On September 14, Napoleon and his army entered a deserted Moscow, where French officers and soldiers temporarily occupied the mansions for rest and leisure. The cavalry stabled their horses in temples, cathedrals, and monasteries (see *In the Assumption Cathedral* [1887–95; Fig. 26]). Shortly thereafter, Russian incendiaries ignited the fires that, in the course of two weeks, would consume 300 churches, 1,500 palaces, 13,800 wooden homes and cottages, and the shops of 6,000 tradesmen.[26] Napoleon took advantage of the light of the conflagration to write one of the several peace proposals he sent to Tsar Alexander, who never responded to any of them. Vereshchagin devotes one painting to a meeting on October 3, when Napoleon, staring desperately at Marshal Lauris-

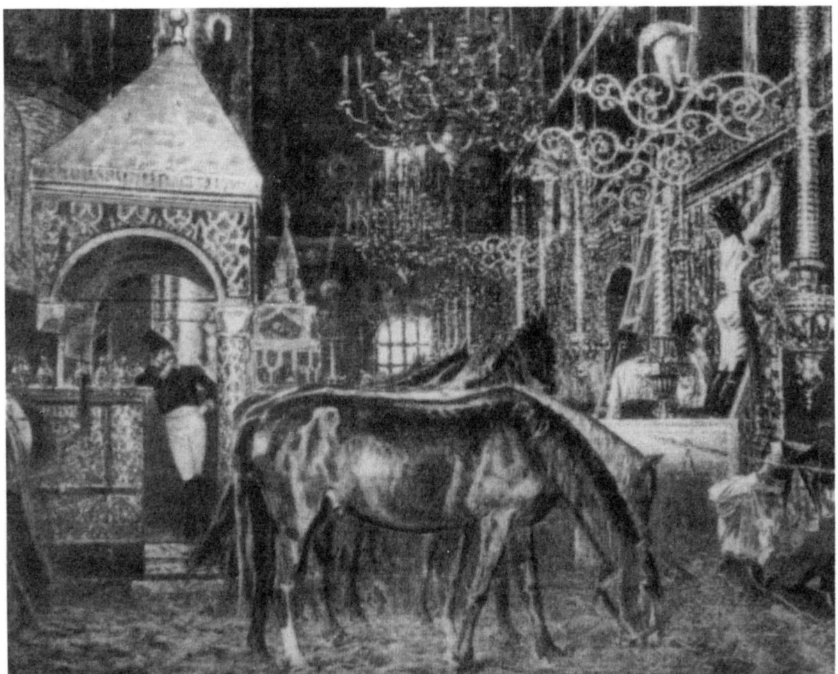

Figure 26. *In the Assumption Cathedral.* 1887–95. Oil on canvas. 132 × 112 cm. Historical Museum, Moscow.

ton, sends him on a peace mission to St. Petersburg (*Napoleon and Marshal Lauriston* (*Peace at All Costs!*) [1899–1900; Fig. 27]). This work may have been influenced by Jacques Louis David's (1748–1825) *Napoleon in His Study* (1812). Lauriston understands only too well the gravity of the situation for Napoleon, who is faced with the terrible absurdity of having conquered a city in ashes. Although Lauriston bends his head to acknowledge Napoleon's request, his expression reveals that his mission will be futile.

Whipped up by a series of cross winds, the raging fires threatened the safety of Napoleon in the Kremlin, which housed a stockpile of explosives, and illuminated the magnificence and splendor of the buildings. Vereshchagin created ten paintings related to the fire in Moscow and Napoleon's stay there. In *The Kremlin is Burning* (1887–98; Fig. 28), a troubled Napoleon, followed by Marshals Davout and Lauriston, among

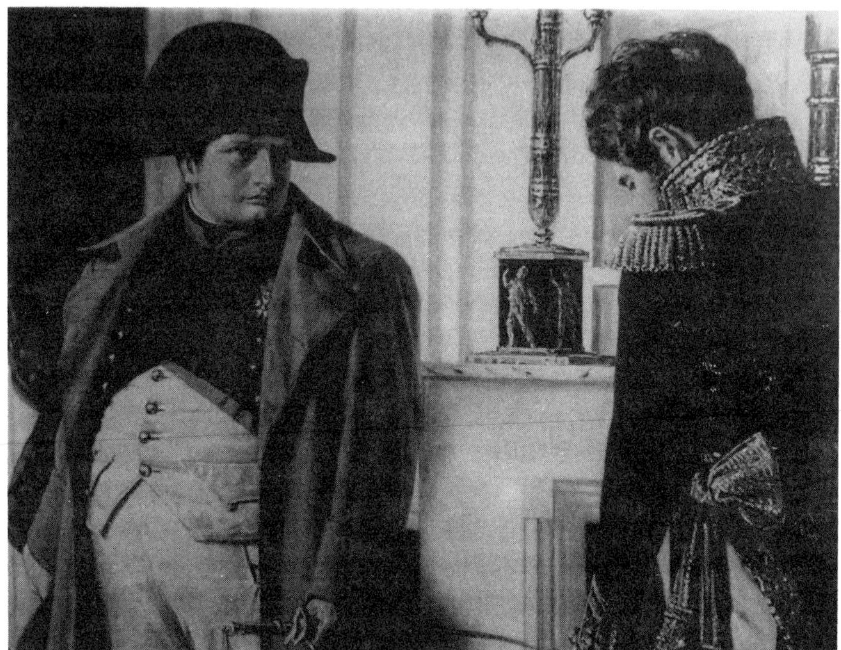

Figure 27. *Napoleon and Marshal Lauriston* (*Peace at All Costs!*). 1899–1900. Oil on canvas. 131 × 146 cm. Historical Museum, Moscow.

others, surveys the fire through an opening in the Kremlin wall. The smoke reaches the Kremlin, the pavement of which is littered with burning debris blown there by swift winds. In the background a group of generals step aside as a piece of flaming debris hurls toward them. Napoleon clearly understands the threat of the holocaust: he must abandon the Kremlin or risk his own destruction.

The French military pondered the intentions of the Russians. Did they destroy Moscow merely to "entangle Napoleon in this catastrophe, that the loss of this man was well worth the loss of the capital? Did they think that the result was of sufficient importance to justify the sacrifice of all Moscow; that heaven, perhaps, in exchange for so great a victory, required so great a holocaust; that this colossus deserved an equally gigantic funeral pyre?"[27] To add to the fury of the conflagration, Russian incendiaries and freed prisoners carrying flaming torches "raced in triumph through the

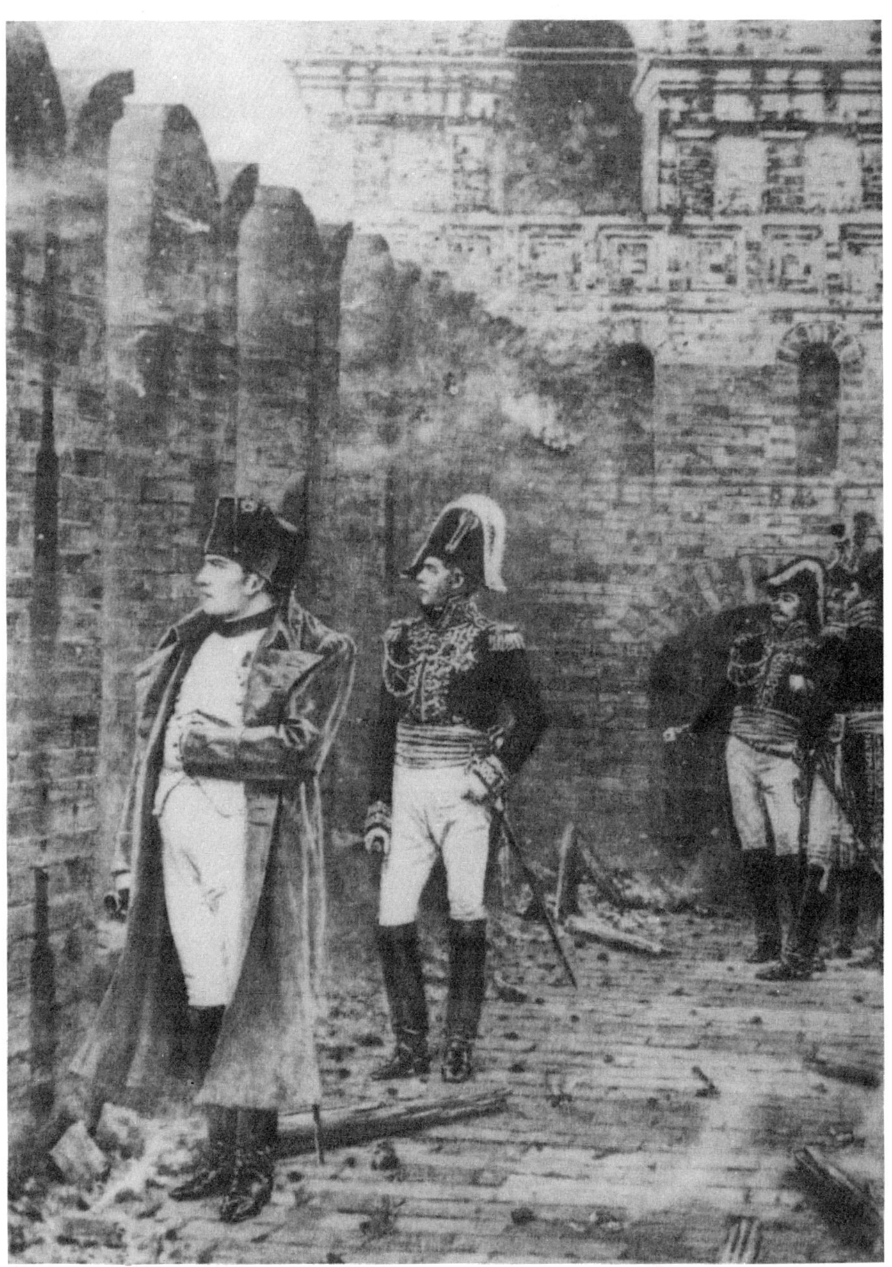

Figure 28. *The Kremlin is Burning*. 1887–98. Oil on canvas. Whereabouts unknown.

blazing streets," setting fire to buildings.[28] French soldiers captured numerous incendiaries and executed them in a Kremlin square, as portrayed in *In Defeated Moscow (Arsonists, or Shooting in the Kremlin)* [1897–98; Fig. 29]. This painting was influenced by Francisco de Goya's (1746–1828) *The Third of May 1808* (1814–15), in which Napoleon's occupation troops in Madrid brutally execute its citizens.

Napoleon left the Kremlin on foot to seek refuge in the Petrovsky Palace, an imperial residence beyond Moscow, but he lost his way and almost perished in the fire.[29] A day later, he viewed the city, which "seemed one vast swirling column of fire, towering into the sky and dyeing it with lurid colors. Sunk in gloomy contemplation, he kept a long mournful silence which he broke at length by the exclamation, 'This forebodes great misfortunes for us'."[30] Vereshchagin's *Return from the Petrovsky Palace* (1895; Pl. 14), probably the most compelling piece in the series, depicts Napoleon's return to the Kremlin when the fires in Moscow were diminishing. The white columns of once-elegant buildings are still ablaze; smoke blackens the pinkish horizon, which reflects the glow of the fires. Household utensils, heaps of ashes, smoldering remains of trees, and bodies of dead Russians lie scattered on the streets. Napoleon's guard of six horsemen leads the procession; behind follow the emperor and his generals. French troops on the left salute as they pass; on the right several soldiers who are looting conceal themselves.[31]

Napoleon, after waiting futilely for Tsar Alexander to respond to his peace offer, began his bitter, humiliating retreat in October with 100,000 troops. Demoralized, and suffering from hunger, fatigue, and cold, they were now driven largely by the instinct for self-preservation. In *Night Bivouac of the Grand Army* (1896–97; Fig. 30), Vereshchagin vividly demonstrates the pathetic struggle of the tragic French soldiers against the relentless, merciless onslaught of Russian winter. By burning Russian villages as he retreated, Napoleon deprived his own men of vital shelter. Their own clothing is completely inadequate to protect them from the bitter crippling cold; they cover themselves with anything they can find—blankets, ragged coats, women's skirts, peasant and clerical garments—and huddle together for warmth like cattle in a barn.[32] Moreover, the French teams "were increasingly unable to haul their guns across country," and thus could offer no resistance to attack.[33] The Grand Army is no

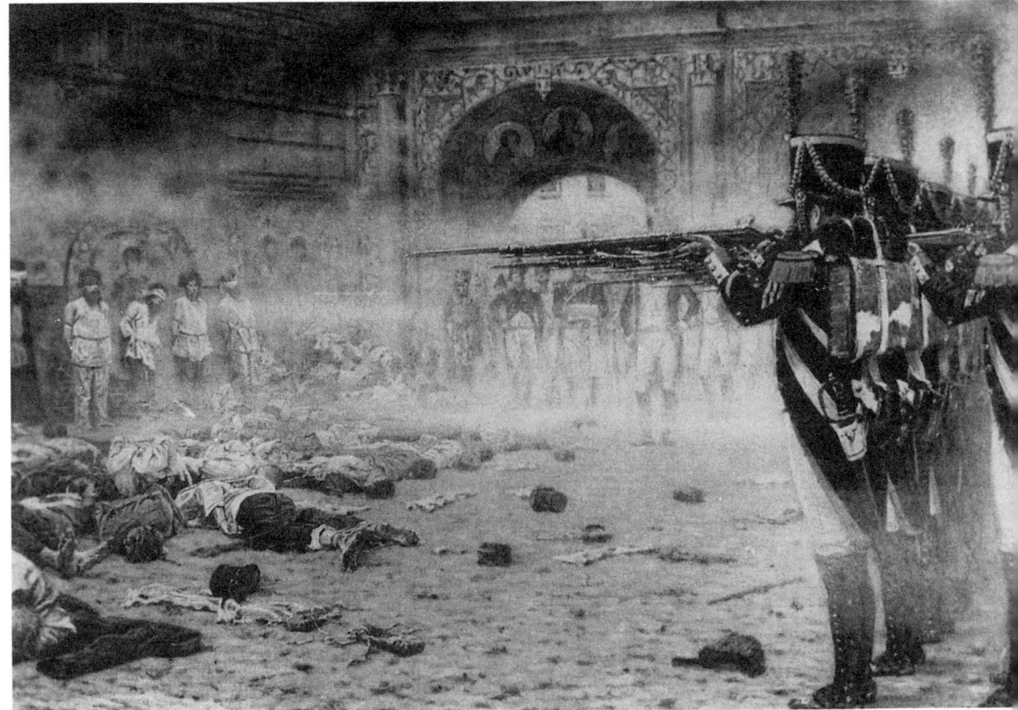

Figure 29. *In Defeated Moscow (Arsonists, or Shooting in the Kremlin).* 1897–98. 86 × 112 cm. Historical Museum, Moscow.

longer able to defend itself against either the Russian army or the Russian winter. Thousands of Cossack Horsemen and Russian peasant guerrillas, in addition to stealing and destroying French food supplies, pounced on retreating soldiers "with ferocious laughter, wounded them, stripped them of everything they had, and left them to perish naked in the snow. These guerrillas, incited by Alexander and Kutuzov, who did not know then how to avenge nobly the country they had been unable to defend, kept abreast of the army on both sides of the road, under the cover of trees. They threw back on the deadly highway the soldiers whom they did not finish off with their spears and axes."[34]

Vereshchagin devotes two paintings to the role of the Russian guerrillas. *Wait! Let'em Come Nearer!* (1887–95; Pl. 15) may very well be the most imaginative and impressive work in the series; it effectively embod-

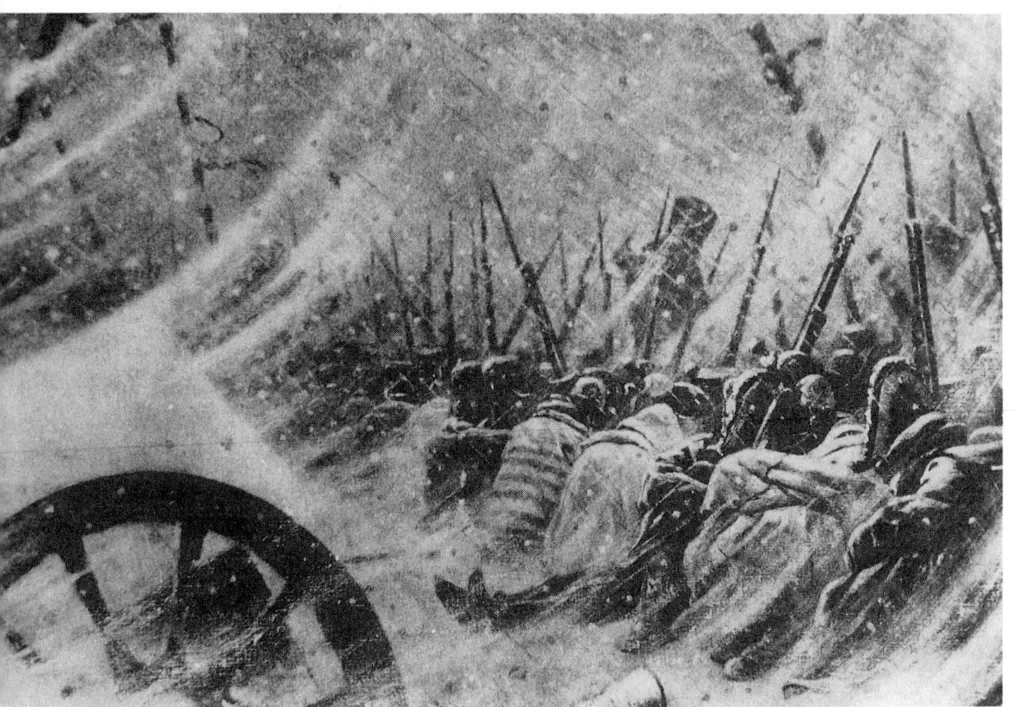

Figure 30. *Night Bivouac of the Grand Army.* 1896–97. Oil on canvas. 100 × 120 cm. Historical Museum, Moscow.

ies Vereshchagin's effort to portray the essential character of the Russian struggle against Napoleon in terms of the patriotism of the ordinary people. A group of guerrillas armed with axes and swords stand behind dense snow-covered shrubs. They resemble the pine trees beside them as, at one with nature, they calmly, confidently wait for the right moment to attack the retreating French army. The sequel to this painting is *Captured with Arms? Shoot Them!* (1887–95; Pl. 16), which depicts three captured guerrillas brought before Napoleon for punishment. The emperor's fury, revealed in his glaring eyes, is part of the process of the mental and physical disintegration to which Vereshchagin inexorably subjects him in the series. Three generals attempt to restrain Napoleon from mad rage, while the partisans, in contrast, bear their fate calmly, heroically.

By the time it left the Russian borders, the Grand Army had been shattered by the pursuit of Kutuzov, the Cossacks, and the guerrillas. In *On*

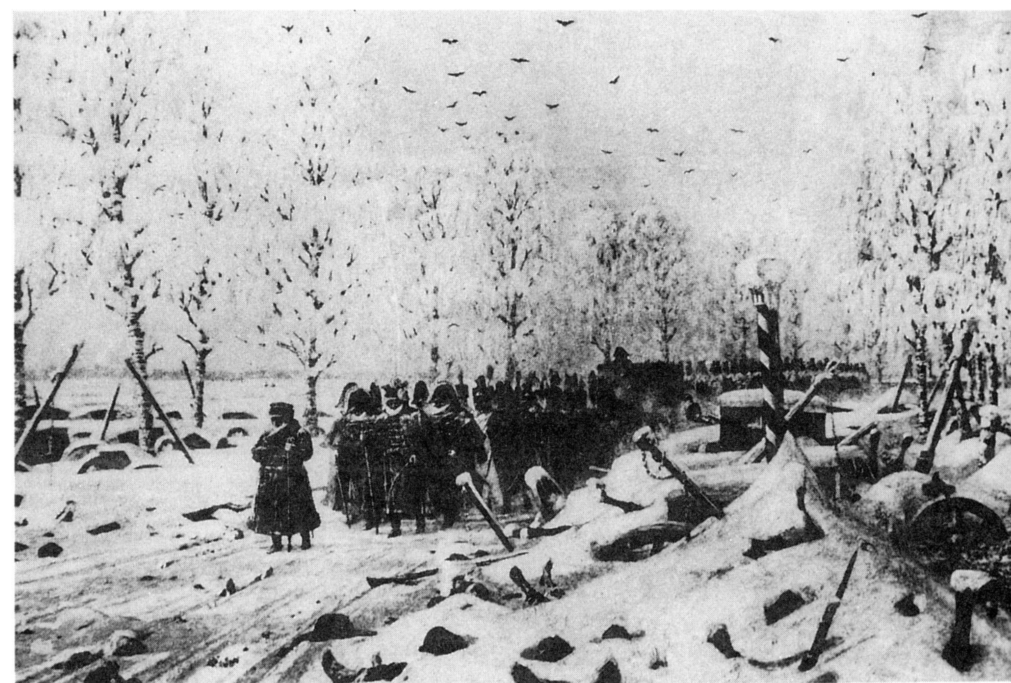

Figure 31. *On the Road. Retreat, Flight.* 1887–95. Oil on canvas. 179 × 303 cm. Historical Museum, Moscow.

the Road. Retreat, Flight (1887–95; Fig. 31), a tiny, vanquished Napoleon slowly leads his helpless army out of Russia in a retreat that resembles a funeral procession. The canes he and his generals carry signify the crippled condition of the army. In contrast, Russian nature, which contributed so much to ravage the Grand Army, now rejoices in all its beauty. Snow covers the dead soldiers and horses and the abandoned equipment that lie scattered on the road, and the frosted trees gleam like beacons, guiding Napoleon and his army out of the land. Vereshchagin summarizes the magnitude of the staggering destruction of the war in human terms for the French forces alone:

> The result of the campaign was the complete annihilation of an army of nearly half a million men. The whole of the artillery,

consisting of 1200 guns and caissons, fell into the hands of the enemy, together with many thousands of wagons and officer's carriages, and an enormous quantity of warlike stores and provisions. According to official accounts, 253,000 bodies were burnt in the provinces of Moscow, Vitebsk, and Mohilef, and 53,000 bodies in Vilna and its immediate neighborhood. More than 100,000 men were taken prisoners. Within historical memory, from the time of Cambyses to the present day, there is no parallel to such a disaster affecting so great a host.[35]

Chapter Six

LAST YEARS

In the 1890s, the Vereshchagins became the parents of three daughters (one of whom died) and one son. The family, which included Lidiia's mother, led a peaceful life in a village near Moscow, where Vereshchagin had built a large wooden home that included his studio, study, and library (Fig. 32). He also had an outdoor studio where he worked in mild weather, as well as a small cottage in the Caucasus. The family's ample staff of cooks, nurses, and governesses in many ways reflected Vereshchagin's childhood household (Fig. 33). The staff often played with the children and took them to nearby fields to pick berries and mushrooms. Vereshchagin and Lidiia would meet with the staff to plan and suggest meals and activities and to discuss the need for various provisions and supplies to be purchased in Moscow. They also read stories to their children, and, when Vereshchagin was away, Lidiia played the piano for them, since he preferred that she not play while he painted (Fig. 34). Vereshchagin disliked the ministration of any form of religious instruction to his children, especially by Lidiia's mother, although the family attended church on major religious holidays.[1] His personal legacy to his children was that they accept and judge others by their spiritual and moral character, not by class origins.[2] He also devoted great attention to the physical development of his children by means of gymnastic equipment in their home.

Vereshchagin was an intensely private person who organized and valued his time. He was the first to arise in the morning, to exercise with his children, and to eat breakfast; then he worked—usually with several breaks—in the studio until sunset. After supper, he would play with the

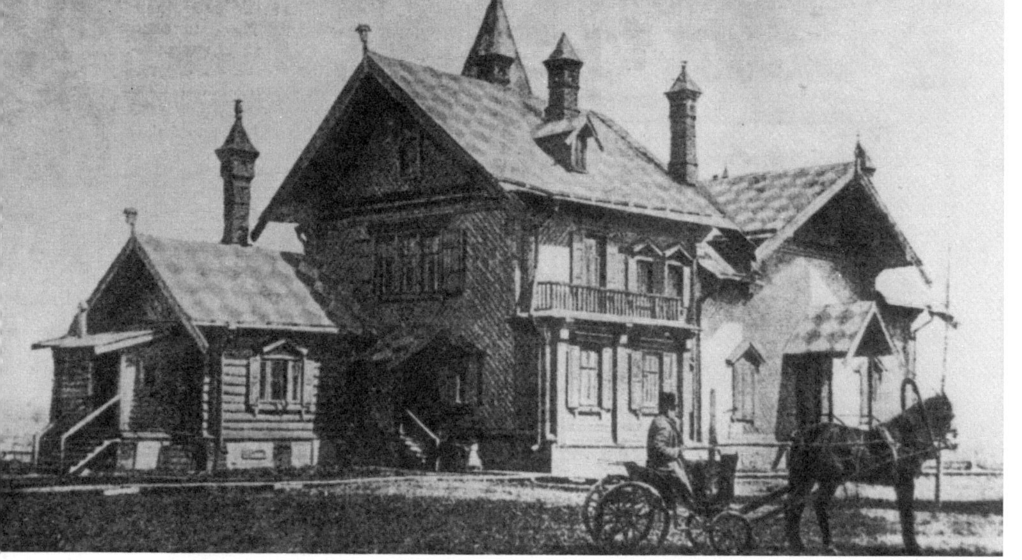

Figure 32. The Vereshchagin home near Moscow. From A. Lebedev and A. Solodovnikov, *V. V. Vereshchagin* (Moscow: Iskusstvo, 1988).

children and tell them of his experiences; after they went to bed, he usually worked in his study, writing letters, tending to his business affairs, or composing his memoirs and other works. Vereshchagin was not merely an observer, but a conscious and active participant in the affairs of his time. During his life, he published about twenty-four books and numerous articles which provided a necessary source of income while he worked on his paintings. This astonishing scope of literary work may be unprecedented for an artist; and it is even more surprising that a complete set of his works has not been published in his homeland, where he is regarded as a classic Russian artist. Because of his extensive literary work, prolific artistic output, and frequent travels, the Vereshchagins rarely if ever entertained guests. The doorman would often tell uninvited visitors that Vereshchagin was too busy to greet them.[3]

Despite his happy family life, Vereshchagin became interested in the Spanish-American War of 1898—the beginning of the American imperial expression of Manifest Destiny—and its effects in the Philippines and Cuba; it was a war that could be given artistic treatment to raise sorely

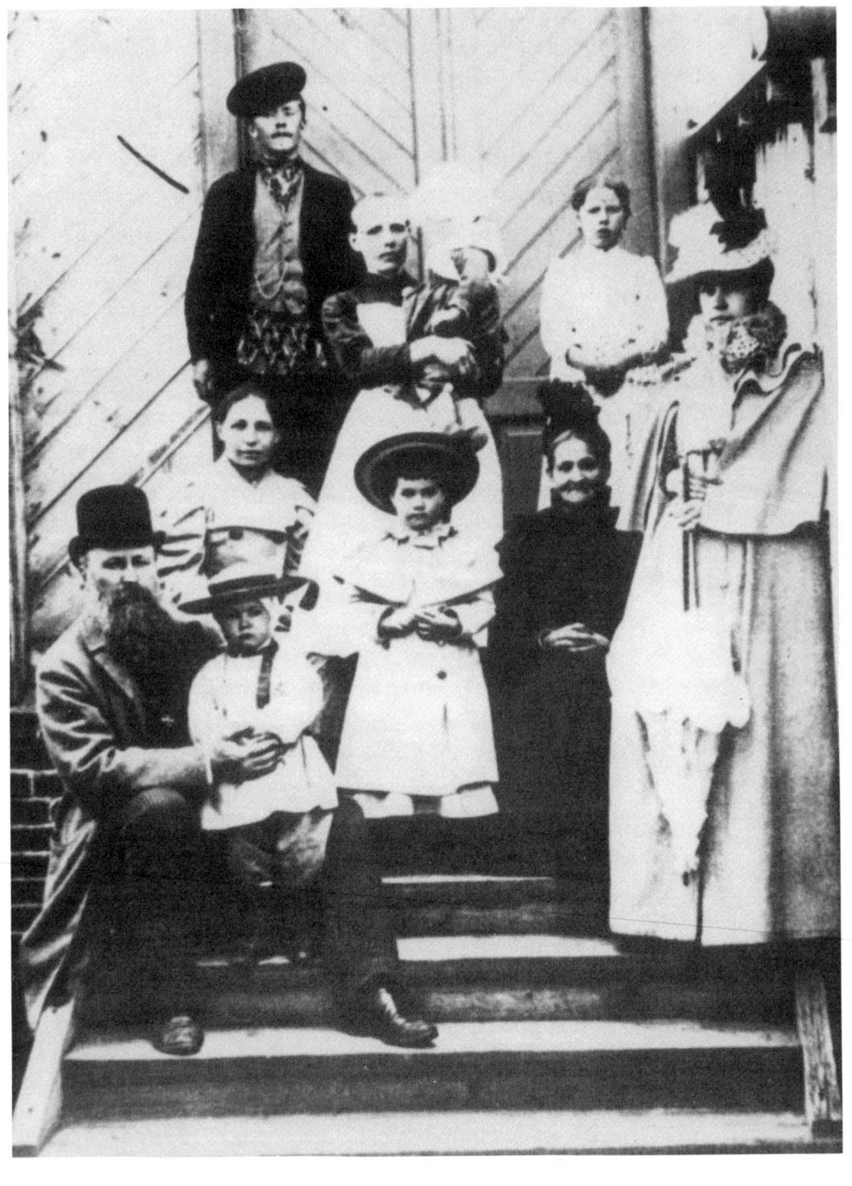

Figure 33. The Vereshchagin family and household staff. From A. Lebedev and A. Solodovnikov, *V.V. Vereshchagin* (Moscow: Iskusstvo, 1988).

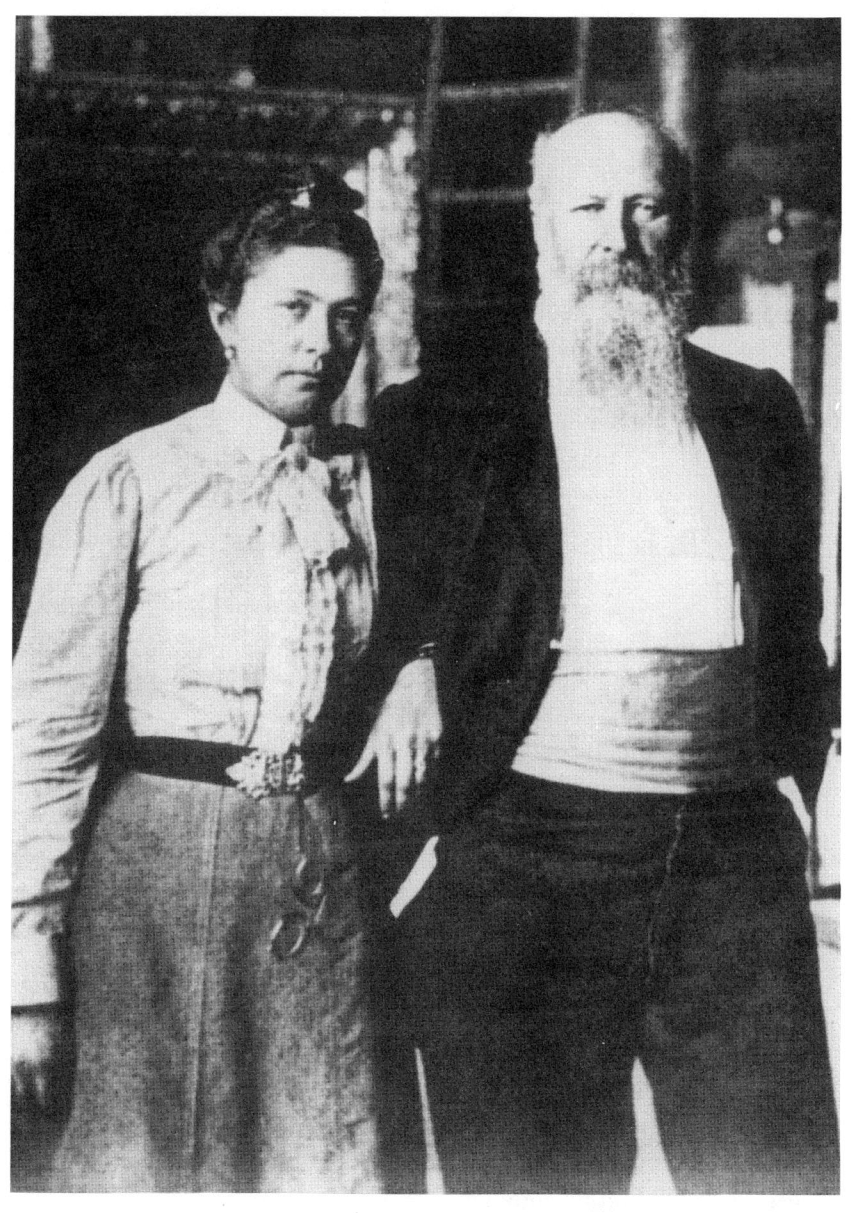

Figure 34. Vasily and Lidiia Vereshchagin, early 1900s. From A. Lebedev and A. Solodovnikov, *V. V. Vereshchagin* (Moscow: Iskusstvo, 1988).

needed money to cover his mounting debts and expenses. In 1901, he spent more than two months in the Philippines, where the Americans had waged for two years a brutal war against Filipino nationalists. There, he completed—among other pieces, which he seems to have sold—a series of five oval paintings about the tragedy of a wounded American soldier who is unable to finish a letter to his mother.[4] This series appears to combine his observations of hospitalized American soldiers and his own experiences as a casualty in the Russo-Turkish War. It portrays the soldier as he announces to his superior officer that he has been wounded; is carried into the hospital; tries, semiconsciously, to express to a nurse a few words for a letter to his mother; loses consciousness; and perishes. The nurse, who appears in four of the paintings, plays a central role in the series: her facial expressions, poses, and gestures mirror the physical condition and fate of the wounded man.

In search of new artistic material and hoping to sell his War of 1812 series, Vereshchagin came to America in late 1901, where he spent a year holding exhibits in Chicago, Washington, D.C., St. Louis, New York, and other cities. On one Sunday, his exhibit drew about ten thousand spectators at the Art Institute of Chicago; it was so successful that "the press not only of Chicago, but also of the entire central belt of the United States were swarming with articles about Vereshchagin and his paintings."[5] During another exhibit, Vereshchagin requested that the admission fee be reduced for children, but the managers responded that, since his works were capable of creating in children an aversion to war, it was "undesirable" to do so.[6] He made two trips to Cuba in 1902 to paint a number of works on the American conquest of that country in 1898. One of his Spanish-American War paintings, *Roosevelt's Capture of San Juan Heights* (1902), was exhibited at the Astor Gallery in New York's Waldorf-Astoria Hotel. Vereshchagin had spoken with President Theodore Roosevelt about the battle and had persuaded him to pose for the painting. Roosevelt not only provided Vereshchagin with advice and photographs of members of his regiment, the Rough Riders, but also kept abreast of the progress of the paintings. When Roosevelt came to New York City on business, he paid a brief visit to Vereshchagin's studio to examine the finished painting. The work depicts a group of soldiers, led

by then-Colonel Roosevelt, charging through a sugarcane field to capture San Juan Hill. Vereshchagin understood the deep symbolic significance of the American flag and portrays one soldier prepared to place the flag on the hill as a mark of conquest. While in New York, Vereshchagin learned that *Procession of Elephants in India*, a painting he had sold for $5,000, had been resold for $50,000.[7]

After the exhibit, Vereshchagin held an auction of thirty-one paintings. One G. Brander bought *Roosevelt's Capture of San Juan Heights* for $18,000, although $25,000 had been expected; he paid another $2,600 for two other works about the American military presence in the Philippines. In view of the country's mood for military glory, Brander planned to exhibit the three works around the country and charge an admission fee. The remaining twenty-eight pieces, many of which Vereshchagin created in the Philippines on the Spanish-American War, brought $23,000—a rather low sum. The twenty War of 1812 paintings were also displayed at the auction but were not for sale, because the Russian government had agreed, after prolonged negotiation, to buy them for 100,000 rubles ($50,000). A small group of speculators were quite disappointed that they had been sold, since they planned to prevent others from bidding on the series in the event of an auction. Aware of the sensation that the series had created in Western Europe, the group planned to return there to auction the paintings, or, possibly, sell them to the Russian government.[8] Most likely, Vereshchagin was aware of the plot and the attendant fragmentation of the series, which is why he tried—successfully—through his agent to sell the series to the Russian government.

In August 1903, Vereshchagin began a three-month visit to Japan to study its culture, art, and architecture for his work and to gain a personal understanding of a potential military adversary of Russia. He had to state the purpose of his visit to Japanese officials, who were suspicious of Russian travelers in view of the growing hostility between the two countries over colonial possessions in Korea and China, particularly Port Arthur, a Chinese port that Japan had captured in 1895. When Russia, Germany, and France forced Japan to evacuate Port Arthur, Russia, seeking a strategic naval harbor for its Pacific fleet, acquired the port on lease from China in 1898. While in Japan, Vereshchagin became aware of her preparations for war against Russia and the systematic cultivation of public opinion

about the inevitability of that war. After touring a wharf, where he may have seen military equipment or activities, he came away convinced of an impending war which an unprepared Russia could not win.[9] He wrote in his notebook that "war with Japan we must try to avoid as aimless, merciless and in any event ruinous."[10]

Vereshchagin was particularly impressed by Japan's natural beauty; he viewed the country as a vast, beautiful, harmonious garden, characterized by order, care, and economy. In a letter to his wife, he noted: "What else to tell you about Japan: there is so much fine craftsmanship here in everything as in no other country except India—the parts, details are extraordinarily good."[11] Vereshchagin captured the beauty of the country and especially the harmony of man and nature in some twenty studies and sketches that he created for subsequent development but which were never completed. Although many of these works were similar to his early ethnographic studies and sketches, some were executed in impasto, a technique in which paint is thickly applied to the canvas, often by means of a palette knife. This method marked a new direction in his art.

With war imminent, Vereshchagin returned to Russia in November 1903 on the very last passenger run from Japan to Vladivostok. He wrote to Tsar Nicholas I that "a terrible war would soon break out" with Japan, but the tsar did not believe him.[12] On February 8–9, 1904, Japan attacked—without a declaration of war—the Russian Far Eastern Naval squadron near Port Arthur (now Lushun) and inflicted heavy damage. However painful, Vereshchagin decided to return to the Far East to be useful to the Russian military and, more importantly, to record the war in his art. He wrote to a friend, the Minister of War, Aleksey Kuropatkin, to make arrangements for him as an orderly in the Far East.[13] Because he had exhausted his funds and incurred debts during his trip to Japan, he asked his close friend, Vasily Kirkor, to help his family should the need arise. Vereshchagin also planned, in cooperation with other Russian artists, to hold an exhibit on the horrors of the war on his return. Before and after he left, he advised Tsar Nicholas, *inter alia,* to be completely decisive and to follow the example of his forefather, Tsar Alexander I; that is, to modernize the Russian navy and to give a professional military officer (i.e., General Kuropatkin) complete command of an army of 500,000 to advance against the enemy.[14] One can only speculate on

Vereshchagin's motives in writing to the tsar. Perhaps he felt obliged to be useful in the light of the tsar's recent purchase of his War of 1812 series. His suggestion that Kuropatkin take command of the Russian army probably stemmed from his experiences in the Balkans, when the tsar attempted to direct the war from St. Petersburg. Perhaps Vereshchagin believed that, as a close friend of Kuropatkin, he could have some influence on the course of the war. Finally, the tsar could be a potential buyer of his works after the war.

On the morning of February 28, Vereshchagin, after breakfast, bid farewell first to his household staff and wife, who was so overwrought that she could not accompany her children to the studio to see their father off. He had promised his wife not to risk his life needlessly; she made no effort to dissuade him from going. Vereshchagin sat in his armchair, gathered his children around him, and hugged them. After a brief moment of silence, he told them in a soft voice that he would be gone for a long time. He asked that they love and obey their mother, that they not fight and quarrel, and that they be honest and always tell the truth; he hugged and kissed each child. As he left the house, he momentarily looked back with tears in his eyes. One of the cooks saw this as a bad omen and remarked: "Oh, that's not good. It doesn't bode well."[15]

Despite his age (sixty-two), Vereshchagin had not lost his enthusiasm for action at sea. That he had been trained as a naval officer made him feel that he had a direct role and stake in the outcome of the battle. When he reached Port Arthur, he inspected the squadron and found it unprepared to challenge the Japanese navy. He met with the new commander of the Russian fleet, Admiral Stepan Makarov, whom he had known during the Russo-Turkish war. Makarov invited Vereshchagin to join him on the battleship, *Petropavlovsk*—the flagship of the Russian fleet in the Pacific—for a series of naval exercises and maneuvers. Built in 1894 and commissioned in 1897, the ship had a water displacement of 11,300 tons, fifty-six guns of various calibre, and six torpedo tubes. In his last letter to his wife, on March 30, Vereshchagin remarked that he had been on the ship and that he was eager to see battle but had seen none for three days. That he sensed where the enemy lurked is evident: "I am prompting Makarov to go further out to sea, but do not know if he will agree."[16]

On the following morning, a few Japanese warships were several miles

at sea, waiting for Makarov to leave harbor and challenge them. On the previous day, the Japanese had sunk two Russian ships near Port Arthur. Makarov tried to persuade Vereshchagin to leave ship in view of a possible duel at sea, but he refused. Accompanied by six warships, the *Petropavlovsk* set out to sea and soon encountered the Japanese ships, which opened fire and then suddenly took flight farther out to sea. Makarov commenced fire and began pursuit, only to discover that he had been lured to a much larger group of Admiral Togo's formidable fleet of twenty-three ships sixteen miles from Port Arthur. Realizing his entrapment and his disadvantage in being isolated from shore batteries and torpedo boats, Makarov immediately turned back to seek shelter in Port Arthur. Admiral Togo made an attempt—perhaps deliberately feeble—to overtake Makarov. Two miles from Port Arthur, Makarov's ship entered a mine bed that had been ingeniously laid between Russian torpedoes the previous evening by Japanese vessels monitoring the sea lanes used by Russian ships in and out of Port Arthur. Makarov had been informed that the Japanese had countermined the Russian channel, but he failed to sweep the area before departing on March 31 and had safely crossed the bed that very morning before he left for sea. Almost immediately, a mine ignited the battleship's ammunition hold, setting off a much greater explosion that ruptured its boilers. Under a cloud of steam and gray-black smoke, the crippled ship rapidly became engulfed in flames. Listing heavily to the right, the enormous battleship appeared to be split as its bow plunged deeply into the sea. Vereshchagin stood on the bridge next to Makarov and sketched the unfolding action. Crew members crowded on to the stern, frantically trying to abandon the ill-fated ship. A third and final explosion doomed the stern, which bared its revolving screws as the *Petropavlovsk* swiftly vanished into the sea with a crew of 700 men "as if it were a fragile, unseaworthy vessel amidst the ocean waves." When the waters had completely swallowed the vessel, a cloud of steam and black smoke cast a shadow over the area in which the ship sank (Fig. 35). Vereshchagin had stayed at his post to the very end. The entire episode took less than two minutes. Seven officers and fifty-two crewmen survived.[17]

The news of Vereshchagin's death appeared in many major newspapers worldwide. Some still held a glimmer of hope that he might be rescued. When, however, his death was officially confirmed, General Kuropatkin

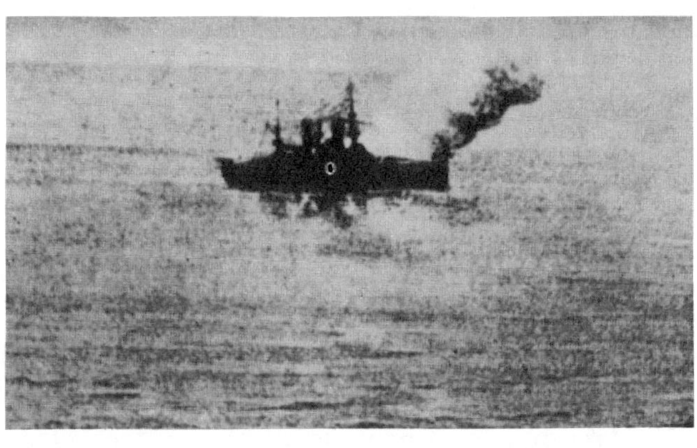

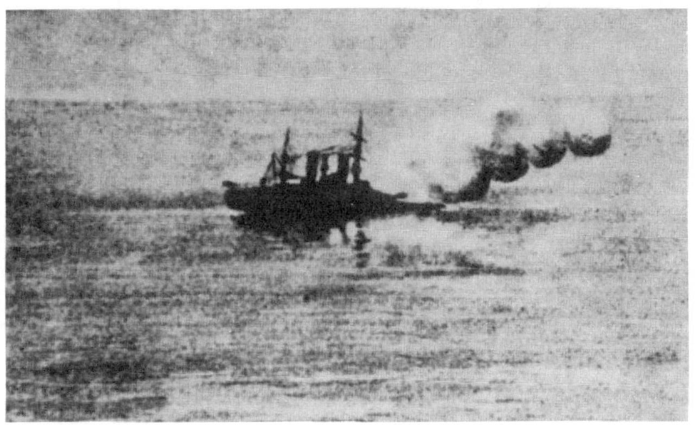

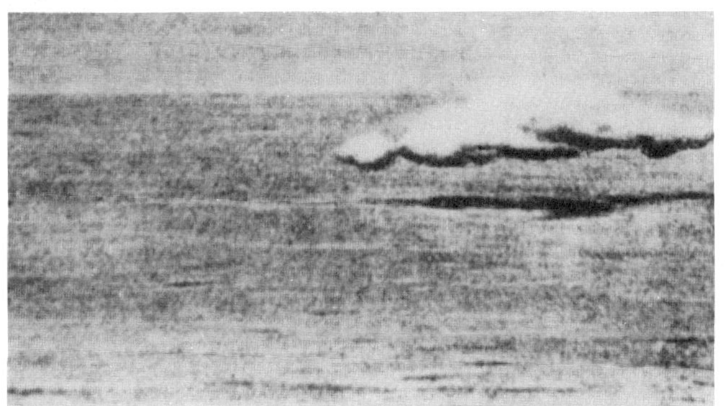

Figure 35. The sinking of the *Petropavlovsk* in 1904. From A. Lebedev and A. Solodovnikov, *V. V. Vereshchagin* (Moscow: Iskusstvo, 1988).

wrote to Lidiia Vereshchagin: "With the whole of Russia I mourn the great artist and the unforgettable battle friend."[18] In many countries—America, Italy, Estonia, Bulgaria, among others—memorial services were held in his honor, poems were dedicated to him, as well as other tributes. A requiem was held in the Kazansky Cathedral in St. Petersburg, but no member of the royal family attended. One Russian newspaper noted the impact of Vereshchagin's death:

> The whole world shook with the news of the tragic death of V. Vereshchagin, and the friends of peace are saying with a painful heart, 'One of the most passionate champions of the idea of peace has passed away. All of Russia is mourning Makarov, the whole world is mourning Vereshchagin. . . .' He captivated, his paintings created a stupendous impression, and all the skeptics had to admit that there was a special power in Vereshchagin's art. That power was *in his feeling*, that power was in the consciousness of the viewer, that in those powerful paintings beats the pulse of a passionate heart.[19]

In his will, Vereshchagin stipulated that there be a posthumous exhibit of his works followed by an auction. After payment of all debts, the family was to live on the annual interest from the proceeds. He granted his first wife, who lived in Munich, one-thousand dollars annually. His funeral was to be simple and nonreligious.[20]

For some time, in view of her deep love and devotion, Lidiia could not reconcile herself to her husband's death; in addition, she could not face the heavy burden of providing for her family, lowering her standard of living, and dealing with her husband's unfinished affairs. The urgent need for money compelled her to sell her home because the children would soon begin their schooling some distance away in Moscow (Fig. 36). Lidiia also sold a painting for 10,000 rubles, which, presumably, liquidated some of Vereshchagin's debts. As for her future income, Lidiia applied to the Academy of Arts for an annual state pension, she wrote: "The death of my husband has found me completely unprepared materially to raise my children. My husband left neither money nor property that produces income. All that he had went to pay his debts, which presently have yet to be settled. I turn to you with the most humble

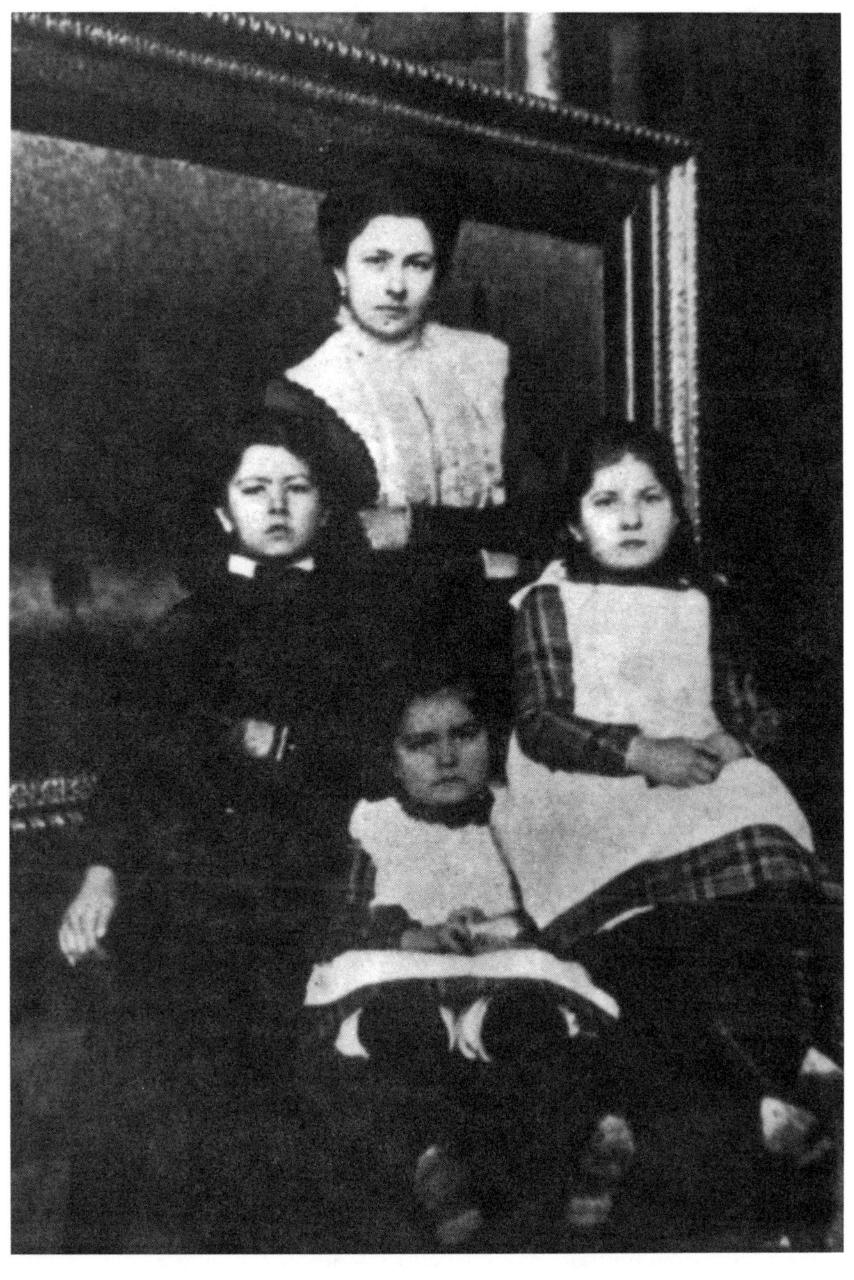

Figure 36. Lidiia Vereshchagin and the children. From A. Lebedev and A. Solodovnikov, *V. V. Vereshchagin* (Moscow: Iskusstvo, 1988).

request to help me in counsel and deed—to petition for a pension." The request came to the tsar's attention, who initially granted her 2,400 rubles yearly but later reduced it to 1,000 rubles.[21]

In fulfilling Vereshchagin's wishes, Lidiia arranged an exhibit of 476 works, consisting of 105 oil paintings and sketches and studies from his earliest works to his latest pieces on the Spanish-American War, the Philippines and Japan. There were about 70 photographs of other paintings. Lidiia had been offered 25,000 rubles ($12,500), for one painting but refused to sell it because Vereshchagin had designated it as a gift to the family. There were also numerous materials related to the craft of painting that went on exhibit to re-create the atmosphere of Vereshchagin's studio (Fig. 37); for Lidiia, this was a way of keeping her husband's memory alive. Art collectors from abroad were invited; some, obviously aware of the value of Vereshchagin's art in Western Europe, arrived even before the exhibit opened.[22] One American industrialist-philanthropist, Charles Crane, a frequent visitor to Russia, probably knew the value of Vereshchagin's works in America when he expressed a strong interest in purchasing them. With the exception of the government or the royal family, very few Russian art collectors could compete against men like Crane and other wealthy Americans who had inquired about the auction.[23]

On November 11, 1904, four days before the exhibit opened, a newspaper article pointed out that many Russians were concerned about the fate of Vereshchagin's collection, and it cautioned against the sale of "the important documents of the talent of the late artist . . . to foreigners." It urged the government to acquire the whole collection.[24] Other newspapers shared this sentiment, which was in accord with Vereshchagin's own wishes that his works remain in Russia, despite his stipulation that an auction be held after the exhibit. Accordingly, on November 25, Lidiia requested in a letter to the tsar's court that, instead of granting her a pension, the government acquire the entire collection of her husband's works, which an academician had recently appraised at more than 150,000 rubles ($75,000) "under normal conditions" (i.e., if he were alive). One cannot determine who established the conditions of the appraisal, for the value of the collection had increased markedly since Vereshchagin's death and, another appraisal indicated that the works could realize 1,000,000 ($500,000) if auctioned. In her letter, Lidiia expressed

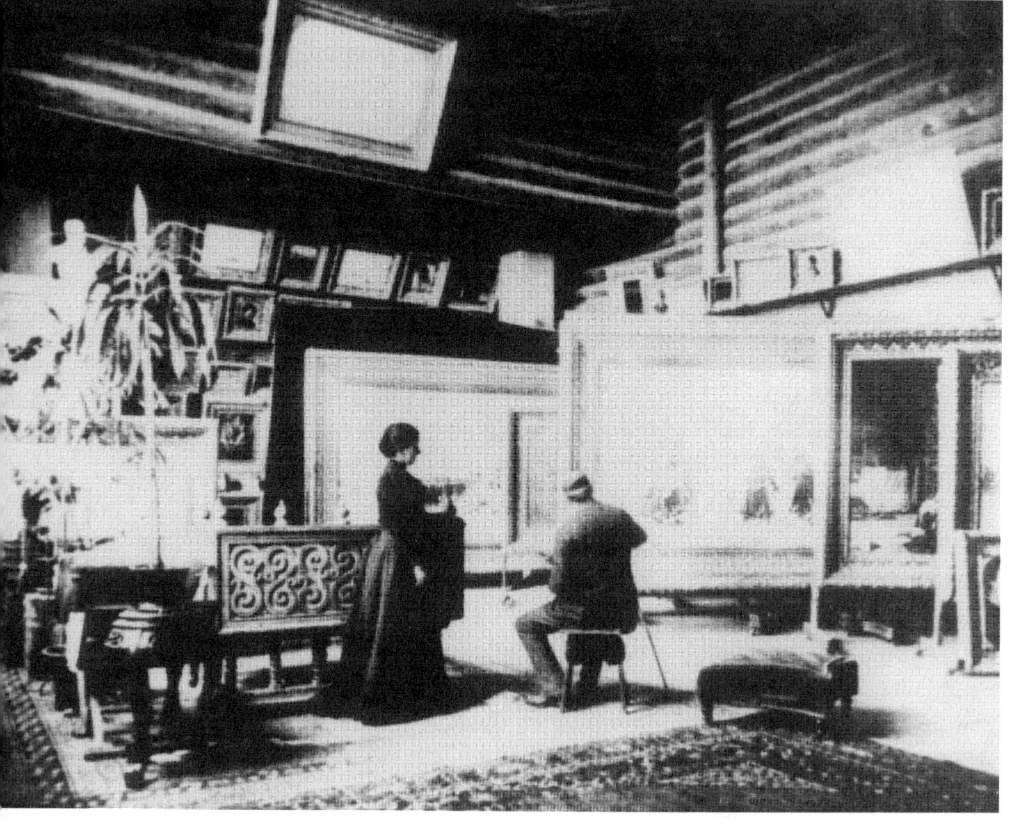

Figure 37. Vereshchagin's Moscow studio. From A. Lebedev and A. Solodovnikov, *V. V. Vereshchagin* (Moscow: Iskusstvo, 1988).

fear that foreign art dealers and collectors would purchase the best paintings: it "would be an extreme pity if such . . . a collection of works is broken up and sold to foreigners."[25] Lidiia was willing to accept 120,000 rubles if the government considered the academician's appraisal excessive. She added that it would be extremely difficult and expensive in the future to establish a museum for her husband's works if foreigners were to buy them. This was an extreme understatement of the problem. Lidiia's suggestion of a museum went beyond Vereshchagin's own wishes and represents a measure of her love, devotion, and sacrifice.

The government failed to respond to Lidiia's letter partly because the tsar had to consult with the head of the Russian Museum in St. Petersburg, where the collection was to be sent. As the auction date (December 12) drew nearer and without any response from the government, Lidiia seemed unable to withstand the pressure of negotiation. On December 4, she wrote another letter to the tsar's court: she was now willing to accept whatever the government would offer for the collection. Tsar Nicholas finally agreed to purchase it for 100,000 rubles, but he refused to accept as a gift those materials and objects that were an integral part of Vereshchagin's studio. The entire collection went to the Russian Museum and was placed in storage, which was perhaps a kind of second death for Vereshchagin and his paintings. Lidiia's modest request that a room be assigned for her husband's studio was relegated to the future, when, she was told, "the curators will give the matter better consideration and find a free place for Vereshchagin's studio."[26] Thus, the government would not even consider a room, let alone a museum, for an artist who had struggled with it for many years. The auction was subsequently canceled. The tsar offered Lidiia's son the opportunity to study at an institution in St. Petersburg at state expense, but Lidiia declined, because she wanted the boy to remain close to the family in Moscow. Until the Russian revolution of 1917, despite its monetary problems, the family kept its financial commitment to Vereshchagin's first wife, although it was under no obligation to do so.[27]

In 1913, a group of artists and prominent social figures, led by the Russian artist Ilia Repin, created a museum in Vereshchagin's honor in the city of Nikolaev in the southern Ukraine. A significant part of the Vereshchagin collection was transferred from the Russian Museum to Nikolaev, to which the Vereshchagin family also sent the materials relating to his studio. A monument to Vereshchagin and an art scholarship in his name were also proposed, but the Academy of Arts failed to approve them.[28] The Tretiakov Gallery reserved four rooms to exhibit the works Tretiakov had purchased from Vereshchagin, and the Russian Museum in St. Petersburg devoted two rooms to the permanent exhibit of Vereshchagin's paintings.[29] In 1957, a monument was dedicated to him in his native city of Cherepovets (Fig. 38), and in 1984 the home in which he was born became a museum. For most of the Soviet period, Veresh-

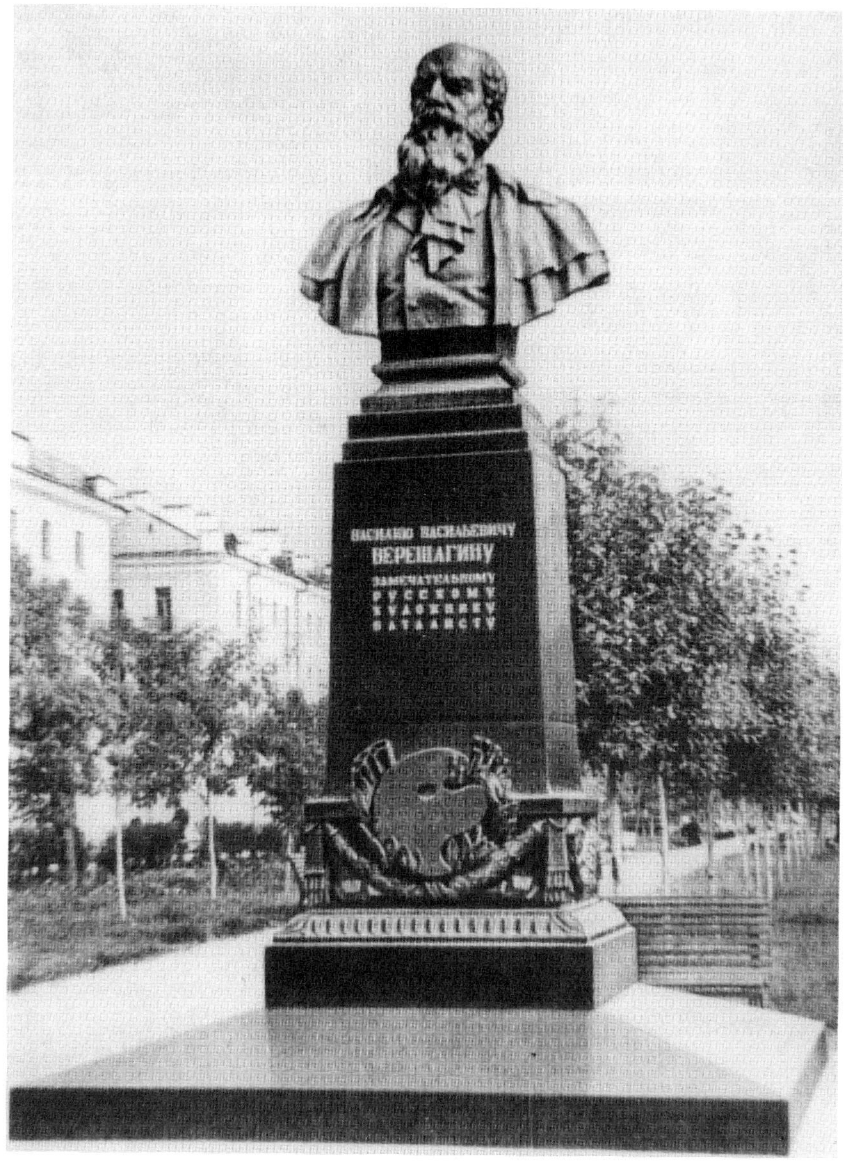

Figure 38. Monument to Vereshchagin in Cherepovets, Russia. From A. Lebedev and A. Solodovnikov, *V. V. Vereshchagin* (Moscow: Iskusstvo, 1988).

chagin's legacy ran counter to Bolshevik ideology of global revolution and totalitarian rule, which he would have condemned as modern manifestations of state violence and thus crimes against humanity. Recently, however, his life and art have been rediscovered and have assumed a special urgency as part of a vigorous Soviet peace offensive both at home and abroad. Hence the very recent publication in the Soviet Union of four books about him.

In the West, however, another constellation of historical factors is necessary to explain Vereshchagin's oblivion since the onset of the twentieth century. The first was economic-political: endemic revolution and war eventually gripped the twentieth century and largely suspended, until quite recently, the active search for peace between East and West. From the end of the nineteenth century, war was generally viewed as an engine of material, social, political, and economic progress by which some form of human and social perfection would be accelerated. As such, war was tolerable, despite the suffering, death, disruption, and turmoil it entailed. For Vereshchagin, however, war was largely unacceptable; it was an immoral and irrational phenomenon that unjustly affected the common masses through universal conscription. The development of industrial technology and the attendant growth of armies; the professionalization, specialization, and mobilization of armed forces; and the conscious planning of armaments for human and physical destruction markedly increased the size and authority of the national-security state in its efforts to organize, develop, administer, and control its armed forces. These developments were not conducive to peace but to conflicting and competing ideological, political, economic and social systems. Massive expenditures for military weapons surely contributed to economic growth, expansion, prosperity (as well as concentrated wealth), employment, and the creation of collateral industries, even if those weapons, particularly in their nuclear manifestations, were never meant to be deployed. Thus, the military-industrial complex—drawing on the eminent leaders from a variety of institutions—and the psychology of war had become woven into the social fabric; rather than improving the human condition, the military-industrial complex had frozen it for some fifty years in the twentieth century. Countries also vied for territorial expansion in terms of cultural aims, and this phenomenon engendered the rise of patriotism and loyalty

to the state in order to promote ideological conformity, unity, and loyalty vital to the war effort in periods of military tension and conflict; to create, manipulate, rally, and channel the latent national mood for war, even though the goal was not so much victory, but the conquest of national and personal alienation, an expression of national pride, a function of national destiny, or the fulfillment of a fantastic historical vision, an opportunity for some form of "liberation," action, participation, demonstration, and assertion. Hence the means of war became ends in themselves. War often includes the passion for something new.[30]

Moreover, the era of "photographic" realism and the moral, ethical, social, or political commentary in art and literature of the previous fifty years, so characteristic of Vereshchagin's paintings, had come to an end in the early twentieth century, when avant-garde movements, often espousing art for art's sake and turning to abstract or nonobjective art, rapidly rose to prominence and became a predominant interest of art historians. Further, during the Cold War, the West elevated some Russian writers to the level of political heroes because of their defiance and opposition to the "Evil Empire," the Soviet State, whereas Vereshchagin's cause of peace was eclipsed and utterly forgotten, largely because in the West he was known, quite ambiguously, as Russia's outstanding "battle painter."

Vereshchagin belonged to an age that took as its fundamental creed the idea of Progress—a steady, gradual advance in improving human life and creating a rational, harmonious social order.[31] The concept, which had supplanted—if it did not compete with—the idea of Providence, assumed that through scientific knowledge and conscious creative efforts, men could determine their own destinies and elevate humanity to a higher plane of existence. Karl Marx's idea of man's ultimate conquest of his environment was perhaps the most utopian manifestation of the idea of Progress. Darwin's *Origin of Species* added scientific validity to such a concept: the laws of development would lead ultimately to perfection. While Vereshchagin was surely a votary of Progress and initially viewed it as an instrument of fulfillment, he eventually came to see war as the enemy of advancement. His war experiences undermined his faith in Progress and led him at the end of the nineteenth century to question the illusion of Progress. His prognosis of human development was now pro-

foundly pessimistic, because the road to Progress, like the "Road to Plevna" and other utopian and totalitarian schemes, was buried under human corpses:

> One often hears arguments that our age is highly civilized and that it is hard to imagine where, in what direction, in what degree mankind can still develop. Isn't it quite the contrary? Isn't it more accurate to say that in all directions humanity has taken only the first steps and that we still live in an era of barbarism? Even if we assume that we are already ashamed of devouring our enemies (i.e. people considered as such at a certain moment), we still have not conceived of another means of ridding ourselves of them or changing their way of thinking when killing and destroying them in tens, hundreds of thousands.[32]

The grim experience of hundreds of wars and mass murder in the twentieth century need not be recounted here to affirm Vereshchagin's statements, for it is only quite recently that we have discovered that society itself cannot remain immune from the disease of war, which breeds violence, crime, and social dislocation. Violence, amply reflected in and promoted by the media, has become so deeply ingrained in the social fabric that it is accepted as a natural, routine condition of daily life. A recent assessment of twentieth-century history confirms Vereshchagin's diagnosis: "In the last fifty years we human beings have slaughtered by our own hands coming on for one hundred million of our species. We all live under constant threat of our total annihilation. We seem to seek death and destruction as much as life and happiness. We are driven to kill and be killed as we are to let live and live. Only by the most outrageous violation of ourselves have we achieved our capacity to live in relative adjustment to a civilization apparently driven to its own destruction."[33]

In the late twentieth and well into the twenty-first centuries, the resurgence of militant, aggressive nationalism will pose an even greater threat of mass annihilation because of the rapid proliferation and accumulation of nuclear weapons by underdeveloped countries. The danger of war will increase if these and other countries do not obtain economic cooperation and/or assistance from, and are not integrated into, the more prosperous

economies of Western nations.[34] This is already happening, however slowly, in relation to the former Soviet Union, where there is a significant potential for civil war or nationalist uprisings against economic backwardness.

Perhaps the time is approaching, as Vereshchagin hoped, when monies are allocated not for instruments of human destruction and preparations for war, but for the war against poverty, hunger, and disease, and for the affirmation of human dignity. Vereshchagin's warning about Russia's war with Japan is still germane: "war . . . we must try to avoid as aimless, merciless and in any event ruinous."

NOTES

INTRODUCTION

1. See I. Repin, "Vospominaniia o V. V. Vereshchagine 1904–1914gg.," in *Repin* (Moscow-Leningrad: Izdat. Akademii Nauk, 1948), vol. 1:338, 340, 343. According to an eminent Russian art historian, Vereshchagin "developed an original and almost photographic technique perfectly appropriate to his needs" (D. Sarabianov, *Russian Art: From Neoclassicism to the Avant-Garde 1800–1917* [New York: H. N. Abrams, 1990], 147). An English critic remarked that "Russia has given to Western Europe a painter both essentially modern and essentially original, whose work should prove epoch-making in our modern history with its unmodern art" (H. Zimmern, "An Eastern Painter," *The Art Journal* 37 [January 1885]: 9). See also V. S. R., "V. V. Vereshchagin i ego proizvedeniia," *Istoricheskii vestnik* 63 (January, 1896): 224.

2. A. Benois, *A History of Russian Painting* (New York: A. Knopf, 1916), 130–31. See also his "Vystavka Vereshchagina," *Mir iskusstva,* no. 10 (1904): 214, in which Benois draws a distinction between Vereshchagin's place in the history of Russian culture and in the annals of Russian art. Although Benois initially "revolted against" Vereshchagin's art because of its "harsh," "amateurish," and "tasteless" orientation, he later felt the need "to change his attitude to the master, and to be engaged in a certain rehabilitation of him. Vereshchagin not only provoked scandals by his daring subjects, but he also possessed the strength of conviction, the will to artistic creation, acute observation and clarity of invention, which, if they do not shape an artist as such, then in that event are the distinctive features of a genuine artist. Other truly vital monuments of their time, created by an artist, are far more valuable than purely 'esthetic achievements in art'" (A. Benois, *Zhizn khudozhnika. Vospominaniia* [New York: Izdat. imeni Chekhova, 1955], 2:145).

3. "Vystavka kartin V. V. Vereshchagina," *Russkii vestnik* 242 (February 1896): 327.

4. V. Sadoven, *V. V. Vereshchagin* (Moscow: Izdat. Tretiakovskoi galerei, 1950), 109.

5. See J. Keegan, *The Face of Battle* (New York: Viking Press, 1976), 296.

6. Quoted in *Gosudarstvennyi Russkii muzei. Putevoditel* (Leningrad: Sovetskii khudozhnik, 1969), 203–4.

7. Ia. Tugendkhold, *Problema voiny v mirovom iskusstve* (Moscow: Izdat. I.D. Sytina, 1916), 150.

8. Ibid.

CHAPTER 1

1. See A. K. Lebedev, V. V. Vereshchagin: Zhizn i tvorchestvo 1842–1904, 2-oe izd. (Moscow: Iskusstvo, 1972), 11; V. V. Vereshchagin, *Detstvo i otrochestvo khudozhnika V. V. Vereshchagina* (Moscow: I. N. Kushnerev, 1895), 1:16; *Sobranie sochinenii V. V. Stasova 1847–1886* (S. Peterburg: M. Stasiulevich, 1894), 2:272–73.

2. Vereshchagin, *Detstvo i otrochestvo*, 1:6–7. See also V. V. Vereshchagin, *Izbrannye pisma* (Moscow: Izo. iskusstvo, 1981), 119.

3. Vereshchagin, *Detstvo i otrochestvo*, 1:25, 111–12.

4. M. S. Anderson, *War and Society in Europe of the Old Regime 1618–1789* (New York: St. Martin's Press, 1988), 117.

5. Vereshchagin, *Detstvo i otrochestvo*, 1:15.

6. Ibid., 1:55–57.

7. Ibid., 1:60.

8. Ibid., 1:65.

9. Ibid., 1:112.

10. Ibid., 1:94.

11. Ibid., 1:128, 132–35, 146, 150, 197–98, 214.

12. Ibid., 1:197.

13. Ibid., 1:265.

14. Ibid., 1:270.

15. T. Kovalenskaia observes that Vereshchagin's fascination with and study of art were tantamount to an escape from the oppressive character of Russian life. *Russkii realizm i problema ideala* (Moscow: Izo. iskusstvo, 1983), 102. But he could have equally taken refuge in the seas.

16. Vereshchagin, *Detstvo i otrochestvo*, 1:287–88, 302–3.

17. Ibid., 303–5.

18. E. Lampert, *Sons Against Fathers: Studies in Russian Radicalism and Revolution* (London: Oxford Univ. Press, 1965), 89.

19. Ibid., 85–86.

20. See ibid., 220.

21. Quoted in E. K. Valkenier, "The Intelligentsia and Art," in *Art and Culture in Nineteenth-Century Russia,* ed. T. G. Stavrou (Bloomington: Indiana Univ. Press, 1983), 160. See also C. A. Moser, *Esthetics as Nightmare: Russian Literary Theories, 1855–1870* (Princeton: Princeton Univ. Press, 1989), 242.

22. See V. V. Vereshchagin, *Listki iz zapisnoi knizhki V. V. Vereshchagina* (Moscow: I. N. Kushnerev, 1898), 1.

23. E. K. Valkenier, *Russian Realist Art. The State and Society: The Peredvizhniki and Their Tradition* (Ann Arbor: Ardis Publishers, 1977), 10.

24. N. Moleva and E. Beliutin, *Russkaia khudozhestvennaia shkola vtoroi poloviny XIX-nachala XX veka* (Moscow: Iskusstvo, 1967), 6.

25. Valkenier, *Russian Realist Art,* 10.

26. Moleva and Beliutin, 19, 23, 33–35.

27. On the artists who subsequently came to be called The Itinerants or The Wanderers (*Peredvizhniki*), see the essays in E. K. Valkenier, ed., *The Wanderers: Masters of 19th-Century Russian Painting* (Austin: Univ. of Texas Press, 1990).

28. E. J. Hobsbawm, *The Age of Capital 1848–1875* (New York: Scribner's & Sons, 1975), 285, 288.

29. For a discussion of the concept of genius in Russian art, see V. D. Barooshian, *The Art of Liberation: Alexander A. Ivanov* (Lanham: Univ. Press of America, 1987), 33, 43.

30. See Vereshchagin, *Izbrannye pisma,* 121–22, 125–27.

31. Ibid., 126.

32. See G. Ackerman, "Gérôme: The Academic Realist," *Art News Annual* 33 (1968): 101–7.

33. See E. J. Hobsbawm, *The Age of Empire 1875–1914* (New York: Pantheon, 1987), 223.

34. H. T. Buckle, *History of Civilization in England,* 2d ed. (New York: D. Appleton, 1887), 3, 5.

35. Vereshchagin, *Izbrannye pisma,* 126.

36. See, for example, F. H. Skrine, *The Heart of Asia: A History of Russian Turkestan and Central Asian Khanates from Earliest Times. With 19 Illustrations from Sketches by Verestchagin* (London: Metheun, 1899).

37. Lampert, 37.

38. See the studies in Lebedev, *Zhizn i tvorchestvo,* 50–51, and in F. Bulgakov, *V. V. Vereshchagin i ego proizvedeniia tvorchestro* 2-oe izd.(S. Peterburg: I. N. Kushnerev, 1905), 43.

39. Lebedev, *Zhizn i tvorchestvo,* 49.

40. For Repin's work and related sketches and studies, see O. Liaskovskaia, *Ilia E. Repin: 1844–1930* (Moscow: Iskusstvo, 1982), 45–67.

41. See *Perepiska V. V. Vereshchagina i V. V. Stasova 1879–1883* (Moscow: Iskusstvo, 1951), 2:271–72.

CHAPTER 2

1. See E. J. Hobsbawm, *The Age of Empire 1875–1914* (New York: Pantheon, 1987), 67. Hobsbawm points out that "between 1876 and 1915 about one-quarter of the globe's land surface was distributed or re-distributed as colonies among a half dozen states" (ibid., 59).

2. Quoted in A. Lebedev, *V. V. Vereshchagin: Zhizn i tvorchestvo 1842–1904,* 2-oe izd. (Moscow: Iskusstvo, 1972), 59.

3. V. Zhelezniak, *Khudozhnik Vereshchagin* (Vologda: Severno-zapadnoe knizhnoe izdatelstvo, 1967), 12.

4. See D. MacKenzie, "Kaufman of Turkestan: An Assessment of His Administration 1867–1881," *Slavic Review* 26, no. 2 (June 1967): 265–69. See also G. Wheeler, *The Modern History of Soviet Central Asia* (New York: F. A. Praeger, 1964), 78–83.

5. See N. Moleva and E. Beliutin, *Russkaia khudozhestvennaia shkola vtoroi poloviny XIX-nachala XX veka* (Moscow: Iskusstvo, 1967), 26–27.

6. Quoted in F. Bulgakov, *V. V. Vereshchagin i ego proizvedeniia,* 2-oe izd. (S. Peterburg: I. N. Kushnerev, 1905), 44.

7. V. V. Verestchagin, *Painter, Soldier, Traveler. Autobiographical Sketches* (New York: American Art Association, 1888), 1–2.

8. Lebedev, *Zhizn i tvorchestvo,* 62.

9. Ibid., 64; V. V. Vereshchagin, *Izbrannye pisma* (Moscow: Izo. iskusstvo, 1981), 129.

10. Vereshchagin, *Izbrannye pisma,* 127–28, V. V. Vereshchagin, "Samarkand v 1868g.," *Russkaia starina* 59 (September 1888): 625, 629, 633.

11. L. N. Tolstoy, *Povesti i rasskazy v dvukh tomakh* (Moscow: Gosizdat. khudozhestvennoi literatury, 1960), 1:67.

12. Vereshchagin, "Samarkand v 1868g.," 629, 634; *Izbrannye pisma,* 127–29; *Perepiska V. V. Vereshchagina i V. V. Stasova 1879–83* (Moscow: Iskusstvo, 1951), 2:209, 322–23.

13. Bulgakov, 52; Vereshchagin, *Izbrannye pisma,* 128; *Perepiska Vereshchagina i Stasova,* 2:320.

14. Vereshchagin, *Izbrannye pisma,* 129.

15. Lebedev, *Zhizn i tvorchestvo,* 76; Bulgakov, 54.

16. Lebedev, *Zhizn i tvorchestvo,* 75–76, 89.

17. Ibid., 119.

18. V. Vereshchagin, "Kitaiskaia granitsa. Nabeg," *Russkaia starina* 64 (October 1989), 165, 168–69, 170–71, 174–76; Lebedev, *Zhizn i tvorchestvo,* 78–81.

19. Quoted in Lebedev, *Zhizn i tvorchestvo,* 90.

20. Ibid., 90; V. V. Vereshchagin, *Vospominaniia syna khudozhnika* (Leningrad: Khudozhnik RSFSR, 1982), 151.

21. "Russia in the East," *The Pall Mall Budget* (October 25, 1872): 4; "The Debate on Central Asia," *The Saturday Review,* 26 April 1873, 535–36; "The Central Asian Question," *The Illustrated London News,* 15 March 1873, 258.

22. Quoted in Lebedev, *Zhizn i tvorchestvo,* 119. I have adjusted the Russian translation of the English version used in the British catalogue to substitute "distrust" for "doubts" and "natural" for "real," which were quoted in English reviews of Vereshchagin's exhibit.

23. "The Agreement between England and Russia," *The Pall Mall Budget* (February 21, 1873): 5. This agreement between the two countries concerned the recognition of territorial boundaries in Central Asia.

24. "Sketches of Central Asia," *The Pall Mall Budget* (April 10, 1873): 12; "Central Asia at the Crystal Palace," *The Times* (London), 9 July 1873; "Sketches of Central Asia," *The Saturday Review,* 26 April 1873, 549–50. See also "Khiva on Canvas," *The Spectator,* 12 April 1873, 470–71; "Central Asian Sketches at the Crystal Palace," *The Graphic* (April 12, 1873): 351; "Basil Wereschagin," *The Illustrated London News,* 23 August 1873, 171; "Dervishes at Khiva," ibid., 3 May 1873, 410.

25. Tolstoy, *Povesti i rasskazy,* 1:172.

26. See A. Shifman, *Lev Tolstoi i vostok* (Moscow: Nauka, 1971), 330.

27. Quoted in *Exhibition of the Works of Vassili Verestchagin: Illustrated Descriptive Catalogue* (New York: American Art Galleries, 1889), 69.

28. On Stasov's relationship with Vereshchagin, see Yuri Olkhovsky, *Vladimir Stasov and Russian Culture* (Ann Arbor: UMI Research Press, 1983), 120–21. Stasov considered Vereshchagin "Leo Tolstoy in art" (ibid., 121).

29. Lebedev, *Zhizn i tvorchestvo,* 128.

30. I. Lazarevskii, "Khudozhnik voiny—V. V. Vereshchagin," in A. Tikhomirov, *V. V. Vereshchagin: Zhizn i tvorchestvo 1842–1904* (Moscow-Leningrad: Iskusstvo, 1942), 88.

31. See V. Sadoven, *V. V. Vereshchagin* (Moscow: Izdat. Tretiakovskoi galerei, 1950), 38.

32. See *Perepiska V. V. Vereshchagina i P. M. Tretiakova 1874–1898* (Moscow: Iskusstvo, 1963), 19–26, 108–9.

33. "Urok russkim khudozhnikam," *Golos*, 23 March 1874.

34. Quoted in Lazarevskii, 92.

35. Vereshchagin, "Kitaiskaia granitsa. Nabeg," 176.

35. *Perepiska Vereshchagina i Tretiakova*, 23.

37. See I. Zilbershtein, "Vystavka khudozhnika V. V. Vereshchagina," in *Literaturnoe nasledstvo* 73, kn. 1 (Moscow: Nauka, 1964), 73:294.

38. Vereshchagin, *Izbrannye pisma*, 35.

39. *Perepiska Vereshchagina i Tretiakova*, 29.

40. Tiutriumov's article is reproduced in Lebedev, *Zhizn i tvorchestvo*, 334–35.

41. *Sobranie sochinenii V. V. Stasova 1847–1886* (S. Peterburg: M. Stasiulevich, 1894), 2:347, *Perepiska V. V. Vereshchagina i V. V. Stasova 1874–1878* (Moscow: Iskusstvo, 1950), 1:287, 289–90. For additional details on reactions to Tiutriumov's attack on Vereshchagin, see ibid., 283–97.

42. See Lebedev, *Zhizn i tvorchestvo*, 132.

43. Quoted in *Sobranie sochinenii Stasova*, 2:349.

44. See Lebedev, *Zhizn i tvorchestvo*, 136.

45. Ibid., 147.

46. Vereshchagin, *Izbrannye pisma*, 34–35.

47. *Perepiska Vereshchagina i Tretiakova*, 24.

48. Ibid., 24–25.

49. *Perepiska Vereshchagina i Stasova*, 1:25–26.

50. Vereshchagin, *Izbrannye pisma*, 37.

51. Ibid., 40–41; Bulgakov, 75.

52. V. Verestchagin, *Painter, Soldier, Traveller: Autobiographical Sketches* (London: R. Bentley, 1887) 1:237–48; Vereshchagin, *Izbrannye pisma*, 36–37.

CHAPTER 3

1. *Perepiska V. V. Vereshchagina i V. V. Stasova 1874–1878* (Moscow: Iskusstvo, 1950), 1:123, 124, 128–30; *Perepiska V. V. Vereshchagina i P. M. Tretiakova 1874–1898* (Moscow: Iskusstvo, 1963), 32, 109.

2. *Perepiska Vereshchagina i Stasova*, 1:123; I. Zilbershtein, "Repin v gody borby Rossii za nezavisimost slavian," in *Repin* (Moscow-Leningrad: Izdat. Akad. nauk, 1948), 1:386.

3. L. N. Tolstoy, *Anna Karenina*, trans. C. Garnett (New York: Random House, 1965), 803–4.

4. D. Mackenzie, *The Serbs and Russian Pan-Slavism 1875–1878* (Ithaca: Cornell Univ. Press, 1967), 100.

5. *Perepiska Vereshchagina i Stasova*, 1:139.

6. M. Pearton, *Diplomacy, War and Technology Since 1830* (Lawrence: Univ. Press of Kansas, 1984), 141. One Russian journal, however, while supporting the war, pointed out that the Russian people would bear the whole brunt of it and anticipated its quick conclusion with a minimum of casualties. Later, after Russian military setbacks, this same journal questioned the right of a "cultured society," in view of its backward economy and the recent liberation of the serfs, to sacrifice its people and resources to the point of exhaustion (see V. Sadoven, *V. V. Vereshchagin* [Moscow: Izdat. Tretiakovskoi galerei, 1950], 54–55).

7. V. Verestchagin, *Painter, Soldier, Traveller: Autobiographical Sketches* (London: R. Bentley, 1887), 2:115; V. V. Vereshchagin, *Izbrannye pisma* (Moscow: Iskusstvo, 1981), 52.

8. A. Zhirkevich, "V. V. Vereshchagin. Po lichnym vospominaniiam," *Vestnik Evropy* 4 (April 1908):498.

9. Verestchagin, *Painter, Soldier, Traveller* (London), 2:138–42; quoted in *Perepiska V. V. Vereshchagina i V. V. Stasova 1879–1883* (Moscow: Iskusstvo, 1951), 2:194.

10. Verestchagin, *Painter, Soldier, Traveller* (London), 2:154–57.

11. The will is reproduced in V. V. Vereshchagin, *Izbrannye pisma,* 221, and provides a significant sum for the promotion of secular education.

12. See A. Lebedev, *V. V. Vereshchagin. Zhizn i tvorchestvo 1842–1904* , 2-oe izd. (Moscow: Iskusstvo, 1972), 169. Tsar Alexander II visited Skrydlov and Vereshchagin at the hospital, wished them a speedy recovery, and awarded the former the Cross of St. George. The tsar's brief comment to Vereshchagin was that he had already been awarded one (ibid.)

13. Pearton, 141.

14. See Lebedev, *Zhizn i tvorchestvo,* 172.

15. Vereshchagin, *Izbrannye pisma*, 57, 62; F. Bulgakov, *V. V. Vereshchagin i ego proizvedeniia,* 2-oe izd. (S. Peterburg: I. N. Kushnerev, 1905), 85.

16. L. N. Tolstoy, *Povesti i rasskazy v dvukh tomakh* (Moscow: Gosizdat. khud. literatury, 1960), 1:34.

17. See "Vospominaniia khudozhnika V. V. Vereshchagina," *Russkaia starina* 64 (December 1889), 789, and *Exhibition of the Works of Vassili Verestchagin: Illustrated Descriptive Catalogue* (New York: American Art Galleries, 1889), 59–60.

18. L. Sobolev, "Poslednii boi za Shipku 1877–1878gg.," *Russkaia starina* 62 (May 1889), 418.

19. Quoted in Sadoven, 66.

20. See Lebedev, *Zhizn i tvorchestvo,* 185–86.

21. Vereshchagin, *Izbrannye pisma*, 73, 229; *Perepiska Vereshchagina i Stasova 1874–1878*, 1:215, 235, 243–48, 250–53, 255, 390–91, 397, 400–401, 404; Bulgakov, 85, Lebedev, *Zhizn i tvorchestvo*, 172.

22. V. Verestchagin, *Painter, Soldier, Traveler. Autobiographical Sketches* (New York: American Art Assoc., 1888), 149–51.

23. Verestchagin, *Painter, Soldier, Traveller* (London), 2: 234–35, 197.

24. Ibid., 237–38.

25. Vereshchagin, *Izbrannye pisma*, 65, 227.

26. MacKenzie, 247.

27. Quoted in ibid., 247.

28. See Lebedev, *Zhizn i tvorchestvo*, 174. The Russian censor deleted this account from Vereshchagin's memoirs of the war.

29. B. Sumner, *Russia and the Balkans 1870–1880* (London: Oxford Univ. Press, 1937), 352.

30. MacKenzie, 247.

31. Sumner, 352.

32. V. Vinogradov, *Russko-turetskaia voina 1877–1878gg. i osvobozhdenie Bolgarii* (Moscow: Mysl, 1978), 224–25.

33. Sumner, 555.

34. L. Stavrianos, *The Balkans Since 1453* (New York: Holt, Rinehart & Winston, 1965), 412.

35. Sumner, 555.

36. Vereschagin, *Painter, Soldier, Traveler* (N.Y.), 170; Lebedev, *Zhizn i tvorchestvo*, 175–76.

37. Vereshchagin, *Izbrannye pisma*, 76–82, 88, 233; Lebedev, *Zhizn i tvorchestvo*, 177, *Perepiska Vereshchagina i Stasova 1879–1883* (Moscow: Iskusstvo, 1951), 2:66, 198, 174.

38. Vereshchagin, *Izbrannye pisma*, 97.

39. *Perepiska Vereshchagina i Tretiakova*, 36–40, 111.

40. See *Sobranie sochinenii V. V. Stasova 1847–1886* (S. Peterburg: M. Stasiulevich, 1894–1906), 2:325.

41. Quoted in ibid., 454–60.

42. *Perepiska Vereshchagina i Stasova*, 2:68–71.

43. Quoted in I. Zilbershtein, "Vystavka khudozhnika V. V. Vereshchagina," in *Literaturnoe nasledstvo*, 73, kn. 1 (Moscow: Nauka, 1964), 306, 335.

44. *Perepiska Vereshchagina i Stasova*, 2:203.

45. See *Sobranie sochinenii Stasova*, 2:461–69.

46. Quoted in Zilbershtein, "Vystavka khudozhnika Vereshchagina," 311.

47. N. Kovalenskaia, *Russkii realizm i problema ideala* (Moscow: Izo. iskusstvo, 1985), 126. See also M. S. Anderson, *War and Society in Europe of the Old Regime 1618–1789* (New York: St. Martin's Press, 1988), 198–204, for an informed discussion of the composition of armies in the eighteenth century and the changes that ensued in the nineteenth.

48. Quoted in *Sobranie sochinenii Stasova*, 2:540.

49. *Perepiska Vereshchagina i Tretiakova*, 38.

50. Quoted in *Sobranie sochinenii Stasova*, 2:550.

51. Quoted in Kovalenskaia, 126.

52. Quoted in Vereshchagin, *Izbrannye pisma*, 238.

53. Ibid., 108, 238.

54. Quoted in Lebedev, *Zhizn i tvorchestvo,* 199.

55. Vereshchagin, *Izbrannye pisma*, 111, 239.

56. Ibid., 111.

57. Ibid., 239.

58. Quoted in *Perepiska Vereshchagina i Stasova*, 2:224–225.

59. Quoted in Lebedev, *Zhizn i tvorchestvo,* 338.

60. Quoted in ibid., 200.

61. *Perepiska Vereshchagina i Stasova*, 2:112.

62. Ibid., 229. See also *Sobranie sochinenii Stasova*, 2:471–86, for other reviews of Vereshchagin's exhibit.

63. *Perepiska Vereshchagina i Stasova*, 2:106.

64. *Sobranie sochinenii Stasova*, 2:538–39.

65. *Perepiska Vereshchagina i Stasova*, 2:99–100.

66. Quoted in Ibid., 302.

67. Quoted in Ibid., 308.

68. Ibid., 229.

CHAPTER 4

1. *Perepiska V. V. Vereshchagina i V. V. Stasova 1879–1883* (Moscow: Iskusstvo, 1951), 2:124.

2. Ibid., 127.

3. Ibid., 116.

4. See V. Sadoven, *V. V. Vereshchagin* (Moscow: Izdat. Tretiakovskoi galerei, 1950), 79–80.

5. Ibid.; *Perepiska V. V. Vereshchagina i P. M. Tretiakova 1874–1898* (Moscow: Iskusstvo, 1963), 124.

6. *Perepiska V. V. Verestchagina: i Tretiakova,* 129.

7. *Exhibition of the Works of Vassili Verestchagin: Illustrated Descriptive Catalogue* (New York: American Art Galleries, 1889), 6–7.

8. *Perespiska Vereshchagina i Stasova,* 2:139.

9. See A. Lebedev, *V. V. Vereshchagin. Zhizn i tvorchestvo 1842–1904* (Moscow: Iskusstvo, 1972), 213–14.

10. *Perepiska Vereshchagina i Stasova,* 2:332, 335, 341.

11. *Perepiska Vereshchagina i Tretiakova,* 69, 126.

12. See *Perepiska Vereshchagina i Stasova,* 2:348.

13. V. Gribayedoff, "A Russian Apostle of Art," *Cosmopolitan Magazine* 6 (1889), 324–25. In Palestine, Vereshchagin discovered corruption and greed among the Greek Orthodox clergy, who were pocketing substantial Russian donations that were specifically intended for schools and shelters ("Vospominaniia khudozhnika V. V. Vereshchagina: Na dalnem vostoke," *Russkaia starina* 63 [August 1889]: 439–45).

14. V. Verestchagin, *Realism* (New York: American Art Association, 1889–90), 17–18.

15. Ibid., 20.

16. See Lebedev, *Zhizn i tvorchestvo,* 221.

17. Verestchagin, *Realism,* 20.

18. Quoted in C. Hibbert, *The Great Mutiny: India 1857* (New York: Viking Press, 1978), 123.

19. See A. Yarmolinsky, *Road to Revolution* (New York: A. Knopf, 1960), 287.

20. Quoted in F. Venturi, *Roots of Revolution* (New York: A. Knopf, 1960), 719.

21. Yarmolinsky, 288–89.

22. Verestchagin, *Realism,* 19.

23. See *Cyclopedia of Painters and Paintings* (New York: C. Scribner's, 1887), 2:273–84.

24. See Verestchagin, *Exhibition of the Works,* 35.

25. "The Verestchagin Exhibition," *The Nation,* 22 November 1888, 424.

26. Verestchagin, *Realism,* 14.

27. See *Cyclopedia,* 4:29–30.

28. Lebedev, *Zhizn i tvorchestvo,* 224.

29. V. Vereshchagin, *Izbrannye pisma* (Moscow: Izo. iskusstvo, 1981), 138, 140–41.

30. Quoted in F. Bulgakov, *V. V. Vereshchagin i ego proizvedeniia,* 2-oe-izd. (S. Peterburg: I. N. Kushnerev, 1905), 98.

31. See Lebedev, *Zhizn i tvorchestvo,* 340, which reproduces the full text of Vereshchagin's reply to Cardinal Ganglbauer.

32. Ibid., 341.

33. Vereshchagin, *Izbrannye pisma*, 140.

34. Ibid., 139–41; Bulgakov, 100; *Khudozhestvennye novosti* 4 (1886): 21; Lebedev, *Zhizn i tvorchestvo*, 225–26.

35. Vereshchagin, *Izbrannye pisma*, 142.

36. Quoted in Lebedev, *Zhizn i tvorchestvo*, 226.

37. Quoted in A. Lebedev and G. Burova, *V. V. Vereshchagin i V. V. Stasov* (Moscow: Iskusstvo, 1953), 33.

38. Quoted in *Khudozhestvennye novosti* 4 (1886): 282.

39. V. Verestchagin, *On Progress in Art* (New York: American Art Association, 1889–90), 3–4.

40. Verestchagin, *Realism*, 23.

41. Ibid., 31, 33.

42. Vereshchagin, *Izbrannye pisma*, 142.

43. "The Verestchagin Exhibition," *The Art Journal* 50 (1887), 382–83.

44. Quoted in Sadoven, 88.

45. *Perepiska Vereshchagina i Tretiakova*, 69.

46. Lebedev and Burova, 66.

47. Lebedev, *Zhizni i tvorchestvo*, 236.

48. B. Macgahan, "Verestchagin and His Work," *Lippincott's Magazine* 44 (1889): 234; Lebedev, *Zhizn i tvorchestvo*, 237.

49. W. Towner, *The Elegant Auctioneers* (New York: Hill & Wang, 1970), 29.

50. R. Williams, *Russian Art and American Money* (Cambridge: Harvard Univ. Press, 1980), 42–43. In 1883, there was a thirty-percent duty, which decreased to fifteen percent in 1890; the duty was lifted from 1894 to 1897, when it was reimposed at twenty percent (ibid.).

51. Towner, 41.

52. Lebedev, *Zhizn i tvorchestvo*, 235.

53. See Vereshchagin, *Izbrannye pisma*, 146–47, and V. V. Vereshchagin, *Vospominaniia syna khudozhnika* (Leningrad: Khudozhnik RSFSR, 1982), 127, which contains a summary of Vereshchagin's will.

54. Vereshchagin, *Izbrannye pisma*, 192; V. Stasov, *Stati i zametki* (Moscow: Izdat. Akademii khudožhestv SSSR, 1952), 1:131–33.

55. Quoted in Gribayedoff, 326.

56. See the New York *Daily Tribune,* 6 January 1889.

57. Quoted in Gribayedoff, 311.

58. Quoted in Towner, 130.

59. Quoted in Lebedev, *Zhizn i tvorchestvo,* 235.

60. *Khudozhestvennye novosti* 6 (1888): 583.

61. "The Verestchagin Exhibition," *The Nation*, 22 November 1888, 423–24. See also "The Verestchagin Exhibition at the American Art Galleries," *The Critic,* 17 November 1888, 246–47.

62. T. Dreiser, *The 'Genius'* (New York: World Publishing Co., 1946), 51.

63. Towner, 131. Bulgakov, 102, states that Vereshchagin received about $73,000. The difference between the two figures may reflect Sutton's commission. *Roman Execution (Crucifixion)* brought the highest bid ($7,500) for a single painting. See Bulgakov, 102, for bids on other paintings.

64. Towner, 130 (emphasis added).

65. Quoted in ibid., 130–31.

CHAPTER 5

1. See I. Lazarevskii, "Khudozhnik voiny—V. V. Vereshchagin," in A. Tikhomirov, *V. V. Vereshchagin: Zhizn i tvorchestvo 1842–1904* (Moscow-Leningrad: Iskusstvo, 1942), 94.

2. Vereshchagin also wrote a book on the war, *1812. Napoleon in Russia*, which is still extremely useful, quite informative, and draws on a wide range of historical materials (some sixty sources). It bears comparison with *Napoleon's Russian Campaign*, a vivid and magistral eyewitness account by Count Philippe-Paul de Ségur, Napoleon's aide-de-camp in that war. Both works have been used here to describe the war and the relationship of Vereshchagin's paintings to the main episodes.

3. B. K., "Mysli po povodu kartin Vereshchagina i kartiny Matveeva," *Russkii arkhiv* 1 (1896): 258.

4. N. K. "V. V. Vereshchagin i ego kartiny," *Novoe vremia*, 21 January 1896; see also "Vystavka kartin V. V. Vereshchagina," *Moskovskie vedemosti*, 25 November 1895.

5. See P. Geyl, *Napoleon: For and Against* (New Haven: Yale Univ. Press, 1949), which deals largely with the views of French historians on Napoleon and his historical significance.

6. See V. V. Vereshchagin, *Izbrannye pisma* (Moscow: Izo. iskusstvo, 1981), 196–200, and A. Lebedev, *V. V. Vereshchagin: Zhizn i tvorchestvo 1842–1904* (Moscow: Iskusstvo, 1972), 261–72.

7. The explanatory notes are in F. Bulgakov, *V. V. Vereshchagin i ego proizvedeniia*, 2-oe izd. (S. Peterburg: I. N. Kushnerev, 1905), 163–91.

8. For a an account of the antagonism between Napoleon and Alexander I, see J. M. Thompson, *Napoleon Bonaparte* (New York: Oxford Univ. Press, 1952), 346–51. Thompson adds: "There can be little doubt . . . that, as in Spain, in Italy, in Austria, in Prussia and in the East, so in Russia, too, the particular reasons in Napoleon's mind for a military enterprise gave way, in the excitement of the event, and as the hope of victory opened out new vistas of adventure and power, to sheer acquisitiveness and the greed to dominate and direct the world: a world in which it became increasingly certain that the Napoleonic Empire could tolerate no rivals" (ibid., 352).

9. J. R. Elting, *Swords Around a Throne: Napoleon's Grande Armée* (New York: The Free Press, 1988), 63–64.

10. Count P.-P. de Ségur, *Napoleon's Russian Campaign*, trans. J. D. Townsend (Boston: Houghton-Mifflin, 1958), 3–4. When Alexander I sent a courier to inquire of the reasons for Napoleon's invasion, Napoleon is quoted as replying that "Alexander is making fun of me. . . . Does he suppose I have come all the way to Vilna to negotiate commercial treaties? I have come to make an end once and for all to the Colossus of the barbarian north. . . . My sword is drawn. These barbarians must be driven back into their Arctic ice-fields . . . so that for the next twenty-five years they shan't come and interfere in the affairs of civilized Europe" (quoted in Thompson, 352).

11. V. Verestchagin, *1812. Napoleon I in Russia* (New York: C. Scribner's, 1899), 55. In France, four printings of this book were published.

12. A. Manfred, *Napoleon Bonapart* (Moscow: Mysl, 1987), 586.

13. Ségur, 6–7.

14. Manfred, 608–9.

15. Quoted in Verestchagin, *1812*, 182.

16. M. S. Anderson, *War and Society in Europe of the Old Regime 1618–1789* (New York: St. Martin's Press, 1988), 196–97. In a letter of June 5, 1812, the Russian Ambassador to England outlined the Russian strategy against Napoleon: "Even if, at first, military operations go against us, we can win, by persistence and retreat. If the enemy begins to pursue us, it is all up with him: for, the further he advances from his bases of supply and munitions into a trackless and foodless country, starved and encircled by an army of Cossacks, his position will become more and more dangerous; and he will end by being decimated by the winter, which has always been our most faithful ally" (quoted in Thompson, 353).

17. Anderson, 197.

18. Ségur, 51. One Englishman (Sir Robert Wilson) described Kutuzov (age seventy-four) as "a *bon vivant*, polished, courteous, shrewd as a Greek, intelligent as an Asiatic, well instructed as a European"; the general was also "so fat that he

had to be driven about the field" (see Thompson, 355). On the Russian paintings of the battle of Borodino, see *Borodino: 1812* (Moscow: Mysl, 1987).

19. Ségur, 59–60; Elting, 522. See Elting, 521–26, for a description and analysis of the social composition, structure, strengths, and weaknesses of the Russian forces.

20. Quoted in Verestchagin, *1812*, 229.

21. Quoted in Manfred, 617; see also Lebedev, *Zhizn i tvorchestvo*, 259.

22. See Verestchagin, *1812*, 230.

23. Ségur, 96.

24. The Speaker, "Verestchagin," *Living Age* 220 (1899): 464.

25. Ségur, 90–91, 95; Elting, 277.

26. Verestchagin, *1812*, 210.

27. Ségur, 109.

28. Ibid., 111.

29. "Vystavka kartin V. V. Vereshchagina," *Russkii vestnik* 242 (Feb. 1896): 325.

30. Ségur, 115.

31. On retreating from Moscow, one French Sergeant looted the following: "a woman's chinese silk dress, several gold and silver ornaments, amongst them a part of the silver gilt casing of the great cross of Ivan the Great (in its centre a solid gold cross about a foot long), a woman's riding cloak lined with green velvet, two silver pictures in relief, one of the Judgement of Paris, the other of Neptune in a chariot drawn by sea-horses, several lockets, and a Russian prince's spittoon set with brilliants; in a large pouch hung at his side by a silver cord was a crucifix in silver and gold, and a Chinese porcelain vase." Provisions, weapons, and ammunition were also included in his knapsack (Thompson, 364–65).

32. See Bulgakov, 191, for Vereshchagin's explanatory notes for this painting.

33. Elting, 263.

34. Ségur, 177.

35. Verestchagin, *1812*, 175. "Accounts of the retreat of the *Grande Armée* from Russia in 1812 are all so full of horror of the snow and frost, the moral collapse, the disintegration of the army, the starvation and the cannibalism, that one is amazed that anyone at all survived" (A. Collis, "Some Survivors of the Russian Campaign," *History Today* 21, [November 1971]:796).

Chapter 6

1. V. V. Vereshchagin, *Vospominaniia syna khudozhnika* (Leningrad: Khudozhnik RSFSR, 1982), 50. This book by Vereshchagin's son appears to be the only source of information about Vereshchagin's family life.

2. Ibid., 46.

3. Ibid., 39.

4. See A. Lebedev and A. Sododovnikov, *V. V. Vereshchagin* (Leningrad: Khudozhnik RSFSR 1987), pls. 49–54.

5. V. Mak-Gakhan, "Prodazha kollektsii kartin Vereshchagina v New Yorke: 1," *Moskovskie vedemosti*, December 10, 1902.

6. V. V. Vereshchagin, *Izbrannye pisma* (Moscow: Izo. iskusstvo, 1981), 193–94.

7. A. Lebedev and G. Burova, *V. V. Vereshchagin i V. V. Stasov* (Moscow: Iskusstvo, 1953), 205; V. Mak-Gakhan, "Prodazha kollektsii kartin Vereshchagina v New Yorke: 2," *Moskovskie vedemosti*, December 11, 1902.

8. Mak-Gakhan, 2.

9. Vereshchagin, *Vospminaniia syna khudozhnika*, 115–16. See also "V. V. Vereshchagin," *Novoe vremia*, 13 April 1904.

10. Quoted in A. Lebedev, *V. V. Vereshchagin: Zhizn i tvorchestvo 1842–1904*, 2-oe izd. (Moscow: Iskusstvo, 1972), 281.

11. Vereshchagin, *Izbrannye pisma*, 203.

12. See *The London Times*, 15 July, 1904.

13. Vereshchagin, *Izbrannye pisma*, 206.

14. See "Pisma V. V. Vereshchagina Nikolaiu Romanovu," *Krasnyi arkhiv* 2, no. 46 (1931): 167–71.

15. Vereshchagin, *Vospominaniia syna khudozhnika*, 120–21.

16. Vereshchagin, *Izbrannye pisma*, 210.

17. Vereshchagin, *Vospominaniia syna khudozhnika*, 177; Lebedev and Burova, 161; Lebedev, *Zhizn i tvorchestvo*, 286–87; B. Ostrovskii, *Admiral Makarov 1848–1904* (Leningrad: Molodaia gvardiia, 1951), 388–91, A. Sorokin, *Oborona Port-Artura: Russko-iaponskaia voina 1904–1905* (Moscow: Izd. Min. VSCCR, 1948), 58–59; "Voina. Telegraf i telefon," *Russkie vedemosti*, 4 April 1904; "The Story of the Sinking of the Petropavlovsk," *The Nation*, 21 April 1904), 303.

18. Lebedev, *Zhizn i tvorchestvo*, 287.

19. Quoted in Lebedev and Burova, 160. An American writer in Boston echoed this sentiment: "With the ill-fated battleship perished not only the intrepid Makaroff . . . but one of the most remarkable figures in the whole world of art, the greatest of war-painters, Vassily Vasilievich Verestschagin" (R. Newmarch, "Vassily Verestschagin: War Painter," *Living Age* 242, [1904], 129).

20. Vereshchagin, *Vospominaniia syna khudozhnika*, 126–27.

21. See Lebedev, *Zhizn i tvorchestvo*, 290.

22. A. V. S-n, "Po povodu auktsiona veschei V. V. Vereshchagina v Peterburge," *Russkie vedemosti*, 29 November 1904. A highly interesting

description of Vereshchagin's studio was published in V. Sizov, "V masterskoi V. V. Vereshchagina," *Russkie vedemosti*, 11 September 1904.

23. N. Kravchenko, "Vystavka V. V. Vereshchagina," *Novoe vremia*, 29 November 1904.

24. See A. V. S-n, "Posmertnaia vystavka V. V. Vereshchagina," *Russkie vedemosti*, 11 November 1904.

25. Quoted in Lebedev, *Zhizn i tvorchestvo*, 290. After the Russian government acquired the collection, many counterfeit paintings bearing Vereshchagin's signature appeared in St. Petersburg and Moscow. Once Vereshchagin noticed such a painting in a Moscow store, he cut it to pieces with his pen knife as others looked on (see "Khudozhestvennaia khronika," *Novoe vremia*, 16 December 1904).

26. Quoted in Lebedev, *Zhizn i tvorchestvo*, 290.

27. Ibid., 347.

28. Ibid.

29. See L. Lord, "Some Modern Russian Painters," *Art and Archaeology* 7 (1918): 304; *Gosudarstvennyi Russkii muzei. Putevoditel* (Leningrad: Sovetskii khudozhnik, 1969), 203–5.

30. On war in the nineteenth and twentieth centuries, see M. S. Anderson, *The Ascendancy of Europe. Aspects of European History 1815–1914* (London: Longman, 1966); M. S. Howard, *War in European History* (London: Oxford Univ. Press, 1976); and "The Art of the Tat," *Times Literary Supplement*, 9–15 Feb. 1990, 138; E. H. Carr, "Preface," *The New Society* (London: Macmillan, 1957).

31. E. H. Carr, *What is History?* (London: Macmillan, 1962), 113. See also J. B. Bury, *The Idea of Progress: An Inquiry into Its Origin and Growth* (New York: Macmillan, 1921).

32. V. V. Vereshchagin, *Listki iz zapisnoi knizhki khudozhnika V. V. Vereshchagina* (Moscow: I. N. Kushnerev, 1898), 82.

33. R. D. Laing, *The Politics of Experience* (New York: Pantheon, 1967), 49.

34. See the penetrating article by A. C. Janos, "Social Democracy, Communism, and the Dynamics of Political Change," *World Politics* 44 (October 1991), especially p. 111.

SELECTED BIBLIOGRAPHY

WORKS BY VASILY VASILEVICH VERESHCHAGIN

Detstvo i otrochestvo khudozhnika V. V. Vereshchagina (The Childhood and Youth of the Artist V. V. Vereshchagin). Moscow: I. N. Kushnerev, 1895.

1812. Napoleon I in Russia. New York: C. Scribner's, 1899.

Exhibition of the Works of Vassili Verestchagin: Illustrated Descriptive Catalogue. New York: American Art Galleries, 1889.

Izbrannye pisma (Selected Letters). Moscow: Izo. iskusstvo, 1981.

"Kitaiskaia granitsa. Nabeg" (The Chinese Border. The Raid). *Russkaia starina* 64 (October 1889):157–81.

Listki iz zapisnoi knizhki khudozhnika V. V. Vereshchagina (Pages from V. V. Vereshchagin's Notebook). Moscow: I. N. Kushnerev, 1898.

On Progress in Art. New York: American Art Association, 1889–1890.

Painter, Soldier, Traveler. Autobiographical Sketches. New York: American Art Association, 1888.

Painter, Soldier, Traveller: Autobiographical Sketches. 2 vols. London: R. Bentley, 1887.

Perepiska V. V. Vereshchagina i P. M. Tretiakova, 1874–1898 (The Correspondence between V. V. Vereshchagin and P. M. Tretiakov, 1874–1898). Moscow: Iskusstvo, 1963.

Perepiska V. V. Vereshchagina i V. V. Stasova, 1874–1878 (The Correspondence Between V. V. Vereshchagin and V. V. Stasov, 1874–1878). 2 vols. Moscow: Iskusstvo, 1950–51.

"Pisma V. V. Vereshchagina Nikolaiu Romanovu" (V. V. Vereshchagin's letters to Nicholas Romanov). *Krasnyi arkhiv* 2, No. 46 (1931):167–71.

Realism. New York: American Art Association, 1889–1890.

"Samarkand v 1868g." (Samarkand in 1868). *Russkaia starina* 59)September 1888):617–41.

Turkestan: Etiudy s natury (Studies from Nature). S. Peterburg: A. Begrov, 1874.

"Vospominaniia khudozhnika V. V. Vereshchagina: Na delnem vostoke" (Recollections of the Artist V. V. Vereshchagin: In the Far East). *Russkaia starina* 63 (August 1889):439–45.

BOOKS

Anderson, M. S. *War and Society in Europe of the Old Regime, 1618–1789.* New York: St. Martin's Press, 1988.

Barooshian, V. D. *The Art of Liberation: Alexander A. Ivanov.* Lanham: University Press of America, 1987.

Benois, A. *A History of Russian Painting.* New York: A. Knopf, 1916.

——. *Istoriia russkoi zhivopisi v XIX v.* (A History of Russian Painting in the XIX Century). S. Peterburg: Znanie, 1902.

Berlin, I. *Russian Thinkers.* New York: Viking Press, 1978.

Borodino: 1812. Moscow: Mysl, 1987.

Buckle, H. T. *History of Civilization in England.* 2d ed. New York: D. Appleton, 1887.

Bulgakov, F. *V. V. Vereshchagin i ego proizvedeniia* (V. V. Vereshchagin and His Works). 2-oe izd. S. Peterburg: I. N. Kushnerev, 1905.

Bury, J. B. *The Idea of Progress: An Inquiry into Its Origins and Growth.* New York: Macmillan, 1921.

Carr, E. H. *The New Society.* London: Macmillan, 1957.

——. *What is History?* London: Macmillan, 1962.

Curran, M. "Vladimir Stasov and the Development of Russian National Art." Ph.D. Diss., University of Wisconsin, 1965.

Cyclopedia of Painters and Paintings. 2 vols. New York: C. Scribner's, 1887.

Dreiser, T. *The 'Genius.'* New York: World Publishing Co., 1946.

Elting, J. R. *Swords Around a Throne: Napoleon's Grande Armée.* New York: The Free Press, 1988.

Geyl, P. *Napoleon: For and Against.* New Haven: Yale University Press, 1949.

Gleason, A. *Young Russia: The Genesis of Russian Radicalism in the 1860's.* Chicago: University of Chicago Press, 1983.

Gosudarstvennyi Russii muzei. Putevoditel (State Russian Museum. Guide-Book). Leningrad: Sovetskii khudozhnik, 1969.

Gray, C. *The Great Experiment: Russian Art 1863–1922.* New York: H. N. Abrams, 1962.

Hibbert, C. *The Great Mutiny: India 1857.* New York: Viking Press, 1978.

Hobsbawm, E. J. *The Age of Capital 1848–1875.* New York: Scribner's & Sons, 1975.

——. *The Age of Empire 1875–1914.* New York: Pantheon, 1987.

Howard, M. S. *War in European History.* London: Oxford University Press, 1976.

Keegan, J. *The Face of Battle.* New York: Viking Press, 1976.

Kovalenskaia, N. *Russkii realizm i problema ideala* (Russian Realism and the Problem of the Ideal). Moscow: Izo. iskusstvo, 1983.

Krupskaia, N. *Vospominaniia o Lenine* (Recollections of Lenin). Moscow: Izdat. polit. literatury, 1957.

Laing, R. D. *The Politics of Experience.* New York: Pantheon, 1967.

Lampert, E. *Sons Against Fathers: Studies in Russian Radicalism and Revolution.* London: Oxford University Press, 1965.

Lebedev, A. *V. V. Vereshchagin.* Moscow: Iskusstvo, 1968.

——. *V. V. Vereshchagin. Zhizn i tvorchestvo 1842–1904* (V. V. Vereshchagin. His Life and Art 1842–1904). 2-oe izd. Moscow: Iskusstvo, 1972.

Lebedev, A., and Burova, G. *V. V. Vereshchagin i V. V. Stasov* (V. V. Vereshchagin and V. V. Stasov). Moscow: Iskusstvo, 1953.

Lebedev, A., and Solodovnikov, A. *V. V. Vereshchagin.* Leningrad: Khudozhnik RSFSR, 1987.

Liaskovskaia, O. *Ilia E. Repin 1844–1930.* Moscow: Iskusstvo, 1982.

MacKenzie, D. *The Serbs and Russian Pan-Slavism 1875–1878.* Ithaca: Cornell University Press, 1967.

Manfred, A. *Napoleon Bonapart.* Moscow: Mysl, 1987.

Moleva, N., and Beliutin, E. *Russkaia khudozhestvennaia shkola vtoroi poloviny XIX-nachala XX veka* (Russian Art School of the Second Half of the XIX Century to the Beginning of the XX Century). Moscow: Iskusstvo, 1967.

Moser, C. A. *Esthetics as Nightmare: Russian Literary Theories, 1855–1870.* Princeton: Princeton University Press, 1989.

Novitskii, A. *Istoriia russkago iskusstva s drevneishikh vremen* (A History of Russian Art From Ancient Times). 2 vols. Moscow: Izdat. V. I. Lind, 1903.

Olkhovsky, Yu. *Vladimir Stasov and Russian Culture.* Ann Arbor: UMI Research Press, 1983.

Ostrovskii, B. *Admiral Makarov 1848–1904.* Leningrad: Molodaia gvardiia, 1951.

Parker, F., and Parker, J. *Russia on Canvas: Ilya Repin.* University Park: Penn. State University Press, 1980.

Pearton, M. *Diplomacy, War and Technology Since 1830.* Lawrence: University Press of Kansas, 1984.

Sadoven, V. *V. V. Vereshchagin.* Moscow: Izdat. Tretiakovskoi galerei, 1950.

Sarabianov, D. *Russian Art: From Neoclassicism to the Avant-Garde, 1800–1917.* New York: H. N. Abrams, 1990.

de Ségur, Count Ph-P. *Napoleon's Russian Campaign.* Translated by J. D. Townsend. Boston: Houghton-Mifflin, 1958.

Shifman, A. *Lev Tolstoi i vostok* (Leo Tolstoy and the East). Moscow: Nauka, 1971.

Skrine, F. H. *The Heart of Asia: A History of Russian Turkestan and Central Asian Khanates from Earliest Times. With 19 Illustrations from Sketches by Verestchagin.* London: Methuen & Co., 1899.

Sobranie sochinenii V. V. Stasova 1847–1886 (Collected Works of V. V. Stasov 18497–1886). 4 vols. S. Peterburg: M. Stasiulevich, 1894–1906.

Sorokin, A. *Oborona Port-Artura: Russko-iaponskaia voina 1904–1905* (The Defense of Port Arthur: The Russo-Japanese War 1904–1905). Moscow: Izdat. Min. VSCCR, 1948.

Stasov, V. *Stati i zametki* (Articles and Notes). 2 vols. Moscow: Izdat. Akademii Khudozhestv SSSR, 1952–54.

Stavrianos, L. *The Balkans Since 1453.* New York: Holt, Rinehart & Winston, 1965.

Sumner, B. *Russia and the Balkans 1870–1880.* London: Oxford University Press, 1937.

Thompson, J. M. *Napoleon Bonaparte.* New York: Oxford University Press, 1952.

Tikhomirov, A. *V. V. Vereshchagin: Zhizn i tvorchestvo 1842–1904* (V. V. Vereshchagin: His Life and Art 1842–1904). Moscow-Leningrad: Iskusstvo, 1942.

Tolstoy, L. N. *Anna Karenina.* Translated by C. Garnett. New York: Random House, 1965.

——. *Povesti i rasskazy v dvukh tomakh* (Tales and Stories in Two Volumes). Moscow: Gosizdat. khudozhestvennoi literatury, 1960.

Towner, W. *The Elegant Auctioneers.* New York: Hill & Wang, 1970.

Tugenkhold, Ia. *Problema voiny v mirovom iskusstve* (The Problem of War in World Art). Moscow: Izdat. I. D. Sytina, 1916.

Valkenier, E. K. *Russian Realist Art. The State and Society: The Peredvizhniki and Their Tradition.* Ann Arbor: Ardis Publishers, 1977.

——, ed. *The Wanderers: Masters of 19th Century Russian Painting.* Austin: University of Texas Press, 1990.

Venturi, F. *Roots of Revolution.* New York: A. Knopf, 1960.

Vereshchagin, V. V. *Vospominaniia syna khudozhnika* (Recollections of the Artist's Son). Leningrad: Khudozhnik RSFSR, 1982.

Vinogradov, V. *Russko-turetskaia voina 1877–1878gg. i osvobozhdenie Bolgarii* (The Russo-Turkish War of 1877–1878 and the Liberation of Bulgaria). Moscow: Mysl, 1978.

Volodarskii, V. *V. V. Vereshchagin.* Leningrad: Khudozhnik RSFSR, 1962.

Vucinich, A. *Darwin in Russian Thought.* Berkeley: University of California Press, 1988.

Walicki, A. *A History of Russian Thought from the Enlightenment to Marxism.* Oxford: Oxford University Press, 1980.

Wheeler, G. *The Modern History of Soviet Central Asia.* New York: F. A. Praeger, 1964.

Williams, R. *Russian Art and American Money.* Cambridge: Harvard University Press, 1980.

Yarmolinsky, A. *Road to Revolution.* New York: A. Knopf, 1960.

Zabel, E. *Wereschtschagin.* Leipzig: Velhagen & Klasing, 1900.

Zavadskaia, E. *V. V. Vereshchagin.* Moscow: Iskusstvo, 1988.

Zhelezniak, V. *Khudozhnik Vereshchagin* (The Artist Vereshchagin). Vologda: Severno-zapadnoe knizhnoe isdatelstvo, 1967.

ARTICLES

Ackerman, G. "Gérôme: The Academic Realist." *Art News Annual* 33 (1968): 101–7.

"The Agreement between England and Russia." *The Pall Mall Budget* (February 21, 1873): 5.

"Basil Wereschagin." *The Illustrated London News* (August 23, 1873): 171.

Benois, A. "Vystavka Vereshchagina" (The Vereshchagin Exhibition). *Mir iskusstva*, no. 10 (1904): 213–14.

Bowlt, J. E. "Russian Painting in the Nineteenth Century." In *Art and Culture in Nineteenth Century Russia*, edited by T. G. Stavrou, 113–39. Bloomington: Indiana University Press, 1983.

"Central Asia at the Crystal Palace." *The Times* (London), July 9, 1873.

"The Central Asian Question." *The Illustrated London News* (March 15, 1873): 258.

"Central Asian Sketches at the Crystal Palace." *The Graphic* (April 12, 1873): 351.

Collis, A. "Some Survivors of the Russian Campaign." *History Today* 21 (November 1971): 796–802.

"The Debate on Central Asia." *The Saturday Review* (April 26, 1873): 535–36.

"Dervishes at Khiva." *The Illustrated London News*, May 3, 1873: 410.

Gribayedoff, V. "A Russian Apostle of Art," *Cosmopolitan Magazine* 6 (1889): 311–26.

"Inostrannoe obozrenie: Gibel *Petropavlovska*" (Foreign Review: The Destruction of the *Petropavlovsk*). *Vestnik Evropy* (May 1904): 355–60.

Janos, A. C. "Social Democracy, Communism, and the Dynamics of Political Change." *World Politics* 44 (October 1991): 81–122.

"Khiva on Canvas." *The Spectator* (April 12, 1873): 470–71.

B. K. "Mysli po povodu kartin Vereshchagina i kartiny Matveeva" (Thoughts Concerning Vereshchagin's Paintings and a Painting by Matveev). *Russkii arkhiv*, no. 1 (1896): 257–59.

N. K. "V. V. Vereshchagin i ego kartiny" (V. V. Vereshchagin and His Paintings). *Novoe vremia*, January 21, 1896.

Kravchenko, N. "Vystavka V. V. Vereshchagina" (The Vereshchagin Exhibition). *Novoe vremia*, November 29, 1904.

"The Late M. Verestchagin." *The Illustrated London News* (April 23, 1904): 598.

Lazarevskii, I. "Khudozhnik voiny—V. V. Vereshchagin" (Artist of War: V. V. Vereshchagin), in A. Tikhomirov, *V. V. Vereshchagin: zhniz i tvorchestvo* (V. V. Vereshchagin: His Life and Art). Moscow-Leningrad: Iskusstvo, 1942: 87–100.

Lord, L. "Some Modern Russian Painters." *Art and Archaeology* 7 (1918): 301–12.

Macgahan, B. "Verestchagin and His Work." *Lippincott's Magazine* 44 (1889): 232–37.

MacKenzie, D. "Kaufman of Turkestan: An Assessment of His Administration 1867–1881." *Slavic Review* 26, no. 2 (June 1967): 265–85.

Mak-Gakhan, V. (Macgahan, B.) "Prodazha kollektsii kartin Vereshchagina v New Yorke: I" (The Sale of the Collection of Vereshchagin's Paintings in New York: I). *Moskovskie vedemosti*, December 10, 1902.

——. "Prodozha kollektsii kartin Vereshchagina v New Yorke: II." *Moskovskie vedemosti*, December 11, 1902.

Newmarch, Rosa. "Vassily Verestschagin: War Painter." *Living Age* 242 (1904): 129–36.

Repin, I. "Vospominaniia o V. V. Vereshchagine 1904–1914gg" (Recollections of V. V. Vereshchagin 1904–1914). in *Repin*, vol. 1. Moscow-Leningrad: Izdat. Akademii nauk, 1948: 335–46.

R., V. S. "V. V. Vereshchagin i ego proizvedeniia" (V. V. Vereshchagin and His Works). *Istoricheskii vestnik* 63 (January 1896): 217–29.

"Russia in the East." *The Pall Mall Budget* (October 25, 1872): 4.

S-n., A. V. "Po povodu auktsiona veshchei V. V. Vereshchagina v Peterburge" (On the Auction of V. V. Vereshchagin's Pieces in St. Petersburg), *Russkie vedemosti*, November 29, 1904.

——. "Posmertnaia vystavka V. V. Vereshchagina" (The Posthumous Exhibition of V. V. Vereshchagin). *Russkie vedemosti*, November 11, 1904.

Sizov, V. "V masterskoi V. V. Vereshchagina" (In V. V. Vereshchagin's Studio). *Russkie vedemosti*, September 11, 1904.

———. "V. V. Vereshchagin: Po lichnym vospominaniiam i pismam" (V. V. Vereshchagin: From Personal Recollections and Letters). *Russkie vedemosti*, May 28, 1904.

"Sketches of Central Asia." *The Pall Mall Budget* (April 10, 1873): 12.

"Sketches of Central Asia." *The Saturday Review* (April 26, 1873): 549–50.

Sobko, N. "Battle and Travel." *Magazine of Art* 7 (1884): 184–91.

The Speaker. "Verestchagin." *Living Age* 220 (1899): 463–65.

Starr, S. F. "Russian Art and Society, 1800–1850." In *Art and Culture in Nineteenth-Century Russia*, edited by T. G. Stavrou, 87–112. Bloomington: Indiana University Press, 1983.

"The Story of the Sinking of the *Petropavlovsk*." *The Nation* (April 21, 1904): 303.

"Urok russkim khudozhnikam" (A Lesson to Russian Artists). *Golos*, March 23, 1874.

Valkenier, E. K. "The Intelligentsia and Art." In *Art and Culture in Nineteenth-Century Russia*, edited by T. G. Stavrou, 153–71. Bloomington: Indiana University Press, 1983.

"The Verestchagin Exhibition at the American Art Galleries." *The Critic* (November 17, 1888): 246–47.

"The Verestchagin Exhibition." *The Nation* (November 22, 1888): 324–24.

"The Verestchagin Exhibition." *The Art Journal* 50 (1887): 382–83.

"Voina. Telegraf i telefon" (War. Telegraph and Telephone). *Russkie vedemosti*, April 4, 1904.

"Vystavka kartin V. V. Vereshchagina" (Exhibition of Vereshchagin's Paintings). *Moskovskie vedemosti*, November 25, 1895.

"Vystavka kartin V. V. Vereshchagina" (Exhibition of Vereshchagin's Paintings). *Russkii vestnik* 242 (February 1896): 323–27.

Zhirkevich, A. "V. V. Vereshchagin: Po lichnym vospominaniiam" (V. V. Vereshchagin: From Personal Recollections). *Vestnik Evropy*, no. 4 (April 1908): 496–532.

Zilbershtein, I. "Vystavka khudozhniva V. V. Vereshchagina" (Exhibition of the Artist V. V. Vereshchagin)." In *Literaturnoe nasledstvo* 73, kn. 1, Moscow: Nauka, 1964: 291–336.

Zimmern, H. "An Eastern Painter." *The Art Journal* 37 (January 1885): 9–12; (May 1904): 38–42.

INDEX

Note: Numbers in italics refer to illustrations (figures or color plates).